New Urban Development

New Urban Development

Looking Back to See Forward

CLAUDE GRUEN

RUTGERS UNIVERSITY PRESS

NEW BRUNSWICK, NEW JERSEY, AND LONDON

LIBRARY OF CONGRESS CATALOGING-IN-PUBLICATION DATA

Gruen, Claude.
    New urban development : looking back to see forward / Claude Gruen.
      p. cm.
    Includes bibliographical references and index.
    ISBN 978–0–8135–4793–0 (hardcover : alk. paper)
    1. Cities and towns—Growth.   2. Housing policy.   I. Title.
    HT371.G7128   2010
    307.76—dc22

                                        2009043152

A British Cataloging-in-Publication record for this book is available
from the British Library.

Visit our Web site: http://rutgerspress.rutgers.edu

Manufactured in the United States of America

To Nina
My muse and critic (not necessarily in that order)

CONTENTS

PREFACE

It's not unreasonable for you to ask right here and now: What is this book about? It's about intentions, it's about objectives aimed at achieving those intentions, and it's about the decisions made to result in the intended objectives. Rarely do intentions, objectives, and decisions all align in any field of endeavor. The field of endeavor in this book is urban development.

I wrote this book to help urban land-use policymakers align their intentions, their decisions, their objectives, and what results. The results are determined by the way the rules and actions of elected officials and their staffs affect the economics of the urban areas they govern and serve. That is why it was necessary for me to begin by looking back to enable you to understand the way public laws and actions have influenced the economics of urban America in the past. Based on what we observe in the past, you and I can better see ahead so we can suggest the necessary changes in the laws and planning practices that shape the use of land.

To observe how real estate regulations and planning practices interact in urban places with the economics of those places, I looked through two "scopes." One scope was in the form of the writings of the many scholars from whom I learned so much about urban economics and planning practices. My academic education and the resulting debt I incurred to those who provided it began at the University of Cincinnati under the wise and patient tutelage of professors Robert Wessel, Alfred Kuhn, and the other professors in the department of economics, as well as Dean William L. C. Wheaton, under whom I taught at the University of California, Berkeley.

The other scope that enabled me to see into the workings of regulatory authorities and urban economic activity resulted from my forty-five years as an urban economic consultant. The insights provided by our clients, the many other land use professionals we have worked with, and my colleagues at Gruen Gruen + Associates (GG+A) together brought into clear focus the many nuances of urban economics behavior and the way planning laws are written and administered. Examples of what my personal experiences as a consultant and unrepentant "city guy" have enabled me to see I share with you in the chapters of this book.

In the ten years that I wrote this book, I have not only played the author's trick of stealing time from my family, but I often interrupted Nina, my professional partner and my wife, to get the benefit of her surgically precise insights to clear confusion away from my own view of urban phenomena. Aaron Gruen and Andrew Ratchford have borne the burden of answering questions and conducting analysis for this book in addition to their work at GG+A. Judy Lofton has been in charge of preparing the manuscript as it went through many changes. I have long benefited from discussions about suburban development and other urban issues with my friend Robert Bruegmann, professor of art history, architecture, and urban planning at the University of Illinois at Chicago. Nevertheless, in substantiation of the dictum that good deeds rarely go unpunished, I imposed the reading of an early draft of this book on Robert; his suggestions greatly improved the next draft. I owe a particular debt to George Lefcoe, University of Southern California Law School, who drew on his encyclopedic knowledge of urban legal literature to answer my questions and point me toward relevant literature, whether or not he shared my view on the subjects at hand. My good friend Leanne Lachman's insightful views of changes in demographics and real estate institutions kept me in focus on those matters. Mark David Menchik, formerly a staff member of the Office of Management and Budget (OMB), currently working at the National Research Council, and John Wilkins, artistic director of Last Planet Theatre and senior adjunct professor of English at the California College of the Arts, read and provided very useful comments on early drafts. Professor John M. Quigley, Department of Economics, University of California, Berkeley, read a revised draft and provided suggestions that were all reflected in the book you now read.

This book benefited from the suggestions of Susan M. Bielstein, executive editor at the University of Chicago Press, and two faculty members who read one of the earlier drafts. Professor Joseph Gyourko, director of the Zell/Lurie Real Estate Center, The Wharton School, generously provided data and answered questions on the "Superstar Cities" study of housing prices discussed in chapter 1, and Professor William A. Fischel, Department of Economics, Dartmouth College, answered questions on his valuable work, which is in discussed in chapter 3.

Marlie Wasserman, director of the Rutgers University Press, and her staff made many useful suggestions as they shepherded the publication of this book. But her most helpful recommendation was that I engage the services of Mike Elia to assist in the reorganization and developmental editing of the manuscript. Mike's editing was as brilliant as Marlie said it would be. The way he prods an author to do what is most effective for the reader makes me suspect that he had an earlier career at the prow of a ship rowed by galley slaves. The final draft of this book would be considerably less readable without the good works of copy editor Patricia Bower and classics professor Nicholas Humez, who polished the prose and prodded me into what I can only hope clarified my intent. Nick also compiled the index.

Authorship is an act of ego satisfaction. Those who have helped me complete that act have prevented many errors of thought and writing; those that remain are my own.

New Urban Development

1

Constraints on Housing Additions Escalate Prices

The owner of any vacant land on your block, or in your neighborhood, or elsewhere in your city and county cannot build on that land without the permission of those you elected to govern your town and county. Even if you own the house you live in, you cannot remodel it or tear it down and rebuild without the approval of your local government. Your home may be your castle, but how you can change it, what it can look like, and where you can build a new one are dictated by the building codes and zoning ordinances of your local jurisdiction.

Your local jurisdiction produces maps comprising zones. Each zone specifies that what you do with your property within that zone must be in conformity with the general laws laid out in the codes and ordinances. The zoning ordinances specify details for buildings, such as the allowable density (or number of units per acre or square foot of land), the allowable maximum height, the ratio between floor area of building and area of land it will occupy, and the setback (how far back from the street), among many other specifications that apply to proposed changes to the built environment. In other words, these maps indicate how much and what type of space you can build on, whether your development or redevelopment plans conform to a list of conditions, and architectural rules. Fees are imposed by the public planning bodies that review applications for permits to build, remodel, or demolish real estate.

Causes and Consequences of Housing Price Increases

Since about 1965, the odds that the owners of vacant land would be allowed to build have been decreasing in the regions housing demands have been driven up by growth in employment and newcomers. And since about that same time, there have been cutbacks in federal and state expenditures for roads, utilities, drainage, and other improvements needed to make vacant land accessible so that home builders could obtain enough land to build sufficient numbers of single- and multifamily units to satisfy consumer demands for new homes.

The cost of vacant land that could be approved as a site for development— on the block where you live or anywhere in your community, town, or city—has increased. Consequently, the price or rent of your home and all the other houses, apartments, and condominiums in your area has increased and has continued to increase (although during the years before the end of the past century, there were a few very brief interruptions in the progressive increases). This price escalation was particularly great between 2001 and 2007 and came to be referred to as the "housing price bubble."

When elected officials of the federal government saw housing prices climbing at a much faster rate than consumer incomes, they became concerned about the slowdown in the rates of homeownership. Fewer households could afford to make that first purchase that would make them homeowners. To counter the potential drop in the number of first-time home buyers, the federal government began chopping away at safeguards that had been put in place to discourage lenders from providing mortgage loans to borrowers who could not pay back. These safeguards were part of the New Deal of President Franklin D. Roosevelt during the Great Depression of the 1930s.

Starting with the administration of Jimmy Carter and continuing through the presidency of George W. Bush, lending standards were relaxed. Housing prices continued to escalate. Americans began take for granted that housing prices would always rise. It was inevitable, sort of like a financial force that only lately began to exert itself.

The timing of when Americans began to act on their belief in this inevitability was wonderfully serendipitous for lending institutions. Here is what happened: Americans were buying more from overseas than they exported—the result was an outflow of U.S. cash to the foreign nations we were buying from greater than the inflow of foreign currency to us. With their excess of U.S. dollars, countries such as China, among other exporters of goods to the United States, were purchasing U.S. bonds and other securities, effectively sending back U.S. money to us. The dollars we send overseas to pay for the foreign-made goods we buy return to finance Washington's deficits and soak up Wall Street's securities.

Never at a loss for ingenious ways to marry lenders to borrowers, and to make profits from the marriages, Wall Street invented securitized mortgages. Banks and mortgage brokers issued mortgage loans to individual home buyers, and then sold these mortgages to investment bankers and mortgage companies for a little less than the face value of the mortgages. The buyers of the individual mortgages packaged them into securities that could be sold to investors. The packaged securities were subdivided into groups of mortgages considered to be of similar risk. These groups, or "tranches" (from the French word for "slice"), were sold as individual securities or as securities containing several tranches of mortgages. Repackaging and subsequent resale of these tranches was not uncommon.

So far, you should be able to see how more mortgage money became available from lenders. Much of the newly issued mortgage money was lent to homeowners who were still paying off their existing mortgages but who saw the opportunity to "cash in" on the escalating value of their homes. The difference between the balance on the existing mortgage on a home and the new and higher market value of that same home is called equity. If the home that was bought for $100,000 was now worth $300,000, the homeowner could now use the $200,000 equity in the home as collateral against a new loan. This refinance gave the homeowner cash to pay for remodeling the home, buy a new car, pay for a child's college education, or any other major expenditure.

Some of the flood of dollars available to American investment bankers and mortgage companies were loaned to households whose credit history and incomes made it very likely that they would repay the loan. Such loans on housing are referred to as prime mortgages, whose issuance would be considered prudent by third-party evaluators. The prudence of loans made to households with a shaky credit history and without proof that they had enough income to make it possible for them to pay off the loan would be questionable. Such questionable or higher risk loans to home buyers became known as subprime loans. The due diligence or underwriting process by which the applicants of such loans were qualified was often driven more by the desire to make such loans than by carefully gauging the ability of the borrower to make the stipulated payments.

Not only were the long-term interest rates on subprime loans higher than on mortgages issued to "prime" borrowers, the up-front fees charged were also higher. These higher fees made subprime mortgages particularly lucrative for lending institutions. Therefore it should have come as no surprise that mortgage brokers and employees of mortgage companies, including those who entered the rapidly expanding real estate lending industry, would enthusiastically sell subprime mortgages to home buyers. As we will discuss later, the federal regulatory barriers that would have made the issuance of the subprime mortgages difficult, and in many cases illegal, were removed as housing prices increased. Furthermore, little regulatory control constrained investment bankers as they wrote and marketed contracts called derivatives that promised protection from mortgage defaults or changes in prevailing interest rates. Over time, as the scale of mortgage lending grew, an increasingly large percentage of subprime loans were included in the securitized packages traded in the financial community.

The heavy, long-term burden of paying off subprime loans was hidden from borrowers through interest teaser rates that were very low in the early years of the mortgage but adjusted upward in later years. Private mortgage insurers, including those that had once been part of the national government, such as the Federal National Mortgage Association (Fannie Mae) and the Federal Home Mortgage Corporation (Freddie Mac), were encouraged by members of Congress and occupants of the White House to continue insuring such loans. As long as housing prices continued to escalate, strapped mortgage borrowers could refinance their homes, perpetuating an ever-rising sequence of rising prices and mortgage debt.

For some time, this "too good to be true" sequence appeared to bestow a self-replenishing piggy bank on all homeowners. But by 2007 prices reached a level that made many prime mortgage borrowers and those lucky enough to have paid off their mortgages think, "I am glad I bought my house when I did because I couldn't afford to buy my own house today."

Sure enough, "if it's too good to be true, then it isn't true" was proven as housing prices stabilized in 2007 and began to dive in 2008. Initially, subprime mortgages and then some overextended prime mortgages began to go into default. As those defaults grew into news events, more and more banking and investment imprudences—and worse—became known.

The Beginning of Mortgage Defaults

From July of 2006 to January of 2009, when what was termed the *housing price bubble* had burst, the median price of homes in the United States fell by 26 percent. Disposable income during this period had grown by 9 percent. As a result, housing costs relative to income dropped below what they had been in 1968.[1] This sudden drop in what homes were worth was, in effect, a drop in the nation's wealth and became a bomb that crippled our economy and threw the banking system into a catatonic state.

The Obama administration came into office facing both a major economic recession and a financial panic. The word *recession* is used to indicate a period of negative growth in both jobs and income. When this negative growth reaches the point of very large-scale losses of jobs and decreases in economic activity, such as occurred during the 1930s, the state of the economy is referred to as a depression.

The rise in mortgage defaults caused a drop in the value of the mortgages included as assets on the balance sheets of banks and other financial institutions that are mortgage lenders. Mortgages that had been considered good assets turned into "toxic" assets. As bankers always do, once they sense the boat is tipping, they all rush to the other side of the boat. That is what happened when toxic assets were identified on the books of private lending institutions and such loan-insuring organizations as Fannie Mae and Freddie Mac. Banking institutions went from lending too much to lending too little.

Builders who recently had no trouble selling close to 2 million newly constructed homes a year had seen their inventories of unsold homes grow since late 2007. By mid-2008, construction of new homes had slowed to a crawl. This reduction in economic activity threw the employees and suppliers of builders out of work; even harder hit were the legions of real estate finance specialists who had been busily selling and paving the way for mortgages to buyers. Thus, the end of the very long period of soaring housing prices directly brought a significant section of the economy to its knees as housing production dropped.

Even more disastrous was the freezing of the capital market as lenders who had poured money into sound and unsound mortgages and other forms of borrowing grew fearful of making loans—even to financially sound households and businesses having the wherewithal to pay back the loans. After only a few months in office, President Barack Obama's secretary of the treasury, Timothy Geithner, made available up to $2 trillion from the U.S. Treasury to back the buying up of the bad loans, now classified as toxic assets, from banks and other financial institutions. This was done with the hope that such strengthening of bank balance sheets would encourage these institutions to get back into the lending business. In a direct effort to reverse the downward trend of the nation's economy, the Federal Reserve Bank, under Chairman Ben Bernanke, also bought billions in long-term Treasury bonds. This was the modern-day equivalent of printing money. Toward that same end, the president and Congress authorized a huge stimulus package of spending.

The frightening economic instability that history will record as the recession and banking panic of 2007 is only one of the unintended wrongs that resulted from the restrictions that the folks at city halls placed on development in our most economically vital urban places. Driving the price of shelter higher than it would be if local governments had permitted the building industry to supply enough new single- and multifamily houses to stay ahead, or at least even, with growth in demand has also forced up the cost of labor in the United States without enabling the higher paid workers to obtain a higher standard of living. By raising the bar of what constitutes a living wage, overly restrictive local housing rules and the failure of Washington to pay for the infrastructure supports of urban growth have downgraded the ability of America's industries to compete globally.

The same regulatory spirit that brought us the housing price bubble has also frozen the layout of urban development as well as made it difficult to replace obsolete buildings and locations. The inability of urban places to keep up with the technology of the times has curtailed America's ability to innovate, which it needs to do to compete with fast-moving businesses around the world. Perhaps worst of all are the barriers to upward social mobility and the maintenance of a large middle class, which the wrongs of local urban land-use policy have created. All these consequences of urban policies will be discussed further in this book.

By urban policies, we mean the decisions made by local governments about what can be built, rebuilt, and changed on the grounds of urban places, that is, on the land of urban places. Urban policies also include the decisions made at the federal and state levels about what local governments can decide as well as where and what state and federal governments pay to benefit urban places. These policies lay out the laws that governments enforce and under which they act.

The term *political economy* refers to the decisions made by representatives of the public that influence the inputs of private businesses and consumers into the information-processing systems called markets. The resources that we think of as having been allocated by markets are actually the result of the "votes" registered in markets by both private and public decision makers. When viewed solely from the perspective of urban development, the political economy is the sum result of urban public policy in action.

Local Political Economies Boost Housing Prices

On both coasts, communities with strong economic growth that seemed to spur migration from other parts of the country as well as immigration into the United States, thereby increasing housing demand, were the first to adopt the more restrictive policies born of the changing civic attitudes and legal environment ushered in during the 1970s. By the end of the following decade, both the effects and the political power behind the new supply-restricting regulatory policies were becoming evident.

In 1990 the Urban Land Institute supported a study of development regulations in the metropolitan jurisdictions of Sacramento, California; Nashville, Tennessee; and Orlando, Florida.[2] With regard to housing affordability, the study estimated that in 1989, development regulations in the various jurisdictions of Sacramento County added about $26,000 to the cost of a typical home, about a fifth of the median new home sales price, which was $131,000 at that time.

All three sites, according to the results of the study, had "recently experienced rapid population growth and residential development that strained the capacity of existing infrastructure and public service systems and raised issues of growth management, public finance, and environmental protection. Each site has followed a different path of regulatory response to growth-related problems." At that time, only a few jurisdictions in the Nashville area were found to "have gone beyond traditional subdivision and zoning ordinances." In Florida at that time, local governments were found to generally favor growth while local neighborhood organizations were not usually influential in project reviews. Sacramento County was reported to be devising powerful instruments to "limit, channel, and tax" residential development. Furthermore, the study reported that in Sacramento, neighborhood organizations not accountable to the local voters and taxpayers were active in planning matters. The authors of this early study of the regulatory environment that began to exist in the 1970s concluded that "municipal policies usually are designed to protect the interests of existing residents, not prospective ones."[3]

Local economic downturns and the increasing laxity and volatility of mortgage financing did create some hiccups in the price trend of regions within which jurisdictions adopted the newly politicized land-use regulations, but overall the trend of prices for housing in such regions was well ahead of price trends for other goods and services. In these regions, those who already owned houses found that the wealth creation long associated with homeownership was escalating; those who did not own housing found their access to wealth creation and upward social mobility denied.

Restrictions and Elasticity

By 2005 the restrictive, price-raising effect of the land-use regulations imposed by an increasing number of jurisdictions was apparent to those economists who studied the housing prices and the difference in housing supply elasticities between U.S. metropolitan areas. The term *supply elasticity* refers to a measure of the responsiveness of producers (the suppliers) to changes in the price of their product. That measure estimates a point on the supply curve defined as the percent change in supply divided by the percent change of price. A price change that induces proportionally more supply is referred to as more elastic supply (the percentage change in supply is greater than the percentage change in price); a price change that induces proportionally less production is referred to as less elastic supply (the percentage change in supply is less than the percentage change in price).

A careful study of forty-five U.S. metropolitan areas by John M. Quigley and Steven Raphael of the University of California, Berkeley, presented at the American Economic Association meeting in 2004, found that "estimates of the price elasticity of supply varied substantially from place to place. Metropolitan areas that were heavily regulated, according to the measure developed in Malpezzi (1996), always exhibited low elasticities." Their reference is to an earlier study done by Stephen Malpezzi, Gregory Chun, and Richard Green of the University of Wisconsin.[4]

The jurisdictions in California have been leaders in land-use regulation subject to politics. Commenting on the rise of housing costs in their home state of California, Quigley and Raphael noted that "during the past three years, housing prices in five coastal counties increased by more than 60 percent." They noted, too, that in California cities are free to set their own land-use rules with little oversight from state or other authorities.

Superstar Cities Study

A study called "Superstar Cities" by Joseph Gyourko and Todd Sinai of the Wharton School at the University of Pennsylvania and Christopher Mayer of the Graduate School of Business at Columbia University, examined differences in house prices and income growth across fifty U.S. metropolitan areas between 1950 and 2000.[5] During those fifty years, the number of families living in all U.S. metropolitan areas doubled. Nationally, housing prices were found to have increased by 1.5 percent per year faster than the consumer price index (CPI). But the rate of housing price growth was not spread evenly across the fifty metropolitan areas studied; there were wide gaps between the housing prices of cities. The inflation-adjusted prices of housing in cities that were experiencing economic prosperity, although they restricted housing development, far outpaced the rate at which prices grew in places that did not restrict the production of housing. That is, despite rising housing demand, land-use regulations followed the new pattern of restricting growth; restricted growth made the supply of housing more inelastic, causing land prices to soar and driving up the price of housing.

The study pointed to the San Francisco primary metropolitan statistical area (PMSA) as an example of fast housing price appreciation. San Francisco had an annual average housing price increase of 3.5 percent between 1950 and 2000—more than 2 percentage points per year greater than the average of all the PMSAs. San Francisco's inflation-adjusted housing prices grew 458 percent between 1950 and 2000. The Gyourko study noted that while San Francisco and Los Angeles were among the first major areas to limit housing production, areas such as Boston and New York were regulating their housing production to make it more inelastic between 1970 and 1990. The five areas that the study found to contain the fastest inflation-adjusted appreciation in housing prices between 1950 and 1980 were San Francisco, San Diego, Los Angeles, Oakland, and Seattle. All of these areas enjoyed economic growth and had significantly lower price elasticities of supply imposed by regulatory policies. Not surprisingly, given the high cost of living in the affected regions, the "Superstar Cities" study found that these cities attracted more higher-income households.

This study also evidenced that housing prices did not rise in places with strong demand but without supply restrictions. As an example of this, the study compared the population growth and housing prices experienced by San Francisco and Las Vegas. Between 1960 and 2000, the population of San Francisco grew by only 44,000 families, but housing prices between 1970 and 1990 grew between 3 and 4 percent per year. During that same period, Las Vegas grew explosively from fewer than 50,000 families in 1960 to 117,538 families by 2000. Las Vegas encouraged builders to compete in housing production so the elasticity of housing supply was high. The run-up of housing prices that followed the surge of easy credit and subprime loans accelerated both housing prices and housing production in Las Vegas during the beginning decade of the twenty-first century.

But between 1970 and 1990, Las Vegas housing prices appreciated at only about half the national average, or about .08 percent per year.

Pro-Growth City

In considering the determinants of housing prices, keep these three economic truths in mind: (a) housing markets are local; (b) capital markets are national or international; and (c) prices are always set at the margin of sales—that is, the last sale in a market. Until very recently, when the U.S. Bureau of Land Management started rationing out its vast land holdings, Las Vegas was a pro-growth city. Developers bought land at prices below what it cost to prepare the lots for development, and they built whenever they thought housing prices were high enough for them to make a profit. That is, the housing supply was very price elastic in Las Vegas.

The city's economic prosperity was boosted as it attracted workers who came partly because homeownership was affordable and left money in the budget for other expenditures. My wife and I remember eating at a restaurant in Las Vegas and talking with a waitress who asked where we lived. When we told her San Francisco, she said, "That's where I am from. I grew up in Noe Valley" (a San Francisco neighborhood). We asked her why she left San Francisco, and her answer was, "Here in Las Vegas my husband and I could afford a nice house where we could keep a dog—that's something we would never have been able to do if we stayed in San Francisco."

The competition among builders, facilitated by that city's pro-growth policies, kept sales high because home prices in Las Vegas took only a small bite out of the budgets of working couples. Housing prices went down even further as builders fought for customers who obtained subprime mortgages When too many subprime buyers in Las Vegas found they could not keep up their payments, along with the overbuilding that occurred after years of high demand and good profits, the inevitable happened—mortgages began to go into default and the price of land dropped. Builders were stuck with finished lots they could not sell for what it had cost them to bring utilities up to the lots.

Other fast-growing, economically prosperous places whose land-use regulations did not get on the supply-restricting bandwagon maintained both prosperity and affordable housing prices. The Superstar Cities database indicated that between 1980 and 2000, the inflation-adjusted housing appreciation rate was 1.8 percent in Austin, 0.07 percent in Dallas, and 2.2 percent in Atlanta. All three regions had enjoyed strong growth in jobs and population but did not impose market-neutering constraints on the housing supply. As would be expected, places with weakening economies saw housing price increases at a much slower rate than the national average. Furthermore, the study emphasized the effect that increasingly inelastic housing markets were having by making it affordable only to the rich.

TABLE 1.1

Real Annualized House Price Growth, 1950–2000

1950 Population over 500,000

Top 10 MSAs by price growth		Bottom 10 MSAs by price growth	
San Francisco	3.53	San Antonio	1.13
Oakland	2.82	Milwaukee	1.06
Seattle	2.74	Pittsburgh	1.02
San Diego	2.61	Dayton	.99
Los Angeles	2.48	Albany (NY)	.97
Portland (OR)	2.36	Cleveland	.91
Boston	2.30	Rochester (NY)	.89
Bergen-Passaic (NJ)	2.19	Youngstown-Warren	.81
Charlotte	2.18	Syracuse	.67
New Haven	2.12	Buffalo	.54

Source: Gyourko, Mayer, and Sinai, "Superstar Cities."

Table 1.1, reproduced from the Superstar Cities report, lists the real annualized housing price growth (that is, in prices that have been adjusted to take out the effect of inflation to make the prices comparable over time) of the metropolitan statistical areas with populations over five hundred thousand, which had the fastest and slowest inflation-adjusted annual housing price appreciation between 1950 and 2000.

Scottsdale, Land-Use Regulations, and Housing Prices

Gyourko's study provides strong empirical evidence of the relationship between land-use regulations and the increase of housing prices in U.S. metropolitan areas. In 2005, lawyers representing Scottsdale, Arizona, engaged my firm to conduct a study to provide the basis of my testimony in court as to the effect on the value of land that the city's removal from development of virtually all of the remaining vacant land (to create a large park) had on land next to the gateway to the park. The city had taken one-half of a large parcel of land that had recently been acquired by Toll Brothers Builders, who intended to create that gateway. At issue was the value of the land the city was taking from Toll in a condemnation action. To gauge the effect of the removal of land where development would have competed with Toll's development, we conducted an empirical analysis of the effect that supply reductions in the submarkets of a single jurisdiction had on the price of housing within that jurisdiction relative to housing prices within its broader metropolitan region.

A submarket, which in the case of urban places is usually a neighborhood, refers to a geographic area within which the price of similar products, goods, or services tends to be very similar. But because housing buyers and renters prefer to live in some submarkets more than in others, the prices of similar housing units differ from submarket to submarket.

The City of Scottsdale authorized the use of eminent domain in 1995 to acquire 36,340 acres of land, about one-third of the city, for a public park called the Preserve. These acres contained all of the vacant land in the city, except for a few in-fill sites. Most of the land in the southern two-thirds of Scottsdale had been developed with housing or other uses by 1998. The Preserve that the city decided to develop on the upper one-third of Scottsdale had been previously zoned for at least 9,813 housing units. Although there was some question about the city's ability to actually pay for all the land that would fall within the Preserve's boundaries, by 1998 voter approval of funds had convinced most developers that the Preserve lands would no longer be in the potential supply of housing lots.

To gauge the effect of this perceived reality, we used data on the median sale price of single-family houses in Scottsdale and the metropolitan region for each year from 1982 to 1998. From this data we calculated the trend of relative prices between the city and the wider region. In 1982 the median sales price of new detached single-family homes in Scottsdale was $79,456. In that same year, the median price of all new detached single-family houses sold throughout the Phoenix metropolitan area was $67,600. That is, in 1982 prices for new detached single-family homes in Scottsdale were 117.5 percent of the median price of detached single-family houses throughout the Phoenix metropolitan area. The trend of relative prices for both new homes and preexisting or resold homes continued upward all the way to 2003. Figure 1.1 shows this trend of relative prices for both new and resold detached single-family houses. Note that the line representing the relative price of new homes seems to break upward in 1998 while the price of resold or existing homes sold each year follows the previous trend without a break.[6]

We calculated the equation of the relationship between the relative price of new single-family detached homes in the city and the region from 1982 through 1998; we perceived the trend broke in 1998, which suggests that a change in the underlying relationship occurred at this time.[7] The equation of the trend from 1982 to 1998 was then used to forecast the relative price of new single-family detached housing from 1999 through 2005. The results of that forecast were then compared with data on new home sales in Scottsdale and the region for that same period. The difference between the relative price forecast from the 1982 to 1998 trend and the relative price calculated from the actual sales of such

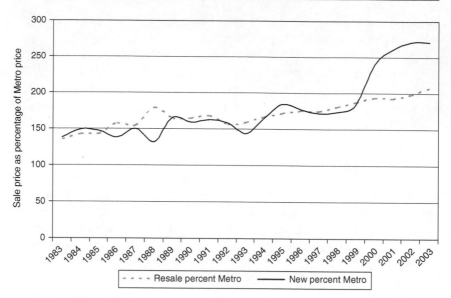

FIGURE 1.1 Scottsdale single-family median sales price as a percentage of Phoenix metropolitan area price

new houses in the years from 1999 to 2005 is an indication of the effect that removing the Preserve lands from the potential supply of housing had on the relative price of new houses in Scottsdale as compared to the entire region. Table 1.2 summarizes these calculations and compares the actual premium paid for new single-family detached houses in Scottsdale from 1996 through 2005.

The statistical analyses suggest that the removal of the potential residential lands and the addition of recreational benefits of the new park and preserve were together expected to raise the relative price of new single-family detached homes in Scottsdale by approximately 30 percent by 2005. I testified to that effect in the Arizona court.

IF YOU REMEMBER THE LESSONS taught in your introductory economics class, you will not be surprised by either the nationwide or single metropolitan area studies summarized. Although urban markets may be complex, they do not violate the laws of supply and demand. No matter how good the motives underlying regulatory actions, they restrict the potential ability to develop and redevelop in one or more areas without offsetting such restrictions with equally great increases in the potential supply within similar submarkets. The net effect is to drive up the price of the precluded land-use type.

You can distinguish the neighborhood where you live from other neighborhoods in terms of how they appeal to you as a place to live. This ability of people to distinguish and prefer some areas over others is what makes neighborhoods submarkets. As the price of housing in one submarket changes to make the

TABLE 1.2

Estimated Scale of Price Effect

Year	Actual single-family median sale price		Actual Scottsdale premium %	Premium predicted using data from 1982 to 1998* %	Single-family median sale price based on predicted premium $	Percent supply effect from 1982 to 1998 %
	Phoenix Metro Area $	Scottsdale $				
1996	130,750	231,650	177.2	180.6		
1997	136,130	233,320	171.4	183.5		
1998	139,070	240,980	173.3	186.4		
1999	146,710	270,260	184.2	180.6	264,996	1.9
2000	150,770	362,280	240.3	183.5	276,671	23.6
2001	156,560	409,045	261.3	186.4	291,803	28.7
2002	159,990	433,335	270.9	189.3	302,803	30.1
2003	173,240	469,885	271.3	192.1	332,868	29.2
2004	195,000	569,095	291.8	195.0	380,293	33.2
2005	251,795	716,670	284.6	197.9		

Sources: Compiled by Gruen Gruen + Associates and Johnson & Zaddack using data from *Arizona Business Monthly* and the ASU Housing Study.

*Equation using 1982–1998 data: $P = -5574.88 + 2.879196 \times year$. $R^2 = 0.6561$.

houses within it more or less affordable, the effective demand that consumers generate for that neighborhood and the houses in other neighborhoods is changed.

That housing prices cannot go up forever became apparent in 2007, when even the rich felt that housing prices were over the top. In 2008 local housing markets saw prices implode as subprime mortgage holders could no longer keep up their payments.

Confirming the Superstar Cities Study

In July 2008, three noted housing scholars, Edward L. Glaeser of Harvard University and Joseph Gyourko and Albert Saiz, both of the Wharton School at the University of Pennsylvania, reviewed housing prices in various metropolitan areas from 1982 through 2007.[8] Their study confirmed the conclusion of the Gyourko "Superstar Cities" study: We can know from economic theory and common sense that differences in supply conditions, whether the housing supply is price elastic or inelastic, account for a significant portion of the differences between price behaviors in different local markets. The Glaeser, Gyourko, and Saiz study also suggested that although prices escalated in virtually all markets, the length of time that prices escalate is less when elastic or unconstrained supply conditions exist than when political constraints make local conditions inelastic. One conclusion drawn from the study's extensive review of housing data is that during a rapid price escalation "bubble," price increases will be larger in metropolitan areas that are more inelastic and will be both shorter and rarer in more elastic areas.

Using data from 2000 from the Office of Federal Housing Enterprise Oversight (OFHEO), adjusted to 2007 dollars, the three scholars created an estimate of the median price of housing in metropolitan areas, which they compared with an estimate of the minimum profitable production cost of housing in each of those areas. Their study confirmed that the gap between housing prices and the cost of profitably producing housing was much greater in metropolitan areas where the supply was inelastic than where permits were still easy to obtain.

In the Orlando-Kissimmee metropolitan area, where the housing supply is elastic, the median price was estimated at $230,099, with production costs at $154,597, suggesting a gap of $75,502. The median estimated house price in the inelastic San Francisco–San Mateo–Redwood City market was $721,694 and the production costs were $209,922, a gap of $511,772. These data confirm what theory predicts, which is that land prices escalate whenever and wherever competition decreases. These results further confirm that decreasing construction costs can make only a small dent in the price of housing in comparison to the effect of opening up access to the efficient use of vacant and underutilized land.

The higher housing prices that resulted from supply restrictions reduced the ability of Americans to become homeowners. This is reflected in the lower rate at which homeownership has grown in states such as California, which have led the nation in market-stifling planning regulations. But overall, until 2007, homeownership continued to increase in spite of rising prices because of the availability of inexpensive and abundant credit. Faith in the long-run investment worth of housing spurred demand in communities with healthy economies, despite rising prices. Readily available credit also encouraged demand from investors seeking the benefits of the appreciation in market value of a single-family home.

The long period of housing price increases fed on itself, as the effective demand for housing was propelled above sustainable levels by the toxic mixture of unrealistic consumer expectations and the imprudent mortgage loans to home buyers. With rising house prices—the topic at virtually every gathering of people in regions blessed by economic and population growth—renters able to obtain mortgage financing rushed to become homeowners to get in on the housing wealth train.

Housing Equity and Consumer Spending

Many existing homeowners tapped into the rising value of their housing equity to raise cash for other expenditures. The November 8, 2007, *New York Times* chronicled the high-spending ways of Marshall Whittey, whose wedding on "a sumptuous private estate in the Napa Valley" and a honeymoon in Tahiti, were among the expenditures paid for with money from refinancing his home. When the value of this home dropped, Mr. Whittey started to economize. Reminiscing about the days when the value of his home was soaring, Whittey, aged thirty-three, was quoted as saying: "It used to be that if I wanted it, I'd just go and buy it and finance it."

Mr. Whittey's high-spending ways ended, and the unsustainable migration of renters into the ranks of homeowners came to an end when the support of overly risky and imprudent mortgage lending was withdrawn. By the spring of 2007, housing sales and prices dropped. Hardest hit was less expensive housing where sales had been financed with subprime mortgages.

The Housing Meltdown

Because of the role that housing equity had come to play in financing a broad variety of consumer expenditures, the "housing meltdown" had a greater recessionary impact than had been the case during earlier housing production slowdowns. A paper written by James Kennedy and former Federal Reserve Chairman Alan Greenspan was quoted in the *New York Times* as estimating that "from 2004 through 2006, Americans pulled about $840 billion a year out of residential real estate, with home-value backed lines of credit and refinanced mortgages. These so-called home equity withdrawals financed as much as $310 billion a year in personal consumption."[9]

Like a drug that can save lives if taken in moderate doses but can cause death if too much is consumed, mortgage credit can help access homeownership and build wealth. If loan payments fall within the income capability of borrowers, mortgages permit the building up of personal wealth over time. But what happened over time was that lending practices, encouraged by ever-rising house prices and lax governmental regulation, included initial low-interest teaser loans. The interest on these loans subsequently was increased, requiring payments beyond what homeowners' incomes could allow. Many such borrowers did not anticipate this. They expected that ever-rising house prices would permit refinancing to cover their income shortfalls.

The 1930s Great Depression

Like medicines taken wisely, credit can be beneficial to consumers and the economy. Consumer credit, the ability to borrow in order to buy, has probably provided the greatest boost to economic growth and expansion since the invention of money freed buyers and sellers from the need to identify and barter mutually desirable items. Even after the United States became an urban nation, most of the home loans available were short-term, interest-only mortgages that usually required high down payments. The difficulty of obtaining mortgage loans contributed to the prevalence of renters among the inhabitants of the urban places of the eighteenth and nineteenth centuries. The "weak" form of credit would be a factor contributing to the Great Depression, during which more than 250,000 Americans lost their homes each year between 1930 and 1935 to foreclosures on loans of this sort.

The census for 1930 indicated there were slightly fewer than 30 million homes in the United States that year. This suggests a foreclosure rate of about eight-tenths of 1 percent, or 0.8 percent, per year, with around 4 percent of all homes foreclosed by 1935. Default rates were much higher. David C. Wheelock of the Federal Reserve Bank of St. Louis found that as of January 1, 1934, 43.8 percent of urban, owner-occupied homes with a first mortgage were in default.[10] At the end of the first quarter of 2007, Standard & Poor's reported that just under 1 percent of all residential mortgages were in foreclosure. At that same quarter, 3.71 percent of all residential mortgage holders were delinquent, that is, behind on one or more payments, while subprime loans had a delinquency rate of 18.79 percent.[11] While the United States housing credit situation was dire during the 2008 recession, it was not nearly as bad as what occurred in the depression of the 1930s.

The economic debacle of the Great Depression burned banks as well as homeowners. As a result, the American mortgage system was reinvented by Franklin D. Roosevelt's New Deal. The federal government stepped in, initially to buy defaulted mortgages to be subsequently resold as government-insured securities. Fully amortized mortgages that required borrowers to pay off principal along with interest during the twenty-year or longer life of the loan became standard for decades. After 1945, with the end of World War II, further liberalization of mortgages to returning G.I.s lowered down payments and interest rates, causing the proportion of Americans who owned rather than rented to escalate dramatically. According to the prewar 1940 census, 43.6 percent of American households owned their homes. The 1980 Census of Population and Housing reported that 64 percent of Americans lived in a housing unit to which they held title.

During the 1980s, starting on a small scale, American banking and financial entrepreneurs revolutionized mortgage lending in a way that would come to dwarf the impact of how federal insurance eased the availability of mortgage credit. Mortgage insurance was privatized, and more significantly, the United States' investment banking community figured out how to borrow money from all over the world in order to buy packages of mortgages. The kind of borrowing from local banks portrayed in *It's a Wonderful Life*, with Jimmy Stewart playing the role of small-town banker George Bailey, became a thing of the past, even though the movie is still played on television every Christmas season. Mortgages were packaged in risk-similar tranches and then sold to investors over the world.

Packaged Mortgages and the New Intermediaries

Not coincidentally, the Wall Street invention of packaged mortgages became increasingly popular during the last two decades of the twentieth century as the United States' trade deficit put trillions of U.S. dollars in the hands of foreigners. America's foreign creditors preferred reinvesting in the world's most secure economy rather than purchasing its goods and services. The resulting vast increase in supply of mortgage money drove interest rates down. It also created a new group of mortgage intermediaries, including banks that no longer lent their depositors money but served as middlemen between homeowners and those who sold securities backed by mortgages. As long as housing prices kept rising, mortgage money became available to households with less income and fewer assets than had previously been required by mortgage lenders. By the mid-1990s, the securitization of mortgages—packaging mortgages into investment securities—worked in combination with the success of the Alan Greenspan–led Federal Reserve system in holding down inflation to bring mortgage rates to historic lows.

Stifling the Threat to Growth of Homeownership

In 1995, because they saw rising prices as a threat to the further growth of homeownership, President Bill Clinton's secretary of Housing and Urban Development (HUD), Henry G. Cisneros, worked with mortgage lenders to implement a national homeowners' strategy that would make mortgage funding available to an even higher proportion of Americans. The president and his secretary of HUD were right to strive toward the goal of expanded homeownership as a foundation for individual and civic welfare. Perhaps the most convincing and succinct argument for homeownership as an important step up the ladder to wealth and social mobility was written by Harvard professor Henry Louis Gates Jr. in a November 18, 2007, *New York Times* op-ed piece. In considering the broadening class divide among African Americans, Gates reported, "I have been studying the family trees of twenty successful African Americans, people in fields ranging from entertainment and sports (Oprah Winfrey, the track star Jackie Joyner-Kersee) to space travel and medicine (the astronaut Mae Jemison and Ben Carson, a pediatric neurosurgeon). And I've seen an astonishing pattern: 15 of the 20 descend from at least one line of former slaves who managed to obtain property by 1920—a time when only 25 percent of all African-American families owned property." He went on to say: "The historical basis for the gap between the black middle class and underclass shows that ending discrimination, by itself, would not eradicate black poverty and dysfunction. We also need intervention to promulgate a middle-class ethic of success among the poor, while expanding opportunities for economic betterment." Gates suggested a program similar to Margaret Thatcher's program in Britain, which allowed 1.5 million residents of public housing projects in that country to become homeowners in the 1980s.

Neither Gates nor I are suggesting that homeownership alone is all that is required for familial social and economic success. Clearly, individual initiative, feasibility, and opportunities always play a role. Gates notes, for example, that ten years after slavery ended, Oprah Winfrey's great-grandfather Constantine Winfrey bartered cotton he had picked on his own time for eighty acres of prime bottom land in Mississippi. This was a man who taught himself to read while accumulating that cotton. Clearly, Oprah's great-grandfather was admirably unique in many ways, but his success at becoming a property owner played an important role in moving his descendents well up the ladder of economic and social success in America.

Henry Cisneros had a sincere and deep commitment to increasing homeownership rates, particularly among minorities. I met Cisneros a few times in 1978, when he was on the City Council in San Antonio and I was preparing an analysis of the fiscal impact of the alternatives being considered by the city for its first citywide general plan. In addition to a report, my work provided the city with a model that could be used to compare the costs and revenues likely to result from alternative growth scenarios. On the day I made my final presentation to the San Antonio City Council, my summary of the report seemed to be understood and well received. But when I tried to explain the purpose and methodology of the model, the looks on the faces of some council members made it clear that my presentation was not faring well. As I tried, but failed, to recover during the question period, Councilman Cisneros rose to his feet. In a quiet but clear and 100 percent accurate description of the purpose and methodology of my model, Cisneros did superbly what I had been unable to accomplish. At that time, Cisneros led the fight to give the long neglected, mostly Hispanic South San Antonio area an even break in terms of city services. He subsequently became mayor of San Antonio.

As the head of HUD, Cisneros successfully campaigned for billions of dollars in mortgage insurance for first time home buyers as a part of his National Homeownership Strategy. The number of years of stable income required for mortgages that could be insured was lowered from five to three years, and lenders were allowed to hire appraisers directly, rather than depend on a government panel for appraisals of home value. In an October 19, 2008, article in the *New York Times*, Cisneros argued that it was impossible to know in the beginning that the federal push to increase homeownership would end so badly. The article indicates Cisneros felt that once the housing boom got going, "laws and regulation barely had a chance." He is quoted as saying: "You think you have a finely tuned instrument that you can use to say: Stop! We're at 69 percent homeownership. We should not go further. There are people who should remain renters. But you really are just given a sledge hammer and an ax. They are blunt tools."

The Great Depression had taught that the regulatory barriers to mortgage lending, and therefore homeownership, must be kept up. When those barriers were torn down through the efforts of well-meaning homeownership advocates such as Henry Cisneros, only the bursting bubble of housing prices could stop the explosion of imprudent but seductive lending.

Home values exceed the value of all mutual funds and pensions. As Gretchen Morgenson wrote in an April 8, 2007, column in the *New York Times*, once the government encouraged the middlemen who sold mortgages to make them more affordable, "lenders were off to the races." Housing prices were dramatically escalated by the financial push created by the purveyors of mortgage funds in conjunction with the supply-constraining efforts of councils and planning commissions in many regions where demand was high. By 2004 the value of all homes owned by American households reached $17 trillion—this amount exceeded the value of all corporate equity held by mutual funds and pension funds.[12]

Buoyed by supply restrictions in some of the fastest growing regions, and by the ready availability of cheap credit everywhere in the United States, housing prices rose continuously from 1995 through most of 2005. The recession of 2001 failed to interrupt this increase.[13] But by then the scale and profitability of mortgage lending led to a great increase in the number of firms and individuals in that business. As the competition between lenders with ample proceeds at their disposal intensified, the debacle of subprime mortgages picked up steam.

By 2001 the flood of easily obtainable low-interest loans acted as a stimulating drug that kicked the trend of rising prices well above the rates of increase caused by supply restrictions alone. By the end of 2005 these price increases had slowed sales and, in many markets, led to an actual decline in prices. By 2006 these slowdowns and price decreases were being referred to as a bursting "housing bubble." But to the extent that this term was apt at all, it should have been accompanied with the clarification that what blew up the bubble to the bursting point was the surge of demand created by the availability of easy mortgage loans. Subprime loans with terms that included low teaser rates that would escalate in subsequent years became a lucrative part of lenders' portfolios. A significant portion of those who used such subprime mortgages to become homeowners lost their homes through foreclosures in 2006 and 2007. But the focus on the short-term, cyclical effect of overly aggressive mortgage lending obscured the long-run effect of the supply inelasticities induced by the new political economy introduced into an increasing number of regional markets.

You already read a few pages earlier that much of the capital scooped up by mortgage securitization would not have been available except for the willingness of exporters to the United States to finance the huge trade deficit that resulted. Year after year, there was a huge gap between what American consumers bought and what American firms exported. Had the countries that produced the shiploads of goods bought in U.S. stores, or had the suppliers of oil and services not been willing to lend us back what we had paid them, interest rates in the United States would have soared and the U.S. economy would have soured. Instead, because U.S. capital markets were loaded with dollars, interest rates plummeted and the economy was bolstered. In combination with rising housing prices, the availability of new sources and new types of mortgages had pushed American mortgage debt from 20 percent of total household income in 1949 to 73 percent of total household income and more than 60 percent of the nation's gross domestic product (GDP) in 2006.[14]

Righting the Wrongs

The prevailing social culture in America is not willing to navigate a U-turn and return the helm of decisions about land use to an unfettered market. Nor is there a need to throw out the use of tools, such as zoning, exactions (fees paid by a developer to proceed with plans to build), or design controls that determine what style and architectural details will be allowed, or to abandon the public capital budgeting process. But if these tools are to be used in a manner that does not restrict the amount of housing that is built or stop needed changes in the buildings and pattern of development within built-up areas, they must be redirected. The redirection I will suggest in the last chapter of this book will permit needed change and expansion. Most importantly, planning rules and practices must be redirected to encourage and facilitate, rather than restrict, competition among private land developers, builders, and those who finance their efforts. If allowed to compete, the private sector would produce the amounts and types of residential and nonresidential additions and modifications to urban space needed to increase the living standards of residents and the effectiveness of local businesses.

Local plans must allocate sufficient lands and grant builders the right to the development densities that would allow them to build more housing per square foot of land to ensure that developers will not only be able to respond to the demands of residents and businesses but they—not only developers but investors and builders as well—will be forced to do so under competitive conditions. The rules emanating from local and regional political bodies should open urban frontiers by facilitating the competition that will hold down the price and increase the quality of urban residential neighborhoods and workplaces.

The next chapters of this book revisit conditions in the urban land-use markets as they existed under a now-vanishing political economy that empowered free markets to make decisions. The land economics that operated under the old capitalistic system will be discussed here, not to replicate those rules but to learn how the market operated within the capitalistic laboratory. Even though such an unrestrained market is not likely to return, those who set plans and policies aimed in the direction of such an economy have a great deal to learn from this history. To reset local land-use rules beneficially to influence rather than replace the market requires an understanding of how development markets function.

There is a silver lining in the dark clouds of recession caused by the bursting housing price bubble. The fact that housing is more affordable today than it has been in approximately thirty years creates an opportunity. The final chapter of this book presents suggested changes in urban policies that can keep housing from once again taking larger and larger bites out of household incomes. Because there would then be more household income for other purposes, living standards would rise and the American workforce would become more cost competitive. I also suggest changes in the way cities currently freeze obsolete buildings and clusters of buildings in place. Allowing appropriate change rather than seeking to preserve all that exists will release the full economic power of the urban environment.

2

Vitality from Growth and Freedom to Change

Tearing Down City Walls Releases Constrained Energy

Business Energy, Civic Energy, and Creative Energy

You know from chapter 1 that when housing production is constrained in cities or towns with the potential for growth, homes in those places become less affordable. Rising housing costs lower the living standards of residents and make it more difficult for renters to become owners. Working men and women react by seeking higher wages and moving to areas where costs are lower, especially housing costs. Lowering housing affordability and its quality per dollar also lessens the ability of local businesses to attract workers with the skills they require. So constraining housing production in an area increases the price of housing in that area, which motivates workers to relocate. All three effects together worsen the competitive strength that the local labor market contributes to the economy of that area.

Higher housing prices squeeze the budgets of locals who do not already own a home. Labor is more costly and skilled workers and professionals harder to find. But what happens in the local labor market is only a part of the story of what happens to the regional economy when the frontiers of urban places start to close. Consider the following frontier-closing, growth-restraining restrictions on the use of land:

- Barriers on outward expansion
- Limits on housing density
- Refusals to allow changes in existing structures
- Restrictions on the conversion of land from one use to another
- Time-consuming approval policies for commercial and industrial uses

- Limits on the amount of building per year
- Special development fees not related to the actual costs of induced public services

All of these restrictions make it harder to keep the space occupied by the drivers of the local economy attuned to technological advances and location-related efficiencies. In the fast-moving arena of the twenty-first-century's global economy, the office and industrial complexes of the nation's cities and suburbs must not be deprived of innovation-encouraging clusters of activities, or of production-enhancing efficiencies, lest they seize like the moving metal parts of a machine deprived of lubricant.

Because the whole of the nation's economy is the cumulative result of the economic activities of its urban places, closing the frontiers of urban places greatly weakens the ability of the nation to compete in the global economic battleground.

Stockholm and Barcelona

The advantages of open urban frontiers within cities and at their edges can be observed by looking at the tremendous burst of industry and wealth in medieval Europe, when walls no longer limited the geographic expansion of cities. Consider Stockholm in the seventeenth century. It had been until 1627 a small village with a population of about 12,500. That year, the government of Sweden allowed the wall and gates of the city to be torn down so that the surrounding land and islands could urbanize, prosper, and grow. Soon after, Stockholm became a trade and ironworks center, growing into an economically powerful city of more than 60,000 people over the next century.

Barcelona is another example of the way urban places grow in productive power when they are allowed to expand and change. Spain's central government refused to give Barcelona permission to tear down and expand beyond its medieval walls. When it tore down the walls in 1854, clusters of textile and other industries grew in size and efficiency. By the end of the nineteenth century, newly industrialized Barcelona was one of Europe's three most populous and cosmopolitan urban places. The economic surge that resulted from the expansion of Barcelona's development base gave birth to the Catalan renaissance of art and culture.

The chief city planner of mid-nineteenth-century Barcelona was Antonio Raira. He did a magnificent job of laying out the new districts of the expanding city. Buildings such as the Church of the Sagrada Familia, designed by the great sculptor and architect Antonio Gaudi, continue to this day to attract admirers from around the world. (Although the church is not yet completed, and will not be for several decades, the use of materials and extent of completion fascinate professional builders as well as those who simply come to see it.) Wealth, art, and culture flowered in that city from the lifting of the restrictions on the growth of Barcelona in 1854 until 1939. In the latter year, the oppressive national regime under the leadership of the dictator Francisco Franco crushed the civic life of Barcelona. When today's tourists, as well as Barcelona's natives, stroll down the beautiful, pedestrian-friendly Rambla Boulevard and admire the city's architecture, they are enjoying what happened when urban growth and change were allowed to flourish.

The Effect of Land Restrictions on the Building Industry

Most American households have never lived in a new house for the same reason that many Americans have always bought used cars. "Previously owned or occupied" houses tend to be cheaper than newly constructed houses, just as used automobiles usually do not cost as much as this year's new models sitting in dealers' showrooms.

Filtration and Gentrification

The name urban economists have given to the process that changes the price and quality of existing houses over time is filtration. Depending on the relationships between housing supply and demand over time, housing prices and quality can filter up, filter down, or remain unchanged.

The prices of all the homes in a neighborhood will move up and down together. Within neighborhoods, differences in house prices will tend to be small, and they are accounted for by differences in the characteristics that consumers see as contributing to housing quality, such as the number of rooms, general condition, and features such as pools or the latest in kitchen equipment and bathroom fixtures. Changes in the region-wide demand-and-supply relationship will tend to push the prices of all the houses within all neighborhoods up or down, but not at the same rate.

Consumers who are seeking to buy a house tend to benefit when the downward movement of housing prices, or "downward price filtration," is accompanied with maintenance or improvement in housing quality. Conversely, when downward price filtration is accompanied by decreased quality, consumers are worse off.

The neighborhood-changing process called gentrification occurs when some housing price increases are induced by housing quality improvements that attract or retain residents with higher incomes than what had previously typified the income levels of neighborhood residents. As the process continues, the neighborhood will provide over time few homes to residents with lower incomes. Only if region-wide additions to housing stock exceed increases in demand will downward price changes provide additional units to lower-income families within some of the region's neighborhoods. Whether quality declines with prices will again be determined by the supply-and-demand relationships in the neighborhoods that serve the less affluent. If there is an ample supply of housing within neighborhoods where prices are relatively affordable, lower-income buyers and renters can choose among alternative sellers, and landlords will have to maintain quality to gain occupants for their units. But if the supply of housing in neighborhoods where prices are affordable to the less affluent is only equal to or less than the quantity of housing sought, then landlords and sellers will not have to maintain properties to find buyers or tenants, and housing quality will decline.

If permitted to do so, builders will rarely stop building houses until they have wrung the last dollar of profit from the opportunities they perceived in the market for new houses. In the past this usually meant that building continued until the number of vacant new units went unpurchased for a long enough time to push prices and rents below what was required for builders to break even on construction. In regions where the new political economy of publicly determined residential land availability has great influence, new construction is stopped by the development approval process before housing prices are weighed down by the scale of competitive building.

Inputs to Housing Production—Costs and Profits

In regions that were not subject to a political economy that controlled the supply of housing rather than supervising what was built, competition in housing markets not only drove prices down but also wrung excess profits out of each of the inputs into housing production. Material costs were hammered down to near their costs of production as suppliers fought for construction business.

Construction labor costs vary greatly with the strength of local unions. Typically, nonunion labor is less expensive than the rates agreed to by builders who have signed union contracts. Some jurisdictions pass laws that require the use of union labor or the payment of hourly wage rates equal to "prevailing rates," which are the equivalent of what is called for in union contracts. Moreover, housing labor unions require work rules in contracts—some are rules necessary for safety; others, perhaps not—although all work rules are costly. But the power of the unions to maintain high wage rates and to demand costly work rules was limited by two threats: nonunion labor and its lower wages; and manufactured components brought to the housing site rather than produced on site by union labor.

Entitlement

Basic economics courses teach that the factors of the production of goods and services are land, labor, material, capital, and entrepreneurship. From the perspective of homebuilders in the increasingly complex, uncertain, and contentious process of obtaining approval for the use of land for residential development in many regions, entitlement has become a sixth factor of production. Entitlement is the term given to the approvals required before a real estate development and construction project can proceed.

Before the recession of 2009, the number of sites entitled for residential development in economically growing regions was below the demand for such sites. As a result, unentitled land, even if it was advantageously located, was worth significantly less than land that had been rewarded with entitlement. Until all the appropriate entitlement granting documents are signed, there is always a risk that permission to build will not be granted. In addition to assuming this risk, obtaining entitlement adds time, costs, and the "brain damage" associated with convincing the neighbors, planners, and elected officials that they should grant the right to build on a specific piece of land. The costs of this effort include paying for mountains of reports, including thick environmental documents and engineering, planning, and economic studies, which are frequently debated in public meetings at great length by speakers who have infrequently actually read all the documents. Courtrooms, too, are crowded with litigants arguing about the accuracy and interpretation of environmental and other studies. During the 1970s, decisions in the courts and by voters in local elections shifted the power to determine the uses of urban land from developers who respond to market signals to local public officials who respond to voters. In their many forms, the entitlement battles that have taken place since 1970 increased the billings of environmental analysts, lawyers, planners, engineers, and even economists.

Once entitlement became a privilege to be granted by a gauntlet of departments, agencies, commissions, and officials rather than a right inherent in the passage of a general plan and zoning document, developers could no longer count on being able to build on land they owned or optioned. The term option refers to a contract under which the owner, or optionor, is paid to grant the optionee a right to buy the land in the future at a specified price. Because unentitled sites are worth less than entitled land and the land owners know that obtaining entitlement is both risky and expensive, the option price is usually small compared to the price put on the purchase of the land. But even if legal control of land is bestowed by outright ownership of an option, developers still need to seek the right to use the land for their intended purpose. That is, they need to obtain entitlement.

The role played by entitlement changed the business dynamics of residential development. The quest for the right to build paved a new lane—the entitlement lane—in the road to profit. The land acquisition managers and entitlement managers within building and development companies became the new princes and princesses of their industry.

Consolidation of the Building Industry

The home-building industry has consolidated largely as a result of these new business dynamics, and due to the increased capital and organizational capability required to successfully meet the challenge of obtaining entitlement from the body politic. There are today fewer companies producing housing than there were in 1970. Many of the smaller local companies that built most of America's housing have been absorbed into behemoth national land-developing and building companies. The common shares ownership (that is, the stock) of most of these companies is traded on national exchanges. These companies usually have a considerable inventory of land under option or purchased and are shepherding this inventory through the regulatory review and entitlement hearings.

The costs of land and entitlement have gone up much more than the costs of the material, labor, or capital inputs into housing development and construction. As the costs of land and entitlement have increased, so also have the profit margins of the builders, but not so for the builders in regions of the country where residential land-use allocation is still left largely to the private sector. During 2004 and 2005, before the slowdown in housing sales that occurred in 2006, national building companies such as Toll Brothers bought large chunks of land. They bought land even in housing markets such as the greater Phoenix area, where housing economics susceptible to politics has only recently begun to replace market economics in determining how much and what type of housing will be added to the existing supply.

By 2007, as the subprime mortgage debacle caromed through financial markets, the entire U.S. economy slowed and housing demand dropped as lenders tightened their rules and speculative investors left the housing market. National builders took large losses because they had to drop the value of the land they had as assets on their balance sheets.

The slowdown in housing demand will not continue forever. And unless local regulatory policies change, residential lands will once again become scarce, causing housing prices to once again escalate.

After reading all I have told you about the costs, uncertainties, and general aggravation of the political process that builders must go through to entitle land, you might expect that the large, nationwide builders would support reforms to this process. Don't count on it. What builders and land developers have learned is that the costly difficulties they put up with do pay off in higher profits. Restrictions on the amount and density of residential development increase housing shortages and drive up prices. The major players in the residential construction industry have learned that higher prices that result from restrictions on supply more than offset the higher costs of obtaining the entitlements that permit them to stay in the game. Put simply, as housing prices go up, the value of entitled land increases by more than the costs of obtaining entitlement.

But first-time home buyers get no benefits from the higher prices they pay. If you and I already own our home, we may think we are better off because of the "wealth effect" of seeing the value of our home increase. But these good feelings are an illusion. What we do not see is the impetus this gives to the higher costs of everything else we buy and the way these prices and the public policies that caused them weaken the vigor of our economy.

Effects on Households

A House Is Not a Retirement Savings Account

Rising house prices benefit some owners, but only in the short run. They hurt all homeowners in the long run. Housing-induced wealth buoyed Americans who, like me, owned a home bought for a price well below its present value. When prices go up, the ownership of a home or homes (many people own more than one home) pushes up net worth and expands credit at the bank or mortgage broker. That wealth from homeownership persisted upward for decades from 1970 until it peaked and began to turn downward by the credit crunch in 2007.

That wealth—the difference between price paid and current market value for a home—is the equity in a home. That equity is an asset; more specifically, it is a home equity asset. The trillions of dollars that these home equity assets added to household balance sheets before the "meltdown" of 2007 is one reason that government statistics during the years of housing price escalation showed a small annual difference between total household incomes and expenditures.

Federal statistics published during the last forty years have shown a declining rate of savings by U.S. households. Since 2008, that rate has started back up. It has become clear that, particularly during the housing boom years of the first part of the twenty-first century, people were cashing in some of their added housing wealth by refinancing their mortgages to take out dollars they could spend. Since the government's statistics did not account for the additions to wealth created by rising home values but looked at savings as being largely the traditional relationship between expenditures and income, the housing-finance upsurge of expenditures appeared simply to be a drop in savings.

Sacrifices and Benefits of Homeownership

Paying a mortgage is no fun. If the payments on a mortgage constitute a large part of the borrower's income, perhaps over 30 percent, the borrower will need to make sacrifices by giving up other important things. As the proportion of income required for mortgage payments is driven higher by rising house prices, the likelihood that households will be willing or able to make those sacrifices decreases. This is particularly likely to be the case for homeowners who live in a region where population and income growth have been high but residential growth constraints have been imposed. For example, in coastal California, where there has been generous mortgage lending and rising home prices, communities have lower rates of homeownership than in the Midwest and areas where decisions on housing additions are still largely in the hands of its buyers and sellers.

The likelihood that both spouses in the household will be employed is greater in communities under the influence of a politically enforced economy rather than a simple free market supply–demand economy. Long commutes to and from work are typical of these communities. In places like the San Francisco Bay region, middle-income families seeking housing they can afford have had to move out beyond growth-controlled open space to communities in the adjoining counties or beyond, where there is little or no control of land use.

California's formerly agricultural communities, such as Tracy in San Joaquin County and Modesto in Merced County, at one time allowed development of housing built on still inexpensive land that was affordable to young families with one or more workers. Before long, those communities adopted the same kind of politically enforced growth restrictions that brought many of their newer residents from closer-in Bay Area communities. Housing prices in Tracy and Modesto soared until the decline started in 2007. But during the years just before, housing in these two communities became unaffordable to prospective home buyers who had incomes similar to the incomes of those who had bought and moved to Tracy and Modesto before the imposition of quotas and restrictions that limited new development.

It was common for first-time homeowners in the decades after 1970 to experience lower living standards—particularly in the longer commutes and the need for additional household members to enter the workforce—factors both due to the higher prices paid for homes. Nevertheless, these homeowners can be considered gainers in the struggle for improved economic well-being in the United States. The losers were households who rented—not out of choice but because they could not afford to buy a home. Also losers in that struggle were the young adults who moved out of the area where they could not afford to buy or rent, leaving their friends and families behind. Lower living standards in these forms will continue unless the planning policies being adopted in response to voter demands are altered to mitigate their supply-reducing effect. Unless the housing supply can be made more responsive—that is, more elastic to rising demand—prices will increase.

The Haves and the Have Nots

The more the rate of homeownership decreases, the greater will be the proportion of economically and socially frustrated "have nots" in the population. The gap between the economically successful and the struggling will continue to widen. Housing prices that climb faster than income-earning opportunities cause particular hardship on immigrants and others with entry-level and low-skilled jobs. That is because they, among all households who cannot even hope to afford homeownership, will be deprived of the upward social mobility and the social cohesion that would come from the gain in economic status of owning a home.

To many Americans, being able to own their own home and build equity in it through monthly payments has long provided a stepping-stone to upward economic mobility. The first home, and perhaps subsequent homes, was usually not a new house. And that was okay. As homes aged, their market values usually dropped, creating opportunities for households who could not afford new homes or simply did not want to pay the premium embedded in the price of a new home. But that all changed where and when regional and local land-use authorities crippled the ability of builders to respond to market signals suggesting that new construction could be profitable.

Not very long ago these older, less expensive houses provided the entry step to homeownership. That step has been superseded by the low interest rates and ready availability of mortgages on flexible, if sometimes risky, terms. But if one lesson is to be learned from the collapse of the subprime mortgage market it is that we cannot continue to provide middle-income Americans access to homeownership via imprudent lending practices.

In regions where there are strong economies and land-use allocation has been delegated to regulators and planners who fail to adopt policies that facilitate competition and sustain demand-responsive housing production, there will be "have" and "have-not" consumers. The "haves" who own homes that fit their lifestyles and aspirations are not likely to want to "trade up." Over time, the "haves" will become a shrinking minority of American households. Democracies cannot survive if the "haves" become a minority and the majority lose the hope of joining their ranks. The people we call the "have nots" will accept that status only as long as they believe they have a chance of moving up the economic ranks. We are all better off if they are given that chance.

Homelessness

Henry George forecast that, because of rising land values, there will be ragged and barefooted children on the streets of San Francisco. (You will be introduced to Henry George and his outlooks on the effects of urban land restrictions in chapter 3.) That forecast seems not yet to have come true. But after more than thirty years of down-zoning that decreased the amount of housing that could be added to the city's stock, there are always homeless beggars on the streets of San Francisco. I continue to encounter them near our San Francisco offices and my home every day, in spite of the more than $200 million the city spends annually in an attempt to reduce the number of people living on the streets.

Although local land-use policies do play a role in the rise of homelessness, there are other reasons why there are increasingly more people living on the streets. When the economy goes sour, more people are without jobs or without other income possibilities. Another reason is changes in the way the mentally ill are treated. Courts were once able to take away the liberty of an individual based solely on the assertions of mental illness made by family members or associates. Public reactions to remedy this grew to the extent that the laws of most states have been changed to make it virtually impossible to force mental health treatment on anyone not actually caught in the act of harming themselves or someone else. The difficulties of requiring anyone to be treated for mental illness are now so extreme that many obviously ill individuals are allowed to remain untreated, on their own, and on the streets.

Even when mental health treatment is acceptable to an individual or when a court is willing to assign a conservator with the power to require treatment, very few institutions are available to treat the mentally ill. The number of beds available in California state institutions for housing the mentally ill tells a typical story. California has been providing inpatient hospital beds for the mentally ill since before 1891. In that year, California had 3,630 beds in hospitals—known as "Asylums for the Insane"—in San Jose, Napa, and Stockton. Treatment often included methods such as shock therapy that today are considered inhumane. In 1950, when California's population had climbed to more than 10 million, there were 31,863 beds in hospitals for treating the mentally ill. In 1957, there were 37,076 beds.

After 1950, even as the population of the state continued to increase, the facilities available to treat the mentally ill, now referred to as developmental centers, began to decline. The drop has been steep since the administration of Gov. Ronald Reagan from 1966 to 1974. As of 2009, the population of California is more 37 million, more than 3.7 times the population in 1957. The California Department of Mental Health reports that today there are just 5,085 beds in institutions that provide treatment for the mentally ill, or about only 14 percent of what was available in 1957.

Another factor that contributes to the rise in homelessness is drug addiction, its consequences, and the failure of society to have any effect on reducing the use of illegal, harmful drugs. Also adding to the street population are the local housing policies that have allowed the removal of old, cheap single-room occupancy structures, commonly known as "flop houses," without replacing them with suitable housing for those who once resided in them.

Higher rates of homelessness were found in cities where there is a shortage of housing on the lower end of the price and quality range. That was the conclusion of an in-depth study of homelessness conducted by John M. Quigley, Steven

Raphael, and Eugene Smolensky of the University of California at Berkeley in 2000:

> Our results suggest that simple economic principles governing the availability and price of housing and the growth in the demand for the lowest quality housing explain a large portion of the variation in homelessness among U.S. metropolitan markets. . . . We find that the incidence of homelessness varies inversely with housing vacancy rates and positively with the market rent for just-standard housing. In simulations intended to assess the magnitudes of these effects, we find that moderate increases in housing vacancy rates and moderate decreases in market rents are sufficient to generate substantial declines in homelessness.[1]

Homelessness and begging are unlikely to ever be eliminated in a free society. But the number of people living on the streets could be greatly reduced if the prices of all houses are not constantly pushed up by supply-restricting local political decisions.

Urban Development's Contribution to Job Growth and Income Growth

The business sections of newspapers often consider residential and nonresidential developments in terms of the role they play in national and regional gross domestic product (GDP). The housing industry's failure to maintain the fast pace of production and sales it had achieved since 2000 was universally blamed for the declining rate of growth in the GDP first observed in late 2006. When residential permits in November 2006 were found to have dropped for the tenth straight month, a situation that was to get much worse, economists quoted in the *New York Times* estimated that the slowdown in home building had caused the rate of economic growth to decline by one full percentage point.

Construction of houses and infrastructure can be viewed as an engine for the creation of jobs and income as well as homes and other facilities. When considered in that light, the beneficiaries of urban development include not only builders and their workers but also the producers of a broad variety of construction materials, home furnishings, and equipment.

The causes of the slowdown in residential construction and sales that were first noticed in 2006 were very different from the causes of the slowdowns that had occurred in previous years. As Allen Sinai, a frequently quoted macroeconomic analyst, observed in the December 26, 2006, *New York Times*: "Past housing induced recessions were characterized by rising interest rates and tight credit, conditions that do not apply in these days of still cheap, easy money."

Mortgage money and housing prices rise faster than incomes. What started the residential construction slowdown in 2006 was something new.

The largesse of mortgage lenders had spurred housing price escalation to the point where it so far outpaced increases in consumers' incomes and their willingness to spend that home sales dropped. There were two causes for the drop: First, there were fewer buyers who could afford to purchase new homes. Second, the speculative investors in housing who had simply made down payments on units purchased for investment rather than as personal residences pulled back from additional purchases and tried to sell units they had recently obtained.

Housing is not a typical economic commodity, but it does have one thing in common with all other goods and services. When the price of an item increases, the number of its buyers decreases. But let's not overlook the reverse. When the price of an item decreases, the number of its buyers increases. The item we are alluding to here is the mortgage to buy a house. The cost of borrowing was obscured by the availability of mortgages that fooled many buyers into believing they could afford to pay more for housing than their incomes allowed. The collapse of the subprime mortgage market and risk of foreclosures revealed the obscured truth that higher prices reduce the quantity of any product that can be sold.

The rising equity value of housing caused many homeowners to extract part of their equity in the form of spendable cash. It has been estimated that about 40 percent of the home equity loans made during the long upward trend of housing values was spent on items unrelated to housing. Similarly, about 28 percent of the capital gains reaped by homeowners who sold residences that had escalated in value was also spent on items unrelated to housing. In the third quarter of 2006, an estimated $380 billion in mortgage equity was drawn out by homeowners. This amount was significantly less than the amount that housing equity extraction had pumped into the economy in each of the years preceding 2006, and it continued to decline in each of the years 2007 and 2008. The slowdown became a meltdown.

Local housing policies created the fuse that finally ignited the explosion of overleveraged, underregulated financial institutions. As the resulting recession spread from the United States to the rest of the world, most of the blame was placed on the financial institutions. Governments expended huge sums to prop up faltering financial institutions and strengthened their regulations to prevent the mistakes that had created those institutional bombs. Massive government funds were also expended to prime the economic pump of consumption and investment to get the economy moving again.

Housing production was among the industries those funds were meant to stimulate. But lost in all the regulatory changes and outpouring of federal funds was any mitigation of the policies that had served as the fuse that set off the bomb of overleveraged, imprudently lending financial institutions. Little attention was given to the source of the initial price escalations, or why prosperous,

growing communities such as Austin, Texas, had never experienced the bal-
looning house prices seen in prosperous coastal communities.

The Multiplier Effect of Housing

Former President Bill Clinton's successful campaign for the presidency was run
under the slogan, "It's the economy, stupid." The message of that slogan runs
continuously in the minds of many of the nation's leaders. This message often
focuses the perspective of the nation's leaders more on the role housing
production plays as a unique generator of jobs and incomes than on its role as
a supplier of homes. Housing is a big-ticket item, and its production spreads
dollars to many sectors of the economy. Most of the dollars paid to workers and
the large network of material, equipment, and service suppliers that serve the
homebuilding industry are spent again by those that receive them. These further
rounds of additional spending are called the multiplier effect of housing, which
can account for as much as 7 percent of economic activity.[2]

The Magic of Agglomeration Economies

Those of us who live and work in large urban areas obtain both advantages and
disadvantages through no effort on our part other than deciding where we live
and work. Because these positive and negative effects are bestowed outside of
our own actions, they are referred to as externalities. Positive externalities that
benefit us are often referred to as amenities while negative effects that we
endure or pay costs to avoid are disamenities.

In his 1980 *Principals of Economics*, Alfred Marshall coined the term
agglomeration economies for the positive economic externalities that large urban
places provide. He identified the monetary and psychic income- and wealth-
generating magic bestowed by large urban places as coming from two sources:
urbanization economies and localization economies. Holding other factors
constant, as metropolitan areas grow, the power of their urbanization and
localization economies increases. Such increases explain the higher land values
one finds in larger urban settlements.

Urbanization economies result from the density and diversity of the
population and economic activity found in large human settlements. The large,
diverse population living within one metropolitan area provides a pool of workers
with the varied occupations and skills needed by differing types of businesses.
The size and range of businesses supported by the labor base also provide each
other with the synergy of a wide range of competitively priced inputs for the
profitable production of goods and services. The size of the population also
helps support many activities, from operas to highly specialized medical clinics.
There is strength and opportunity in numbers.

The second source of agglomeration economies stems from the
clustering of activities within urbanized areas. The offices clustered together in

the downtown cores and suburban activity centers rent for more per square foot than the stand-alone offices at the edge of residential and industrial areas. The owners of these clustered buildings can charge more because they benefit from proximity to other offices, and their clients benefit from the convenience of multipurpose trips for services.[3] Shopping malls and auto rows provide two other examples of localization economies in large urban areas.[4]

Offsets to Agglomeration Economies

Areas with strong agglomeration economies can support higher-cost housing by paying more for labor. But as housing costs rise, the returns to both localization and urbanization economies decline, resulting in a loss to the economic strength of the region. Soaring housing costs in places like the San Francisco Bay Area and Greater Boston have driven the costs of labor to the point where much of the specialty manufacturing that once took place in proximity to their research and design facilities has moved elsewhere. A study of innovative clusters in Europe concluded that "specialization in innovative activity is positively and significantly influenced by specialization in production activity."[5] Since the manufacture of semiconductors has been increasingly automated, there would not have been a push to cut such complementary activities from the agglomeration in Silicon Valley if wage rates had not been pushed to among the highest in the world by the cost of housing in the Bay Area.

Information technology firms report that one incentive of opening new U.S. facilities outside the existing agglomeration in Silicon Valley is that wage costs are 25 percent lower in smaller U.S. cities and towns. According to a survey reported in the February 2005 *San Francisco Chronicle*, "Two out of five residents of the nine-county region have given serious thought to moving away—mostly because of high housing costs."

The parts of the country that do enjoy locational economic advantages, and where land use regulations do not stifle housing production, are attracting workers and jobs. Since the 1990s, despite interest rate decreases and the availability of mortgages requiring little down payment or none, the rate of homeownership in Texas, a state where market decisions about residential land-use allocations still predominate, grew faster than in California.

The Inland Empire

Since the 1990s, the fastest-growing region of California was the "Inland Empire," the metropolitan area composed of Riverside and San Bernardino counties.[6] Residential land prices remained competitively low in the Inland Empire, and builders cranked out affordable housing that attracted a young worker population. The labor provided by this population attracted a job base that kept growing even when job growth was slow or negative throughout the rest of the state.

In a paper on the growth of the Inland Empire, Anthony Downs wrote, "Since 1990, the number of jobs in the Inland Empire has increased 59 percent, compared to an increase of only 16 percent statewide." Downs made it clear that vacant, inexpensive land was the magnet that drew this growth. But he warned that even in the Inland Empire, the specter of land-value-raising political controls could imperil continued growth: "local citizen resistance to higher-density projects could limit population growth."[7]

Balanced Residential and Workplace Growth

Downs's warning applies not just to the fast-growing agglomerations of Riverside and San Bernardino counties. Some communities, such as Austin, Texas, and Denver, Colorado, seem to be continuing to facilitate balanced residential and workplace growth. That balanced growth further strengthens the agglomerations that have been paying off in terms of economic development for these two communities. But rather than "double up" on the initial prosperity brought by agglomeration booms, many regions, such as Greater Boston and Silicon Valley/San Francisco, have constrained the growth of residential development below the demands of an increasing employment base and failed to keep up with needed infrastructure development. Like an airplane that loses power just as it is in a steep climb, the failure to keep growth powered up and balanced causes a stall in the economic lift provided by agglomerations. Housing price increases that drive up the costs of labor, particularly for critically needed skilled workers, along with increasing congestion are causing stalls in agglomerations where economic growth should be on a continual climb.

Alleviating the imbalance in residential growth would have two good economic effects. First, balanced residential growth and workplace growth together would help alleviate rising labor costs and shortages while enabling the living standards of workers to continue rising. Second, residential construction that requires domestic labor and uses a great deal of domestically produced materials provides job and income opportunities that are relatively invulnerable to global competition.

Localization Characteristics

Localization was the term Marshall gave to the second of the two components that provided urban places with the ability to bestow unique economic advantages to the businesses clustered within their boundaries. The first permanent settlements may well have evolved from temporary markets set up for trading along popular routes. Our cities have urban cores that were established as retailers, wholesalers, manufacturers, and those that serve these businesses bid against one another for the limited space in "downtowns" where the action is.

Since the beginnings of the Industrial Revolution, urban cores have developed at the locus of strong transportation linkages because of the ease of accessibility. Concentrated in the urban core, these early agglomerations worked to increase people's material welfare and life spans more than could have been imagined by previous generations. This flourishing is a direct result not only of the built environment but also of the ability to build environments.

Since the 1950s, technologies and development patterns have allowed the locations that benefit from these positive externalities to spread out somewhat more evenly throughout urban regions. The interactions made possible by the spatial proximity of complementary business, cultural, and residential activities create powerful forces for economic development.

Recently developed clusters that provide localization economies to metropolitan regions and the cities within them include the clusters of the high tech industry. Some of these individual clusters or nodes of activity are well known, such as the research and industrial parks, offices, residences, and retail centers that are grouped around Stanford University. The proximity of employment and other gathering places near the university have made it easy for people doing similar work to exchange ideas and create new products and ideas. As the products of what became known as information technology, or IT, grew in importance, additional clusters of related activity formed farther out from the original Stanford node. Today, the multicounty area around Stanford containing many clusters of IT activity is known as Silicon Valley.

An example of a cluster that provided the localization element in the battery of agglomeration economies was concentrated for years around Fortieth Street and Broadway in Manhattan. Emanating from the showrooms and sewing shops near that location were all the specialized activities necessary for the efficient operation of the garment industry. But starting with the movement of manufacturing activities to the southern states in the 1950s, the diversity and scale of mutually supporting nodes of garment production began to leave Manhattan. In time, the critical mass of such activities needed to keep Manhattan a uniquely efficient and innovative location to design, manufacture, and market clothing dissipated. New centers of clothing manufacture spread throughout the world, and Manhattan lost its dominance of that industry.

The cost savings of producing goods and services near supporting or complementary activities, as well as the easier paths to innovation that the agglomeration economies of urban places bestow on local businesses, provide those firms with comparative advantages. These growth opportunities and benefits to the "bottom line" provide business enterprises with an edge over competitors in locations that offer lesser agglomeration economies.

Globalization

Improvements in transportation and communication have greatly reduced the costs and time of moving goods and information all over the world. The friction or hindrance to such movements imposed by geographic distances has been greatly reduced. The result is globalization, which has made the edge provided by strong agglomeration economies a necessity for business survival. Whether the challenges of this "shrinkage of the earth" are great enough to lead to an economic revolution will be answered in the future.

Just as the urban workplaces of the eighteenth and nineteenth centuries determined how well nations responded to the challenges of the mercantile and industrial revolutions, the success of nations in the new global competition will depend largely on the ability of urban centers of activity to spur, apply, and market the products and services of advancing technology. Global competition has the potential to increase the living standards of the world's population and to leapfrog those who have not benefited from previous economic revolutions into the kind of affluence enjoyed in the developed economies. Although there were successful responses to the challenges of past economic revolutions, they did not play out evenly across the geography of urban places. This was true in the past and is likely to be true in the future. There will be urban winners and losers.

The first great cities sprang up from the agricultural settlements that produced surplus food around the riverbeds of Mesopotamia. The mercantile revolution was led by the traders who built powerful commercial enterprises in places such as Venice and Amsterdam. The industrial revolution was initially most successful in English towns such as Manchester.

One unique feature of the current economic changes of globalization is that the places that grow strong, comparative advantage–bestowing agglomerations need not be located on any particular trade route. They can locate anywhere that can provide them with easy access to international transit and communication. But to succeed and grow, most businesses will have to locate in urban places that attract supporting businesses and institutions as well as a skilled labor force. Two famous examples of agglomeration economies that meet these prerequisites are the aforementioned Silicon Valley and the cluster of nodes in the Greater Boston area. But the ability of these two agglomerations, as well as others, to continue to enhance productivity and innovation is being hampered by high housing prices and the subsequent shortage of specialized labor.

Federal and State Foundations for City Building

Thomas Jefferson said, "The mobs of great cities add just so much to the support of pure governments, as sores do to the strength of the human body."[8] He feared the immigrants who fled Europe and clustered in America's cities, and he personally preferred the countryside to urban places. Nevertheless, the foundations for today's urban America were laid under the administration of his presidency. The Louisiana Purchase was undoubtedly one of the greatest land bargains in all history.

Surveying, Recording, Transparency

The ease and transparency of real estate transactions in the United States were made possible by the national land survey of 1787. Jefferson both encouraged and helped devise this measuring of all vacant and unclaimed land in the United States. The survey overlaid a grid of squares encompassing 640 acres each and oriented toward the four points of the compass. The system made it easy to subdivide the squares into smaller, geographically defined areas. This system of organizing land has worked well to facilitate the ownership and transference of real property in the United States. More than two hundred years before the economist Hernando de Soto pointed out the role that widespread land ownership plays in alleviating poverty, the United States was blessed with a sound and simple system for recording land ownership.[9]

Along with Jefferson, many of founders of the republic were engaged in trading and planting. They were also in another business from which they expected big payoffs—they were land speculators and developers. In particular, George Washington, like other Virginians of his day, often spent more time buying, selling, and seeking to develop tracts of virgin land than he spent on the agricultural activities for which he was better known.

To prosper, farms needed be tied to cities. Agriculture could not develop beyond subsistence levels that barely fed the growers and their families unless farms were linked to urban places. Once linked to markets by inexpensive, reliable transportation, and to a legal and financial structure that facilitated trade, it was possible to exchange crops and animals for tools. This resulted in increased productivity of growing and animal husbandry and made available the materials and supplies that improved the life of agricultural families.

Creating links to urban markets requires investment in human capital as well as physical capital. Writing about his early life on a farm in Kentucky, Alben W. Barkley, who served as vice president under Franklin D. Roosevelt, described the building and annual maintenance of "farm to market" roads as a cooperative effort in which all the males of the rural farming community participated. In his autobiography, Barkley wrote:

> Another custom of those days was the system of calling out all the able-bodied male citizens of the community once a year to work on the roads. It was a community enterprise, and no one got paid. A road overseer was appointed for the different districts, and it was his job to see that the men turned out with their own plows, hoes, scrapers, teams, or whatever they could bring, and patch up the dirt roads, which were all we had to serve us.
>
> I began going out with my father on these road-working expeditions as soon as I was old enough to wield the implements. It was a wonderful

experience, a sort of a jubilee, or get-together, for the men. Money or station in life meant nothing, as everyone, rich or poor, turned out. The men would fill in the deep holes and wagon ruts with straw, brush, or sod, then scrape over the surface and cover it with fresh dirt. After working a while, the men would stop to eat and rest, and they would start swapping stories. I would sit quietly and listen, soaking up the yarns I heard the men tell.[10]

Transporting "Moonshine"—This Author's Personal Experience

My own insight into the difference that transportation linkages to urban markets made to farmers came when, as a teenager, a friend and I took a camping trip up the Kentucky River. We were able to navigate the river in our small boat with an outboard engine because the U.S. Army Corps of Engineers had built along the river a series of locks, which in those days they still maintained and operated. We boated past farms with cornfields, and after we made camp we explored the countryside. By then, most farms had dirt-road connections to paved state-built roads, but we did see a few cornfields that even in the late 1940s were only connected to the wider, urban world outside the hills of Kentucky by access to the river. At the end of our trip we pulled our boat out of the river from under a bridge in Harlan County to hitchhike back to where we left our car.

We were lucky to be picked up in the early evening by a driver who could drop us off quite close to where we left our car. The driver also gave us a lesson in how the farmers had coped before the locks were installed along the river. At a roadblock set up by local law enforcement officers near where we were picked up, we learned our benefactor's profession. A sheriff's deputy manning the roadblock leaned into the car and gave our driver a friendly greeting and a quick update on activities of the night. As the car continued down the road, we asked the driver why he was so familiar with the local cops. The driver told us he was the county district attorney, and that the roadblock had been set up in an attempt to slow down the illicit traffic in the local moonshine.

He explained that the cornfields along the river and in the nearby hills had been isolated from the means of transporting their crop until the Corps put in the dams. In the years before the dams and the more recent construction of roads, it was impossible to move the corn to market. Innovating out of necessity, the farmers had learned that concentrating the corn through its distillation into whiskey added value to the corn and made it transportable over Kentucky's paths and early crude roads. By the 1940s the improved roads, which would soon make the locks obsolete, were being used to transport the handiwork of those who still remembered the craft of corn distillation. As I remember, the transport vehicles of choice were souped-up Hudson Hornet automobiles that, with a little luck, could outrun the pursuit of those who sought to enforce the tax on alcoholic beverages.

Infrastructure

It is clear that for the early agricultural economies to thrive, the physical and human infrastructure they depended on also had to grow. It is no different now for the economic activities of urban communities, which depend on the quality and scale of public infrastructure. Such infrastructure includes not only transportation and communication links but also the large number of laws and the financial institutions that facilitate trade, protect the traders, and adjudicate their disputes. The cooperation of volunteers united in a common effort, similar to the road maintenance described by Vice President Barkley, works for small rural or urban settlements. But for there to be larger, effective, and efficient growth, the protection and community services provided by local volunteers are usually insufficient. Instead, some form of governmental organization is usually called upon to guard against predatory forces within and outside the community.

The city of Cincinnati, originally called Losantiville, grew only after the federal government built and staffed a fort, Fort Washington, alongside a few cabins inhabited by settlers along the Ohio River. At that time, the white settlers and their government, working as a unified community, contested the leadership of that area against the same powerful Indian tribes that had fought with the French in the French and Indian Wars. The fort created more safety and protection from Indian raiders for that small settlement than was available to other settlements along the banks of the Ohio River. Much in the same way that clean, graffiti-free streets and parks tell you that an area is safe, the presence of the fort signaled a containment of violence and protection for private investment.

Early in the economic evolution of the United States, the national government and state governments organized the financing of transportation infrastructure that would enable agricultural and urban economies to cut the costs of transporting their products and raw material. In settlements along these transportation arteries, private investment in business activities and public investment in additional infrastructure flourished. In places that were strategically located in terms of markets and resources, the regional economy grew as the complementary infrastructure of housing, public services, and facilities grew, and as they grew, so did the regional economy.

The Erie Canal

As transportation and subsequent public funding provided drainage, water, and other utility infrastructures, they pushed outward the boundaries of urban frontiers. The most dramatic early example of a new transportation artery that kicked off such town- and city-growing production was the opening of the Erie Canal on October 26, 1825. New York governor DeWitt Clinton financed the Erie Canal by issuing bonds to pay for the huge artificially created waterway. The barges drawn by mules along the path beside the waterway carried cargo at a fraction of the cost of wagon transport and provided economic returns to

New York State as well as the other states linked by the canal. Life along this project was characterized then and persists today in folksongs:

> I've got a mule, her name is Sal,
> Fifteen miles on the Erie Canal
> She's a good old worker and a good old pal,
> Fifteen miles on the Erie Canal.[11]

The success of the canal was one of the accomplishments that almost made DeWitt Clinton the first U.S. president with that last name. The canal's construction and financing encouraged other state and federal groups to make grants and financing available to encourage the private construction of roads, navigable rivers, canals, railroads, highways, water drainage, sanitary sewage systems, and other kinds of utilities. All such grants and financing were intended to boost economic activities and facilitate the growth of private investment in rural and urban real estate and businesses.

Knowing which governmental investments and operations are appropriate and who should pay for them are controversies that continue to the present day. How beneficially and fairly they are resolved will continue to shape the future of public development.

Civic Spirit

Government investment in physical improvements made urban growth feasible, and the public investment in how best to survey land and maintain records of titles to land made private ownership possible. Surveying land and recording titles can be considered two types of public infrastructure, which, together with a system of credit and an unimpeded private market for real estate, laid a legal and fiscal foundation for avoiding the poverty-inducing land shortage that Henry George predicted. That foundation was bolstered by a positive civic spirit toward urban development, growth, and change. Throughout the nineteenth century and well into the twentieth century, most cities were under the spell of boosters who saw growth and development as natural and good.

In his brilliant chronicle of Chicago's development into a great city, *Nature's Metropolis*, William Cronon tells of booms followed by busts that failed to discourage the next boom. He wrote: "During the nineteenth century, when Chicago was at the height of its gargantuan growth, its citizens rather prided themselves on the wonder and horror their hometown evoked in others. No other city in America had ever grown so large so quickly; none had so rapidly overwhelmed the countryside around it to create so urban a world."[12]

The fundamental value that growth and expansion were good—if not natural—for Chicago was not confined to the bustling newer places of the west. In 1903 New York mortgage banker and urban scholar Richard M. Hurd wrote: "Whatever the type of city, growth consists of movement away from the point of origin and is of two kinds: central, or in all directions, and axial, or along the watercourses, railroads and turnpikes which form the framework of cities."[13]

Early Urban Expansion

City development has generally expanded outward from the initial center of activity, which was originally the wharves and docks or the railroad stations that linked urban settlements to the world, the same world the workers of those settlements came from, the same world that was partner in trade with those settlements. As the housing around the central workplaces became older and the neighborhoods more crowded, the affluent citizens of the United States developed finer houses farther out in new neighborhoods. They commuted to work, shopping, religious services, and entertainment by foot, on horseback, and in carriages. Since the workers could afford neither finer houses nor horses and carriages, their housing had to be inexpensive and within walking distance of central city workplaces.

As the capacity of transportation grew, becoming more accessible, reaching farther places, and becoming faster and more frequent, the patterns of housing changed to match these new capabilities. From the horse-drawn buggy to the railroad, streetcars, interurban electric railways, and automobiles and trucks, the radius of lands that could be developed stretched out into new neighborhoods. As the urban areas continued to grow, the population of neighborhoods away from the core grew large enough to support their own subcenters of commercial and cultural activities. Stores, restaurants, and businesses to serve neighborhoods and communities began to appear, competing with and replacing some of the same entities that had previously been able to operate only because they had been serving the large number of consumers living in the original urban core.

In towns and cities that have existed for more than a century, structural remnants provide evidence of where the boundaries of residential neighborhoods and both retail and industrial clusters of activity stood during the eras delineated by the transportation changes that have occurred since these towns and cities were first settled. Some older multistoried industrial and warehouse facilities that were once surrounded with buildings for similar uses along with the tenements and boarding houses for the labor employed in those structures have since been converted to loft housing in neighborhoods going through gentrification.

In many older cities, some mansions in the central core are now being used as museums, historic monuments, nonprofit organizations, bed and breakfasts, or funeral homes. They originally housed well-to-do families who traveled by carriage to work, entertainment, and other activities. By the mid-1850s, as horse-drawn rail lines gave working-class people the ability to live farther out from the industrial center, well-to-do families were able to move still farther out to new neighborhoods that became the new prestigious places to live. By the late 1800s through the early 1900s, the electric trolley and, in some places, elevated railways pushed out the boundaries of development still farther.

Older, low-rise apartment buildings were constructed along the paths of trolley tracks. Housing built between 1910 and 1925 is found in the closest city suburbs, where the interurban electric transit, perhaps supplemented by ferries, brought access to lands that could then be developed into new neighborhoods. These transit expansions linked towns and villages of a remote agricultural region to the urban activity centers that had previously only been the destination of rare "trips to town" for the inhabitants of these rural communities. The automobile and particularly the great expansion of highways that followed World War II made it possible to extend the borders of development far beyond anything that had been seen or envisioned before. Between 1947 and 1962, a total of 14,500,000 new single-family homes were built. At least 10,000,000 of them were built in the suburbs, along with 5,000 new shopping centers, 125 of which were large regional malls.[14]

The small rural towns and counties that were being converted into urban places did have regulatory power to guide what would be built on former farms and vacant fields. But during the first decade of the twentieth century through most of the 1960s, local planners and councils were likely to go along with many of the proposals brought before them by private builders and land developers. The major exception was the reluctance of many communities to allow apartments or high-density single-family housing that might attract residents who were less affluent or below middle class. But even here, as demonstrated by well-publicized tract developments such as Levittown on Long Island, New York, some communities were friendly to such residential projects in the late 1940s and early 1950s. In those days, land-use restrictions never included outright restrictions or quotas on annual sales of allowable construction, and rarely included boundaries or so-called greenbelts beyond existing built-up areas.

Until the 1970s, most of the planning restrictions imposed on builders of residential developments, and increasingly on builders of retail and industrial developments, related to the density and design of development rather than excluding large areas from development and limiting the amount of allowed construction. But as suburban expansion continued, some residents within the suburban communities, who had themselves benefited from the availability of this housing, began to lobby for greater local restrictions on what, where, and how much new development would be allowed.

Preservation and Environmentalism

The environmental movement became a popular cultural force and a common cause among suburban residents who sought to control development. Before long, it became clear that the environmental movement was also strengthening the hand of preservationists and others in the older established neighborhoods of the central cities who wanted to slow the pace of growth and stop changes in the scale and character of the urban landscape. President John F. Kennedy's famous line during his Cold War speech at the Berlin Wall, in which he said, "I am Berliner," garnered the United States cheers from around the world. Similarly, politicians and activists opposed to growth and change came to precede their statements with, "we are all environmentalists now." This added to their effectiveness in eliciting the votes of local elected officials against new land uses, and provided an effective social cover for land-use polices that strengthened the power of existing residents over future owners, renters, the poor, and everyone else outside the current ownership "club." This is class warfare—invidious and most effective.

Public decision makers rarely made the doomsday predictions of Henry George come true until the great expansion of housing development in the suburbs called "sprawl." It was not until then that attempts at additional suburban tract housing projects were significantly impeded by the land-use decisions of boards and councils in suburbs that lay in the path of growth. By the 1970s, the slowdown in the ability of houses to be added to the stock of suburban areas in fast-growing coastal regions took place on such a scale that during the following decades the cumulative shortfall in housing production prevented additions to the housing stock from keeping up with the effective demand in those regions.

Another assault on the growth of housing stock that gained momentum in the 1970s was the "slum clearance" movement that started before World War II. The results of slum clearance foreshadowed the unintended consequences of failing to understand and anticipate the cumulative effect of housing supply reductions. What happened should have caused at least a few planners to pause earlier to consider that those effects could happen. By the mid-1960s it was evident that the "slum dwellers" whose lives the redevelopment projects were intended to improve were being hurt by the wrecking balls of public redevelopment.

Even when the unintended consequences of removing thousands of low-priced units from the housing markets of cities were recognized, no broader lessons were drawn. There was no awareness that similar price-raising, quality-lowering market results would follow constraints put on the production of new infill and suburban housing. Ignoring how urban land-use markets work had led public redevelopment in the central cities to create just the kind of negative economic effects that Henry George had predicted private land speculators and property owners would visit on cities. The cumulative effects of the restrictions on suburban development being imposed by the planners and their elected bosses in response to the appeals of the neighborhood activists—now often speaking as environmentalists—who packed the commission and council chambers had similar results. Just as slum clearers decreased the supply of housing by demolishing existing dwellings, the aforementioned speakers reduced the stock of urban housing by limiting the amount of new housing that could be added to the stock of housing. In a clear case of failing to learn from history, change and growth controls in economically powerful coastal cities is to the middle class what the economic disaster of slum clearance was to the poor.

3

Encouraging the Expansion of Land Use . . . and Constraining It

A Land and Building Monopoly Was Foreseen

The streets were not paved with gold in nineteenth-century American cities. But they offered working-class families a chance to earn their way up to a decent standard of living as well as to accumulate the beginnings of some wealth.

In 1871 Henry George, a San Francisco printer and self-taught economist, explained why urban America offered opportunities that acted like a magnet to immigrants from overseas. He attributed these opportunities to the competition among the developers and competition among the owners of urban real estate. In his "Our Land and Land Policy," George told his readers that because the land and building markets of nineteenth-century urban America were competitive, working men and women had opportunities found nowhere in the Old World.

Implicit in his exposition of how land was allocated in American cities was the reality that competitive pressures goaded the owners of real estate into improving the living standards of residents and the capabilities of businesses by building and remodeling structures to take advantage of advances in technology. Consider the changes in the pattern or cityscape of development and buildings that have taken place in the last century. Most of today's urban Americans only know from skits on television and stories told by their grandparents that outdoor toilets were common in the 1920s. Equipping houses with electric fixtures started soon after Edison's invention of the incandescent bulb in 1879, and updates in wiring has paved the way for an expanding array of electric appliances continuing ever since. Central heating has gone from a coal rarity to oil and gas, and now solar energy is coming into wider use.

If we had used the term *shopping center* twenty years after Edison's invention, no one would have understood what we were talking about—much less that it would become a common part of the suburban landscape. Jesse Clyde

Nichols opened the first suburban shopping center, Country Club Plaza, in Kansas City in 1923.

Except for large assembly operations such as Ford's River Rouge plant, most medium to large factories were multistoried buildings with large freight elevators that carried material vertically from one work station to the next. While working my way through undergraduate school in the early 1950s, I visited smaller machine shops with belt-driven equipment connected to electric motors. Shortly thereafter, more efficient manufacturing and processing businesses started to move to industrial and warehouse "parks" built with easy access to recently completed freeways. Today, many of these facilities are considered less than the best because new structures and groupings of buildings are more attuned to contemporary land, air, and sea transportation technology.

The future demands of consumers and businesses will require more innovation-adapting investments similar to those exemplified above. As in the past, the innovations and investments made by competing land developers and builders will be required to enhance the viability of agricultural and urban production while being responsive to changes in consumers' tastes and their ability to pay. Using the term introduced in chapter 2—this will improve the comparative advantages of America's businesses.

Henry George's understanding of how real estate markets were working in the 1870s and 1880s was insightful and optimistic. But he predicted an entirely different view of how real estate markets would operate in the future. He saw the competition that was a powerful and necessary force for economic good being throttled by successful real estate conspiracies. When he looked ahead, George's view of how cities would influence America's economic future and the opportunities they would provide working people turned profoundly pessimistic.

He predicted that urban property owners and developers would conspire among themselves to close the frontiers of urban competition—shutting down competition would tilt in their favor the distribution of income from constrained urban development. He believed that, in time, America's urban landowners and developers would constrain additions and changes to urban real estate, thus raising rents and prices to the point where they could benefit considerably beyond what competing would provide them. George predicted that as competition was throttled by urban landowners and speculators, the same conditions of poverty and despair that led the landless to flee Europe would be reproduced in America.

Nine years after the publication of "Our Land and Land Policy," Henry George explained the primary economic damage done by rising urban land prices. In 1881 he published his magnum opus, *Progress and Poverty*, a best seller in which he restated and stressed that the cost of inexpensive land contributes only a small portion of the prices and rents of buildings: "All that we are proud of in the American character, all that makes our conditions and institutions better than those of older countries, we may trace to the fact that land has been cheap in the United States, because new soil had been open to the emigrant."[1]

From Agrarian to Urban

Today, the American economy and workforce are urban. This makes heeding George's warning more critical now than when he wrote those words. In 1886, when George ran for mayor of New York, 49 percent of the people comprising America's workforce earned their living on farms and ranches.[2] The importance of agriculture in the U.S. economy decreased slowly over the next thirty years. Until 1920, a majority of Americans continued to be employed on farms and ranches. Today, that proportion has dropped to less than 6 percent, and agricultural activities account for only 1 percent of value added to the gross domestic product of the United States.

Nevertheless, a vast array of governmental efforts and dollars are expended each year to maintain more acres in actual and potential agriculture than an efficient agricultural economy needs. The national bill for supporting agricultural prices and paying farm owners to allow land to lie fallow was more than $17 billion in 2006. The total cost to the taxpayers of the farm bill that Congress passed in 2008 was budgeted to be $307 billion over the five years from 2009 through 2014. In the face of evidence that agricultural lands are not in short supply, public policy in America seeks to preserve and expand agricultural land—a quite expensive proposition for maintaining the illusion of an agrarian life long since past.

Yet, going in the other direction in recent decades, public policy has been increasingly restrictive of the use of urban lands, particularly within those metropolitan areas with rapidly expanding population and economic bases. What has been forgotten is the lesson that Charles Abrams wanted us to learn from his 1965 book, *The City Is the Frontier*. Abrams was the chairman of the City Planning Department at Columbia University and was described by *Architectural Forum* magazine as "perhaps the foremost housing consultant in the United States." He wrote: "From 1800 to 1950, the proportion of people living in cities with more than 20,000 people leaped from 2.4 percent to 21 percent. Our civilization is becoming urban, and the advance into cities is one of the most spectacular social phenomena of our time. The city has become the frontier."[3]

Restricting the use of fertile land in times of food shortages both increases the prices of agricultural products and lessens productivity-enhancing and market-responsive changes in farming. In much the same way, restrictions on the use and reuse of urban land drive up the costs of urban space and impair both the quality of urban life and the efficiency of urban production. Closing the agricultural frontier in the early years of the United States would have stunted the country's economic growth and deprived newcomers, by birth or immigration, of the opportunity to enhance their economic status. In contemporary America, housing is the land use most affected by restrictive policies on new construction and the conversion of existing structures. In areas where populations and incomes are increasing, the obvious result is the increase in the price of land where building is allowed, which translates into higher housing prices and rents.

From Encouraging to Controlling the Expansion of Land Use

During the United States' first two centuries, federal and local public policies encouraged expansion and change for both agricultural and urban economic activities. The development and construction of roads, canals, rails, and highways were encouraged to facilitate the expansion of farms, ranches, and cities into the open territory of woods and plains. The damming and diversion of rivers and streams to provide water for power, irrigation, industrial processing, and home use were often financed with government-backed bonds. Public policy encouraged the provision of power to factories, homes, and farms.

In the *Federalist Papers*, Alexander Hamilton and others who shared his views argued for a strong central government possessing, among other powers, the ability to tax and control the private banking system. The antifederalists, including Thomas Jefferson, wanted to leave more control in the several states. The federalists won enough of the debate to convince the constitutional assembly to give the central government broad authority to tax and regulate the banking system. In the generations that followed the passage of the U.S. Constitution, the taxing powers of the central government and the banking system it allowed served the needs of agriculture and industry well. But little was done to lend money directly or indirectly to individual workers or consumers.

The federal government did little to channel mortgage money to private residential markets until well into the twentieth century. But during the second half of that century, the availability of mortgages to individual households more than caught up with the ability of farmers and businesses to borrow. The increase in financing to make mortgage borrowing more available did much to increase the rate of homeownership, which previously had increased mainly in line with the rise in real incomes. Because access to land for agricultural production has never been restricted, agricultural production remains flexible and adaptive. The rapid increase in corn acreage in response to the demand for ethanol provides an example of the continuing responsive capability of farm and ranch land.

There are two reasons why farmers leave their land or stop expanding: The costs of farming, reduced by government farm subsidies, exceed the total revenue from crops and animals, or the price of the land for other uses allowed by local land-use authorities provides more income than does farming and ranching. In neither case is farmland removed as a direct result of public policy. For most of the first two hundred years of America's existence, the same could have been said for most urban uses, and particularly for residential development. But since about 1970 market decisions about land use have been replaced by political decisions in an increasing number of metropolitan regions.

Until the collapse of housing prices kicked off by subprime mortgage defaults in 2007, the rising prices induced by restrictive local land-use policies and imprudent lending created the mentality in nearly everyone in the United States, and probably elsewhere, that housing prices were destined to rise continuously. Those who could not afford to join the homeowners whose homes were increasing in value stood on the sidelines, feeling economically disempowered by the unprecedented increases in the cost of shelter.

Village of Euclid v. Ambler Realty Co.

To the average person involved in land use issues, planning means zoning. Zoning is the shorthand description given to the maps and legal codes that spell out what uses are allowed on the geographically specified lands within the jurisdictions of municipal and county governments. Whether owners will be permitted to do what they want with their land and what category of allowable uses the land falls into will be determined by the local boards and councils that issue the zoning maps and codes. They decide if the intended land use satisfies what will be allowed and where. The power that a local government has with respect to zoning is generally considered to derive from a decision by the Supreme Court in 1926 when it upheld a zoning ordinance adopted two years earlier by the Village of Euclid, near Cleveland, Ohio.[4] The village's zoning had excluded all but single-family houses from development on an area that builders had previously considered as a potential site for apartments and retail uses.

Many people believe that what happened in the Village of Euclid created what came to be the accepted understanding of zoning: the allocation of land by segregating it into districts, specifying for each district the allowable uses within defined building spaces. But actually, zoning in the United States has a history that goes back to at least the early 1900s. It is not unreasonable to consider that zoning evolved from laws that began to be imposed as the U.S. urban population equaled its rural population after the Civil War. The purpose of zoning was to prohibit land uses that demonstrably threatened the health or safety of the public.

In a fascinating history of the cases that led up to the litigation between the *Village of Euclid v. Ambler Realty Co.*, legal scholar Richard H. Chused pointed out that the Supreme Court was convinced to decide as it did by the arguments made in a brief submitted by Alfred Bettman after the Court had heard all other arguments. In his amicus curiae, or "friend of the court," brief, Bettman, a prominent Cincinnati attorney who was a leader of the National Conference on City Planning, zeroed in on the concept that the village should be allowed to outlaw as nuisances uses other than the type of single-family residences already in the neighborhood. The Court stretched its previously allowed limit on the timing during which briefs would be accepted in order to consider what Bettman wrote.

In his written argument, Bettman recognized that the Supreme Court at that time was conservative and therefore unlikely to uphold the zoning if it considered the zoning at issue was being used as a tool for superseding business contracts. Instead of presenting his brief from that perspective, Bettman argued that the broad powers that he wanted the Court to give to local municipalities to limit what use could be made of land were necessary to prevent nuisances that lowered property values. Bettman aimed directly at the prejudices of the sitting judges. He argued that allowing a landowner to develop an industrial building would lower the value of adjoining property. He further argued that zones that allowed mixing land uses that might house different social classes was sufficiently dangerous to property values to warrant granting local officials the right to stop such diversity of land uses. The Court agreed. The justices wrote in their opinion:

> The coming of apartment houses to single-family areas . . . has sometimes resulted in destroying the entire section for private house purposes . . . very often the apartment house is a mere parasite, constructed in order to take advantage of the open spaces and attractive surroundings created by the residential character of the district. . . . Under these circumstances apartment houses, which in a different environment would be . . . entirely unobjectionable . . . come very near to being nuisances.[5]

It's not difficult to get a feel for the judicial climate and perspective of the zoning proponents from Chused's description of this drama that played out in the nation's highest court:

> The Euclid zoning ordinance was drafted by James Metzenbaum. He lived on the town's main street, Euclid Avenue, and was village counsel. The zoning scheme adopted by the town was modeled on the earlier New York ordinance. Euclid simply took the various building type, height, and density classifications of the New York plan and pasted them over Euclid to solidify extant land-use patterns. Euclid Avenue, itself known by some as Millionaire's Row, was lined with mansions as it headed west toward Cleveland. One of the reasons Metzenbaum encouraged Euclid to adopt a zoning plan was to preserve the avenue, which by 1920 had begun to fall upon hard times. Some of its mansions had given way to gas stations or other uses, and a few had been turned into apartments.[6]

Euclidean Zoning

When the Supreme Court, interpreting the U.S. Constitution, ruled favorably for the broad powers implicit in Bettman's perspective on the issue, it gave birth to a baby that would eventually slay the very property rights held dear by the judges who had fathered it. That baby, named "Euclidean zoning" after the court decision that gave it birth, provided municipalities with a power that had previously been invested in the interplay of businessmen and consumers within a market free of direct government control.

The power that Euclidean zoning gave municipalities was so much greater than the past practices and laws they had been accustomed to using that it would take decades for them to use Euclidean zoning. There was also little reason to use this power during the Great Depression. Euclidean zoning had nothing to do with geometry, other than the fact that it would come to impose municipally made development patterns on cityscapes that previously had been market-determined.

Local municipalities began to use the power of Euclidean zoning during the largely suburban development boom that followed the end of World War II. The zoning imposed by growing communities that offered homes to the families of veterans caused vast new suburban developments to use more land and be more homogeneous in terms of uses and types of housing than would have been the case without these zoning ordinances. The general and specific plans published by suburban villages, towns, cities, and counties that were enforced by Euclidian zoning ordinances provided a template of allowable development, which ensured that the neighborhoods of suburbia were homogeneous in lot size, structural type, and demographic makeup—surely more homogeneous in these respects than was possible in the older urban neighborhoods that had arisen before planning decisions effected by the market were superseded and enforced by zoning planning.

Zoning in the Suburbs

Professor Jonathan Levine the University of Michigan has pointed out in his 2006 book, *Zoned Out*, that a variety of zoning-based regulations were used to stop diverse and compact development in the suburbs. The zoning built into the general plans of post–World War II suburban neighborhoods encouraged similar housing on large lots that would fit the budgets of households having similar social status and family characteristics.

As time went on, there were significant criticisms about the role Euclidean zoning played in shaping suburban America. One of the first criticisms was the 1972 book *Land Use without Zoning*, by Bernard Siegan, a practicing Chicago land-use lawyer. He used the example of Houston to argue that low- and moderate-income groups get a better deal without zoning.[7] Siegan argued that the good done by zoning by separating incompatible uses could be accomplished by other means while the bad results of zoning would die with it. Recently other legal scholars, including Chused, have made more extensive arguments against zoning largely based on the observed impact that it has had on enforcing social and land-use homogeneity in suburban development.

Societal and Judicial Bigotry

Partly because of the change in laws and attitudes toward enforced social segregation, there has been increasing awareness for the need to eliminate the zoning in which lurked the pervasive bigotry of the 1920s—the zoning that was accepted by and infected the judges who fathered *Euclid*. One of the most interesting of these arguments to eliminate zoning was presented by Eliza Hall in a *University of Pittsburgh Law Review* article.[8] Rather than use Houston as an example of the good that can come from land-use allocations without zoning, she used the example of Paris, France, citing the beneficial differences between the French and American approaches to planning. She wrote: "In a nutshell, Paris city planning lets owners put their property to virtually any use they want, so long as they do so within structures that are regulated to enhance safety, beauty, and quality of life for everyone. . . . Aesthetically pleasing mixed-use neighborhoods are the natural result."[9]

Like Levine, Hall recognized that zoning spawns what she refers to as sprawl, to which she assigned a host of evils, including social segregation, environmental damage, and "leapfrog" development (development jumping over the vacant land adjacent to existing development in order to build on land further out). She advocated the French system of "zoning for structures, not for uses." Her contemporary perspective was that the *Euclid* decision was contaminated because the temper of the time and the social outlook of the judges were infected with racism, fear of immigrants, and other forms of bigotry. She noted that at the District Court level, Judge David C. Westenhaver was reflecting the conservative judicial bench when he wrote, "The blighting of property values and the congesting of population, whenever the colored or certain foreign races invade a residential section, are so well known as to be within judicial cognizance."[10] Hall pointed out, too, that the same justices who had empowered zoning to restrict what could be built on the land in designated districts had previously shown a willingness to allow the exclusion of racial groups. She based this charge on a 1926 decision of the same court in which the court had endorsed racially restrictive real estate covenants.

The attachment of restrictive covenants to deeds that documented ownership of property was common until after World War II. I have previously mentioned the 1923 development of the first suburban shopping center by J. C. Nichols in Kansas City. Nichols went on to develop a residential community, the Country Club District, adjoining his shopping center. The documents conveying Nichols residential sales in that district all carried a contract, or covenant, excluding African Americans and Jews from occupying the residences—except as servants.

Reformulating Zoning

Contemporary attitudes such as Hall's found firm roots in the America of the 1960s. With regard to social segregation, there is no doubt that the socially homogeneous areas developed in the suburbs after 1945 are much larger than what would have developed in the absence of Euclidean zoning. But with or without zoning, many households prefer living next to those of their own class, and I do mean class, not race.

We Americans are sometimes hesitant to talk or write about class because we do not want to be thought of as snobs or as disavowing the American ideal that all are equal before the law and God. But most of us do know that we differ in the values that influence our behavior and social affect. We do not all talk, act, or dress in the same way; we do not all listen to the same music or raise our children to have the same values. Our social affects—the outward signs of what we are like—are shaped and correlated with our family background, education, occupations, income, and similar characteristics. We can and—whether we admit it or not—we do group people based on these characteristics and outward signs; that is, we group people in these respects into classes.

Race or single characteristics such as income are sometimes used as synonymous with class—but this is never valid, is frequently bigoted, and is always misleading. While President Barack Obama and Sen. John D. Rockefeller are arguably in both the same political party and class, they are not of the same race. But chances are more than likely that high-income basketball stars of the same race as the president or as the senator are not in the same social class as the president or the senator.

Once land is purchased for development and money spent to pay for the costs of putting in needed infrastructure, such as local streets, drainage, and utilities, the interest payable on borrowed money is a ticking clock that makes developers want to build and sell the structures as soon as possible. To do this often motivates them to include in their development as many different types and sizes of residential structures and lots as they can profitably sell. It is easy to see the result of this in the variations in housing types built within just a few blocks of each other in the residential areas of cities built before 1945.

When I was a boy, my family lived in apartments located in the South Avondale and Mount Auburn neighborhoods of Cincinnati. Our immediate neighbors lived in apartment buildings as well. Kids from nearby single-family houses went to the same elementary school that I attended. When my parents could afford and bought a single-family house on a small lot on Edgehill Place, the kids who lived in apartment houses just one block away would come down to our street to play.

Although there were slight differences in the income characteristics of those living in the apartments, we were still similar enough that sociologists would probably have classified most of us as lower-middle- or middle-class families. Only a ten- or fifteen-minute walk, or less than a five-minute drive away, was a neighborhood with very large houses that could be called mansions, built on lots larger than an acre. Many of the occupants of these large houses would be classified as belonging to the upper class or some strata within that group. About a fifteen-minute walk through the woods behind Edgehill Place were streets with newer homes built on lots a little bigger than ours. They included the families of doctors and businesspersons who were more successful than the small store owners who lived on Edgehill, and who would probably have been classified as middle class or upper-middle class. No kids from either of those neighborhoods ever came down to Edgehill Place to play with us.

But from where I lived on Edgehill, or later on Eaton Lane just to the south, it was less than a five-minute drive to either of the other neighborhoods. When I went to high school I met kids from both of those close-by neighborhoods that I had never visited while in elementary school. When I visited some of their homes, I noticed the differences in the way those of us from the three neighborhoods lived and looked at the world.

It has been sixty years since I left the neighborhood. I still stay in contact with some of the friends from all three of these neighborhoods. None of us live in or close to those neighborhoods today; both we and the neighborhoods have changed. But as I look back, I think that we all learned things from each other and that we value the friendships we made while attending the same elementary school and high school.

The residential neighborhoods built in conformity with zoning-enforced general plans of the cities, towns, and villages that had jurisdiction over the vacant land developed in the post–World War II suburban expansions were much larger than neighborhoods of prewar cities such as the neighborhoods where I lived. Acres of land were zoned to accommodate only single-family detached dwellings built on the same size lots. Some communities required large minimum lot sizes for all single-family dwellings and allowed no multi-family or attached single-family dwellings. Although large-scale developments with the same or similar dwelling and lot size characteristics had existed previously, it became much easier to enforce similarities or uniformity over large amounts of acreage with restrictive covenants.

I do have some sympathy with those who want to eliminate zoning, but zoning has become ingrained into the planning and land-use infrastructure of much of America. So rather than eliminate the role of zoning in the planning and land-use allocation process, zoning is one of the things in that process that I suggest altering. We need to reverse the zoning rules so that they will mandate good development instead of facilitating undesirable patterns. Municipalities can use this tool to ensure that development will conform to local design norms and best practices dictated by engineering and environmental sustainability principles.

However, the type of changes to existing zoning that I suggest in chapter 8 will preclude the use of zoning to enforce unnecessarily rigid and uniform standards of development that waste land and override the market to restrict additions to the supply of housing. In chapter 8 I suggest a zoning rule that—rather than force housing to be developed within zones characterized as low density, requiring building on larger lots and thereby making land less expensive per square foot—would require high density to be the rule to which any zoning defaults. With high-density housing zoning, those who want to build on larger lots will be allowed to and would have to buy up several smaller lots to build on. Rather than discouraging mixed uses and transit-friendly development, zoning ordinances can be reformulated to encourage general and specific plans that facilitate mixed uses and easy accessibility to transit. Zoning should have the flexibility to unfreeze the built environment when changes in technology and conditions in the market for goods and services render existing buildings and patterns of development obsolete.

The End of Enforced Segregation

By the 1960s, attitudes against enforced segregation, represented so well in Hall's 2007 article, had become widespread. The loosening ability of residents to affect who would be allowed to purchase housing in their neighborhood raised fears that segregation by class would also be disallowed by law.

From a survey conducted as part of a 1971 study completed for the Miami Valley Regional Planning Commission (MVRPC) my firm found that the desire for a reasonable range of value and income uniformity among neighbors is by no means confined to a single class, race, or ethnic group. Our study was published but only after the validity of its results was intensively examined and determined by staff and commissioners of MVRPC.[11] Homeowners reported many reasons why they felt most comfortable living next to people who shared their views or tastes in everything from music to child-rearing. Not surprisingly, the reluctance of homeowners to accept the development of new housing likely to attract households with less income than theirs was motivated partially by the fear of changes in the level of public services and the decline of property values.[12]

When we reported the results of our study, one question frequently asked was whether "class" was really a surrogate term for "race." Because we and our team of interviewers had talked and listened to the respondents during pretests and the telephone interviews, we were able to reassure the questioners that the respondents to our survey knew the difference. But we were still asked to make a special "run" of the survey results to test the possibility that the responses of middle-class black households differed from the responses of middle-class white households when incomes were used as a surrogate for race. What we found was that middle-class black households wanted to maintain homogeneity in their neighborhood more than middle-class white households wanted homogeneity.

Civil Rights to Environmentalism

The social revolution of the civil rights era brought the full force of the law down on the denial of equal access to housing and other real estate. The success of the civil rights movement in marshaling public opinion against this and other forms of racial, ethnic, and religious discrimination in the marketplace has also helped to encourage the gush of regulations with respect to the environment that also restricted housing development and made it more expensive. Brave marchers and other civil rights activists taught the nation that social change could be legislated and that private property rights could be superseded to achieve social goals.

As books such as Rachel Carson's *Silent Spring* raised societal concerns about the way market-based actions were affecting nature, voters asked their elected officials to rein in the property rights of businesses producing goods and services that harmed the environment. The phrase by Robert Bruegmann in his *Sprawl: A Compact History* that best explains for me the shift in attitude that has occurred since the 1950s is that people now feel they are entitled to obtain the social and physical environment they desire.

Once the concept of controlling race-discriminating and environmentally damaging market actions gained broad acceptance, it was a small step for voters to believe they had the right to ask their locally elected officials to overrule market-based decisions they felt would alter the physical features and social milieu they had grown accustomed to enjoying. The desire of homeowners to protect and, if possible, enhance the value of their homes usually played a conscious or sub-conscious role in motivating them to support restrictive regulations. Economists have their own jargon for such self-serving, anticompetitive attempts to increase the value of an existing property—they call it "rent seeking."

As the pace of technological and social change within the nation increased and Americans seemed powerless to change much of what was occurring inter-nationally, the psychological importance of maintaining neighborhood stability increased. American citizens saw their sons and daughters put in harm's way in Vietnam, and again recently in Afghanistan and Iraq. As more people in the United States felt the world and nation were unstable and insecure, the emo-tional need for safety and stability at home became greater. By the late 1970s, promising to preserve the status quo had become a solid vote-getter for many local and regional politicians.

People who no longer saw the farmlands they once saw from their cars on the way out of town joined the chorus urging a stop to the suburban develop-ment that was referred to in a negative way as "sprawl." The popularity of the antisprawl movement led to the acceptance of a series of additional restrictions on suburban development. The resulting closing of the urban frontiers of regions whose populations were being swelled by births and unprecedented levels of immigration led to leapfrogging development to formerly agricultural communities, far from suburbs at the edges of existing urbanized regions.

Growth Controls

Pressure for public regulations of the housing supply came first and strongest to fast-growing northeastern and Pacific Coast regions. The power to regulate was significantly expanded by two legal rulings that added the ability to control growth to the power to regulate zoning.

A 1972 state court ruling concerning the small jurisdiction of Ramapo, New York, magnified the local power provided by the *Euclid* decision by granting cities the right to impose growth controls.[13] This paved the way for the movements that sought to stop suburban sprawl. One favorite tactic to do this was for the city or county with jurisdiction over the open space and farmland at the edge of existing urban development to place an urban limit line or boundary beyond which no residential development would be allowed.

Often high among the justifications given for such limit lines was that stopping further residential development would enhance local public treasury money by precluding the need to extend public infrastructure to the vacant land. It was claimed that the provision of such infrastructure would cost more than the future taxes to be received from the buyers of the new homes. Rarely was the analysis behind such claims checked because the results of limiting development, justified by such claims, were popular with voters currently living in the already built-up areas. But whether these growth-stopping boundaries were fiscally beneficial or not, they crippled the ability of developers to increase the supply of housing in response to the profit opportunities suggested by the market.

Usually the developers owning or optioning vacant land on the green fields beyond a proposed urban limit line financed campaigns to fight the passage of boundary-setting ordinances. When a developer-financed antiboundary campaign fails, which is usually the case, the passage of the urban limit line ordinance is viewed as a defeat for developers generally. Unfortunately, this view is very wrong. While the particular developer or group of developers who controlled the fields that had been legislated to be forever green may have lost money in the short run, what they gained from limiting opportunities for development of vacant land was decreased competition among builders. Laws that keep the building industry from building enough houses to equal or exceed increases in demand enable those who build to charge more for their products. That is, the effect of urban limit lines and similar techniques turn successful builders into monopolists with the power to charge more for their products than would be possible without the imposed limits.

The creation of monopolies by private parties is a crime under both state and federal antitrust laws. If builders were found guilty of colluding to restrict the supply of housing and to raise prices, as Henry George had thought they would, the builders would be fined and sent to prison. But municipalities are exempt from antitrust laws. Urban limit lines and the other housing supply restrictions imposed by local governments unwittingly create the monopolies that builders could not legally create for themselves. Just as gasoline buyers were the losers when the monopolist Rockefeller controlled the supply of oil, home buyers are the losers when local jurisdictions control the supply of housing.

On the West Coast in 1974, the San Francisco Bay Area city of Petaluma obtained federal court approval to set the rate at which residential growth could take place within its boundaries.[14] I discuss the Petaluma case and a similar case that arose on New York in more detail in chapter 6. These cases were the ground-breaking judicial granting of the rights that existing residents have been using since the 1970s to restrict the house-buying opportunities of future residents.

These examples show that judicial decisions empowered local politicians and their city planners to ignore and override the signals being put out by the market to curtail the amount as well as the type of residential development that would be allowed. I feel compelled to cite just one of the cases that set the tone of what was to follow *Ramapo* and *Petaluma*. In 1974, the highly respected lib-eral Justice William O. Douglas wrote a decision that justified the use of zon-ing to limit the number of unrelated individuals that could live in a dwelling. That decision suggested that zoning ordinances would be valid if they "lay out zones where family values, youth values, and the blessings of quiet seclusion and clean air make a sanctuary for people."[15]

Controls on Urban Land Use Become Increasingly Restrictive

In 1976 my firm conducted a study on the impact of a residential zone change for the City of San Francisco. The change, which became effective in May of that year, lowered the amount of new housing that could be constructed to replace existing units. For practical purposes, the change was "down-zoning," which reduced housing density. By reducing the allowed areas for low-rise, multiunit structures, such as buildings containing three flats or twelve apartment units, the number of single-family and two-unit structures that could be replaced with higher density residences was dramatically reduced. Two areas of San Francisco provided case study examples of different results from this down-zoning.

Tear-Down Feasibility Thresholds

In recent years, the term "tear-downs" has come to mean what happens to older single-family houses in expensive neighborhoods, such as portions of Beverly Hills, as the smaller, older houses are replaced with bigger homes, sometimes referred to as "McMansions." While the term "tear-down" is new, the concept that existing residential structures will be replaced when the real estate eco-nomics of the area make it feasible to tear down is not new. When the purchase price of a new structure in an area is high enough to make it profitable to pay the costs of buying and demolishing the old structure as well as the costs of building the new, then the area (which may be as small as a block or as large as a whole neighborhood) is over the tear-down feasibility threshold.

In 1978 the zoning change that reduced the density of allowable develop-ment, that is, the amount of space and number of units allowed within a specific area, reverted some areas to below the feasibility threshold—the same areas that had been over that threshold according to previous real estate economics. The San Francisco Planning Board did this knowingly. I can say that because my firm had done a case study of what would happen to each of two areas in the event the down-zoning was passed. We reported our results in a public hearing before the board. The U.S. Census Bureau delineates small areas in metropolitan areas on maps and then maintains statistical records for each of those areas, which it refers to as "Census Tracts." We identified the real estate economics of Census Tract 327 in San Francisco's Sunset District neighborhood and Census Tract 109 in the Russian Hill neighborhood of that city.

We found the proposed zoning would have no immediate effect in the Sunset tract because at that time the costs associated with acquiring single-family houses, demolishing them, and then building several units on the site could not be covered by the market value of the new units. That is, the area was below the tear-down feasibility threshold. Conversely, quite a few of the houses in the small area of Russian Hill that we studied were above the tear-down feasibility threshold. Based on the increased number of units that could have been built to replace existing units, Census Tract 109 would have seen a net increase of 1,179 units. But most of those units were never built because the new lower-density zoning disallowed their construction.

In time, some units were torn down and replaced in both areas, but this took decades, during which the prices of all housing in San Francisco escalated. The down-zoning that we studied, and that both the planning board and the board of supervisors approved, was only one of the causes of the escalation in housing prices, but the role played by down-zoning was significant. The new units that were eventually added as the rising tide of prices lifted up the tear-down feasibility threshold everywhere were not added as quickly or in the numbers that would have occurred had the pre-1978 zoning remained in place.

In 2007 I attended a luncheon meeting addressed by Dean Macris, San Francisco's acting planning director. Macris had been the planning director in 1976 and had attended when I gave the report that failed to convince the commission to vote against the proposed down-zoning. A widely respected leader in the planning field, Macris had been called out of semiretirement to lead the San Francisco planning department once again. At the luncheon, he outlined a new plan that, if approved, would dramatically increase the amount and density of housing that San Francisco would allow to be built on land previously zoned for industrial uses in the city's "South of Market" area. The new plan allowed for the construction of towers up to 930 feet in height as well as midrise units.

Macris and his planning team were well aware that even in the midst of a lending capital crunch that had induced a slowdown in housing sales and a slight drop in prices, the high cost of housing in San Francisco was causing severe hardships on the poor. Exorbitant housing prices were also encouraging middle-class homeowners—especially those with growing families—to "cash out" and move to cities where they would have access to more affordable housing and possibly sunnier skies. The only way to allow the city's housing supply to begin to catch up with demand was to solve the problem that Macris referred to in his speech: "The problem with San Francisco is that we don't have enough land."

I suspect that Macris understood that San Francisco had plenty of land, but much of that land was not zoned for residential use, although occupied by obsolete and often vacant industrial structures. Even more housing sites were built with low-density older homes.

The Vicious Cycle of Inclusionary Zoning

Where tear-down development is feasible, developers would quickly rebuild lower-density homes and replace older nonresidential uses with new houses if allowed to do so by zoning. In the area across the street in the middle South of Market neighborhood where I now live, such replacement of old warehouses, obsolete factories, and older homes was feasible for decades before the recession of 2008. Throughout these decades, calls for more affordable housing came from many politicians, civic groups, and citizens. But the construction of a few thousand units of lower-priced new housing by the public redevelopment agency, funded by fees charged to developers who built market housing, produced too few units to make a serious dent in the problem.

In what seemed to be a desirable and worthwhile attack on the problem of affordable housing, an additional provision was added to the zoning ordinance. The provision was an example of what is termed inclusionary zoning, which required that all new housing projects provide a specific proportion of dwelling units at sufficiently lower than market rate prices. These units were to be sold, in the case of condominiums, or rented, if apartments, to households within specified low- and moderate-income brackets.

Like rent control, another land-use policy that eventually exacerbates the problem it intends to cure, the short-term benefits of inclusionary zoning are small compared to the long-run effect they have on discouraging the growth of the housing supply. When originally imposed, San Francisco's inclusionary zoning required that 10 to 15 percent of all new residential projects must be priced to sell well below market to be affordable by very low-, low-, and moderate-income households.

Since originally imposed, the proportion of "below-market" units required has been raised, and the proportion of such units priced to low-income house-holds has increased. Such increases are part of the vicious cycle of inclusionary zoning. The below-market requirement raises the feasibility bar in the real estate economics that determine whether developers can profitably build new units to replace existing structures or on vacant land. When inclusionary zoning fails even to come close to solving the ill of shortages in low- and moderate-priced housing, cities like San Francisco increase the proportion of those units that must be priced to be affordable to low- and very low-income households. Making that paradox understandable is one of the purposes of this book. The following example is one step forward in making it clear and understandable.

In San Francisco, luxury units were selling at very high prices to affluent households from the nearby region as well as from around the world. Regional customers were being drawn from its pool of affluent "empty nesters" and the young high-income earners in the high tech industries. The demand for luxury units as second homes was also being stoked by entrepreneurs and investors who had hit it big in various global industries. In 2007, about 60 percent of the owners of the units in some luxury buildings, such as the residences built on top of the Four Seasons Hotel on Market Street, were part-time residents who had primary dwellings overseas or elsewhere in the Americas. At that time, the selling price was about $1,800 per square foot in residential condominiums in the Four Seasons and other high-end buildings. That was about twice the average $900 price per square foot for less prestigious new condominium projects in San Francisco, and about four times the average $450 price per square foot of new condominiums being built in downtown Oakland. Market prices were kept high for three reasons: the high demand for top-of-the-line luxury units, the shortage of land zoned for relatively high density housing, and the imposition of high fees and long delays for the projects that were approved.

Even for projects that conformed to zoning requirements, the long delays for environmental impact reviews and plan-checking continued to play a role in driving up the costs of developing new housing units in San Francisco. The fees were raised to increase funds for the public construction of affordable housing. And for the same reason that Willy Sutton was said to rob banks, many people believed that developers seemed to be "where the money was." But until the recession of 2008, the lure of profit did keep developers going through the hoops of long delays, inclusionary zoning, and high fees to add to the housing stock.

The surge of supply in the downtown and South of Market areas set up San Francisco for its first housing price decline in decades. When there was no longer the expectation that housing prices would climb forever, the unsold units remained unsold long enough to push prices down. The drop in condo prices offered many households who wanted to live in the city their first big break. However, the price drop was not considered a good thing by the developers—they were left with substantial losses due to the lower prices. Nor was the price drop a good thing for redevelopment agencies. They had counted on a specific portion of tax windfall—that portion referred to as "capturing a tax increment"—from the high-rise units to subsidize publicly sponsored development. The city's redevelopment agencies had intended to use the captured tax increment to build a multibillion-dollar bus and rail terminal plus public housing for low- and moderate-income households.

The Macris-proposed plan, which would allow very high-density residential condominiums to be built in the city, called for the inclusion of moderately priced affordable units in only a portion of the new high-rise buildings. Under the plan, the redevelopment agency would use tax increment funds to subsidize the construction of adjoining low- and mid-rise units that would be rented to low- and very-low income households. The redevelopment agency's one "sales pitch" for the new zoning was that it would not just serve upper-income households but would also directly provide housing for poor and moderate-income households.

It is interesting to note that proponents of the higher density zoning did not even try to explain in their sales pitch that adding new housing at the top of the price range would over time cause housing prices in San Francisco to decline or at least stabilize. This failure struck me as something akin to the "Stockholm Syndrome" under which hostages come to adopt the perspective of their capturers. The steady drumbeat of antimarket rhetoric that for more than thirty years has been used to support actions that install rent control, lower allowable density and heights, increase the costs and time required to obtain building permits, and preserve older, physically obsolete buildings has driven the most basic of all economic concepts out of public discussions. Even developers seemed to have forgotten that the way to drive down the price of all products, even housing, is to increase supply faster than demand.

Since the 1970s, San Francisco had severe restrictions on the height of buildings in downtown zoning districts. But Mayor Willie Brown waged a campaign to show that very tall buildings can be beautiful. "Most effective" was the word that came back after Mayor Brown toured a cadre of influential San Franciscans through downtown Vancouver, British Columbia. The group came back extolling the beauty of the high-rise towers in Vancouver. Macris and his design team played up the aesthetic advantages of allowing high-rise towers in and near portions of the downtown. Still another consideration—that much of the downtown area had few existing residences because that area had been built when San Francisco still had major manufacturing and warehouse land uses—increased the chances that the Macris plan could gain political acceptance.

While I, like most San Francisco residents (I recently moved downtown to a twenty-two-story building on Mission Street), have some quibbles with the specifics of the proposed plan, it could be a step in the right direction. Unfortunately, when the final plan and the regulations that would enforce it had made their way through many debates before the planning commission and the board of supervisors, it was considerably watered down. Older, technically and economically obsolete warehouses and multilevel factories continued to be off limits to developers.

San Francisco and Other Supply-Constraining Places Lead the Way

In 2003 the Lincoln Institute funded a study by urban scholar Eran Ben-Joseph. The purpose was to review what had been published by housing officials and developers concerning subdivision regulations, practices, and attitudes in single-family housing markets. The study reviewed the results of surveys in 1964 and in 1969 by the National Association of Home Builders. That association's surveys had shown that at that time government regulations were not a significant barrier to providing affordable housing.

But all that changed in the 1970s. Ben-Joseph reported: "By the 1970s, a dramatic shift in the relative importance of the problems had taken place. Government regulations, as well as financing difficulties, had become the central problems of the industry."[16] The problem Ben-Joseph was referring to is the problem of providing affordable housing.

Since the 1970s many regional and statewide commissions have been set up to oppose sprawl and to preserve lands adjoining coastal waters and inland waters, agricultural land, open space, and areas that either were or might be designated as wetlands and the habitat of threatened plants or animals. National and state environmental protection acts and agencies, many established since 1970, require reports and a process of hearings and governmental approvals by local, regional, state, and federal boards, agencies, and commissions before development of any scale can proceed.

The actions of these national and state commissions have added a powerful layer of land-use restrictions on top of those imposed by municipal and county governments. The environmental review process mandated now by both the federal government and the states has provided easy access to private parties wishing to enter the arena of public land use regulation in order to stop or modify proposed development projects. The land-use-affecting actions of the public and private forces, whose powers to control the use of land have been greatly enhanced by the changes in laws and public attitudes that have taken place since 1970, work to keep existing buildings from being replaced and to keep vacant land vacant.

Citizen Participation

Elected officials and appointees on planning boards who, for all practical purposes, have become the bodies that decide when, where, and how much the housing supply of urban areas can expand, have tended to be more concerned with the contemporary popularity of proposed projects than with their ultimate impact on the public welfare. Recently a well-respected land-use lawyer sent me an e-mail with a comment relevant to the shift of public policy described in this chapter. I do not want to use his name because to do so would threaten the effectiveness of his appearance before public agencies, boards, and commissions on behalf of clients. He wrote:

> I can attest to this: Far too many zoning boards, plan commissions, and ultimate legislative decision-makers abandon their responsibilities to the greater public good (which they are at least in theory chosen to serve);

and, rather, invite (sometimes literally) "a show of hands" of the hearing/meeting audiences for or against a worthy project—which they often follow blindly, all the while ignoring well-established zoning and planning factors (and the costly evidence given by the developer relevant to those factors) on which they should base their decisions.

Many planning professionals charged with gathering the evidence that municipal officials use to decide the fate of the land use plans and projects rely increasingly on "citizen participation." Unfortunately, citizens who participate are usually unrepresentative of the entire public and biased by the narrow perspective of their own self-interests.

"Visioning!"

The latest approach to land-use planning is called "visioning." Under this approach, a group of self-selected "stakeholders" who live or own property near the area that is the object of current land-use planning are assembled for a series of meetings during which they are queried and they discuss what they would like to see happen and not happen in their area. Rarely, if ever, do the planning professionals who facilitate these meetings moderate the discussions or provide information about the costs, feasibility, or long-run impact of the "planning options and goals." Rather, the participants are asked to invent those options and consider the visions created by what they invented. The resulting visions that are put forward to guide the specifics of the plan rarely suggest changes that could stand the tests of providing the community with a high degree of benefits for the costs likely to result. Often the options they invent are really "wish lists" articulated as goals that are not feasible. Evaluating and discussing the wishes turns out to be time-consuming and expensive and leads to a dead end.

Taken together, both the legal foundations and the planning practices that constitute the new political economy have increased the costs and extended the time of new housing development while dramatically reducing the amount of housing that has been built. The time has come to reformulate the laws and practices by which the municipalities of the American regions with the greatest economic potential manage their lands. Housing is the real estate that has been most affected, but work and recreational spaces of the built environment have also been impacted.

The Powers Granted Property Rights and the Uses of Credit

The rules of economic behavior, including the rules that govern the play in the day-to-day arena of real estate markets, are shaped by societal values at least as much as they are shaped by laws and the court rulings that interpret the constitutionality of those laws. Even totalitarian regimes—societies where the government controls every aspect of the life of its citizens—expend energy to convince their citizens of the "rightness" of their laws, primarily in the form of propaganda, rather than rely exclusively on force to compel compliance with their laws. In representative governments, laws reflect the attitudes, values, and aspirations of the governed.

The attitudes and values of the writers of the U.S. Constitution were drawn from the ancient Greek philosophers as reinvented during the intellectual ferment called the Age of Enlightenment. The writers of the Constitution shared their attitudes and values with the leaders of the people who were to become citizens and voters in the new republic. High on the list of the priorities that emerged from that ferment was the sanctity of private property rights. As Ethan Fishman, professor of political science at the University of Alabama, wrote in an article on Aristotle's *Nicomachean Ethics* and Edmund Burke's *Reflections on the Revolution France*, "Aristotle and Burke supported private property and free enterprise on the basis of the distinguishing characteristic of human beings—the possession of a soul that makes it possible for us to exercise free will and become unique individuals. One of the advantages of private property, they taught, is that it helps us develop and manifest our individuality, as well as to express one of their most cherished ideals, generosity."[17]

When the American colonies cast off the reign of King George, they threw the new country's real estate entrepreneurs—many of whom, like George Washington, were Founding Fathers—into the prizefight ring of real estate markets, where they fought for profits with very little governmental interference. They were warned by referees, both judicial and governmental, who observed in the infighting the low blows of economic fraud and the kidney punches of conspicuously harmful actions or negligence. It was the unrestrained competition among developers, builders, and property owners—including the land speculators among our Founding Fathers and the many who followed in their footsteps—that kept them from having the power to drive up the value of their land and earn excessive profits. Again, when I use the term "excessive profits," I refer the amounts above what would be required to keep developers and builders in business.

As the United States became an industrial power, the titans of industries such as the railroads, steel, oil, and gas often used their size to throttle their competitors and control the supply of what they produced to keep prices high and profits excessive. As mentioned earlier, these predatory practices led Theodore Roosevelt and the "trust busters" who came after him to encourage the passage of antitrust laws that penalized firms and individuals who colluded to control the supply of goods and services to raise prices.

But the antitrust laws that were used to control industrial monopolists did not have to be applied to urban developers. Nevertheless, some developers of new and expanding cities often overhyped what their lots and subdivisions would offer and in some cases built structures that violated the norms of safety. Despite whatever advantages these unfair or even deceitful practices may have provided the cheaters, they were rarely able to cause their competitors to shut down. The land speculators, developers, and builders who built the cities and towns that cradled America's industrial revolution may have wished for the power that Henry George assumed they would come to possess. But their intentions were thwarted by similarly motivated competitors.

The path to profit for urban land developers and builders lay in risking their time and capital to expand urban areas with new development when the demands of increased prosperity and population growth pushed prices past the threshold of profitability. Profit could also be made by modernizing or tearing down and replacing obsolete structures with new buildings that accommodated the latest technology. As a result, residential standards of living as well as workplace productivity continued to rise.

Successive generations of Americans lived more comfortably than their parents did—a comfort that is taken for granted by each successive generation. Supreme Court Justice Sandra Day O'Connor, in a speech shortly after she retired, recounted her life as a young girl growing up on a ranch with no indoor plumbing. Although I grew up in a middle-class city family with an inside bathroom, it was my chore to get up early in the mornings to stoke the furnace with coal so our house would be warm by breakfast time.

At the beginning of the twentieth century, twenty-one years after Henry George published *Progress and Poverty*, only 19 percent of U.S. families owned their own homes, and the average family spent $769 per year. Of these expenditures, 23.3 percent ($179 per year) was spent on housing. In 2002, almost 67 percent of families owned their own homes, and the average expenditure on much-improved housing had climbed to 32.8 percent of expenditures. Housing in 2002 was more expensive in major urban areas with growing economies. In Boston, housing costs constituted 36.5 percent of expenditures, and in New York it was 37.6 percent.[18]

Private property protections were granted in the first ten amendments to the U.S. Constitution, known as the Bill of Rights, in 1789. Until the changes in the law described in this chapter, the Fifth Amendment protected property owners from arbitrary government interference in the use of their land, except in unusual and dire situations. The relevant part of this amendment states that no person shall be derived of "property, without due process of law; nor shall private property be taken for public use, without just compensation."

The 1926 *Euclid* decision was rendered in response to a legal brief that argued that zoning was needed to protect private property from nuisances. But in the light of how this decision has been interpreted ever since, it is clear that the 1926 decision opened a large chink in the armor of protection for private property offered by the U.S. Constitution and court decisions prior to 1926. It took many years, and subsequent court decisions in many jurisdictions, to clarify the way that chink cleared the way for the substitution of public for private decisions.

Even today one sometimes hears some elected members of local government and other attendees at council, planning commission, and similar public meetings express the erroneous opinion that the law will not allow local municipalities and counties to override private decisions made in response to information coming out of local markets about the type, scale, and location of development.

The 1970s brought two court decisions that further expanded the control of local authorities over the use of land: the New York State Court granted the Village of Ramapo the power to impose growth controls restricting the use of property, and the Federal Court of Appeals in California allowed the town of Petaluma to cap the rate of development. These reinterpretations of what the Fifth Amendment to the U.S. Constitution means lay a legal foundation, which has subsequently been confirmed by other courts, expanding the ability of local land-use regulators to turn the control of land use over to urban voters. Thereafter, the political economy in an increasing number of urban places elevates the dictates of the electorate—as they are perceived by their elected officials—over the dictates of real estate markets. In time, other land uses have come to be similarly treated. But it was the housing market that was initially trumped by planning decisions.

An increasing number of court rulings have sanctioned the ability of existing residents to decide how and whether vacant and underutilized property adjoining their homes could be used. Consumers interested in moving to a newly built or to an existing home may still register their demands in the marketplace. But the successful developers of the twenty-first century follow more closely the dictates of the neighbors rather than signals from the marketplace.

Neighborhood Branding

The civil rights movement and, subsequently, heightened environmental concerns have altered the dominant norms of society. Americans accept, and even demand, laws that legislate changes in issues once considered outside the domain of government. Previously, neighborhood segregation by race and class, while rarely sanctioned officially, had been generally accepted as a societal norm.

Coming from a family that had fled the persecution of Nazi Germany and escaped to the United States in 1938, I understood the wrongness of Jim Crow laws. My father joined the NAACP as soon as he could afford the membership fee. He hung his membership card over his desk in the small apparel store he opened in 1939, even though we had few, if any, African American customers in the neighborhood.

In my early years of grade school, my family lived in the South Avondale area of Cincinnati. After almost seventy years, I must confess, I cannot remember the names of many of my neighbors and schoolfellows. But I do remember the names of Jimmy Van Orsdale and Charles Tubbs. Jimmy was athletic, handsome, and popular enough to be elected class president one year. Charley's uncle was a country singer who was frequently on the radio. But that is not why

I remember their names after these many years. What was unique about them in the South Avondale grade school from 1938 to 1946 was that they were white and Christian. The rest of my classmates were from the African American or Jewish families that entirely predominated the South Avondale neighborhood in those years. I never really thought about that, most likely because I never objected to it.

By the time I went to Walnut Hills, a high school that enrolled students from throughout Cincinnati based on test scores, my family had moved to a small single-family house on Edgehill Place, and a few years later to a somewhat bigger house on Eaton Lane. It was then that I got my first introduction to the role that neighborhoods played in determining house values, and the role that demography played in branding a neighborhood with the characteristics that were important to incumbent and would-be residents. I remember going to high school on the first day of school and telling Marilyn Ellman, a socially savvy student in my class, that we had moved from Edgehill Place to Eaton Lane. Her eyes opened wide with disbelief and she asked me, "Doesn't that mean you moved from north of Greenwood Avenue to south of Greenwood Avenue?" I thought about the geography for a second, and then told her, "Yes! So what?" She said "Claude, you have moved from North Avondale back to South Avondale. No one ever does that!"

Marilyn's shock at my family's social naiveté was my first insight into the branding effect of neighborhoods and the role that social and racial discrimination plays in the desirability of that brand. During the 1940s, Realtors showed housing for sale in North Avondale to Jews and white Gentiles. I remember that African Americans were not shown "listings" in North Avondale until the 1950s. When the great University of Cincinnati basketball star Oscar Robertson bought a house, the house was on Eaton Lane, which my high school friend had correctly identified as in South Avondale.

From Racial Branding to Heightened Branding-Based Class Segregation

The accepted codes of neighborhood segregation by race and ethnic background were smashed by the civil rights movement. Deed restrictions and acquiescence to social and business pressures that kept neighborhoods segregated racially and ethnically were made illegal by laws supported by the majority of citizens.

The 1954 *Brown v. Board of Education* Supreme Court decision shattered the illusion of "separate but equal" racially segregated public schools and ultimately led to local court-imposed school busing with the goal of racial integration. Busing had mixed results. Some families of all raced moved to avoid having their children attend school with children of other races, and because of the perceived problem of a decline in discipline in the schools where there was integration.

As always, where the households moved to was limited by their incomes and affected by their priorities for the characteristics of the different neighborhoods and locations where housing prices fit within their budgets. My wife and

I moved our family with five children from a rented home in Berkeley to El Cerrito, a nearby community in the East Bay area of the San Francisco Bay Area. Our children attended a public grade school near home, and later, when they attended high school, they were bused to the public high school in Richmond, California. African Americans were the majority of Richmond High School's students. Asian and Caucasian students were then, and still are, in the minority at Richmond High School. The African American student population includes many children from poor, one-parent families with the lower class characteristics that make it difficult to attain middle-class economic and social status. The city of Richmond has one of the state's highest crime and murder rates.

African American students from the middle- to upper-class neighborhoods attended Richmond High, but because of their color, they had a tougher time socially at the high school than did our own kids. The middle- and upper-class African Americans found themselves called "Oreos"—the cookie that is black on the outside but white on the inside.

Our immediate neighbors were an African American family headed by a physician who had three children—two sons and a daughter. When they reached high school age, the family sent them to a Christian Brothers private school rather than have them attend Richmond High School. They faced the same problems and were reacting similarly to those problems as the attitudes that had been expressed by the middle-class African American respondents whom we interviewed in our study in Dayton, Ohio, "Low and Moderate Income Housing in the Suburbs."

School desegregation gave the loudest and clearest signal that it was no longer acceptable for incumbent neighbors to decide the ethnic makeup or the religious beliefs of who could live next to them and share the same public services. Yet the results of Brown v. Board of Education were by no means the only action that sent this message. Laws against discrimination in housing sales and rentals were passed and enforced on both local and federal levels. Diversity began to be included with all public actions and subsidization of housing production. Discrimination became illegal and, more importantly, culturally unacceptable. When parents pulled their children out of public schools where the racial and class mix had changed, they rarely admitted their true motives, offering excuses such as: "My child has special problems that the public school system cannot be expected to handle."

In the late 1950s, when families started to shift from homes in the center cities to emerging communities in the suburbs, neither they, nor developers, nor real estate sales people ever said that these relocations were attempts to avoid integration specifically or diversity in general. Nevertheless, there were many general plans that set development standards, espousing the desirability of affordable housing and residential diversity in suburban communities. But as farms, ranches, and open space were carved up into new communities, zoning and development standards were set up to ensure that these communities would be accessible only to buyers having a high range of incomes. The first wave of entrants into new subdivisions understood that zoning and development standards were engineered to preclude the entry of lower-income households as the new communities were built out.

Class Segregation and Rent Seeking

One lesson that many Americans learned from the civil rights actions that barred exclusions based on race and ethnic background was the acceptability and heightened importance of income-based class segregation. Such economically enforced segregation was considered by prospective buyers to ensure that there would be good schools, friendly neighbors, and compatible playmates for their kids. Homeowners of all races, religions, and ethnic backgrounds developed an awareness of the role that class segregation played in the creation and maintenance of neighborhood desirability. Even more importantly, they came to feel that every neighbor had the right to share in the engineering and design of programs and policies that would enhance and perpetuate the class status of their neighborhood.

First seen in a few communities on the Atlantic and Pacific coasts, plans and ordinances that reflected the desires of local citizens began to usurp free market decisions on housing. Responding to the desires of local citizens became increasingly popular. The basis of that popularity is not hard to understand—existing, or incumbent homeowners and renters were able to set or preserve local environmental, social, and public service conditions. They felt the satisfaction that comes with feeling that they could have some control over their own residential environment. There is no doubt that the objective of controlling what was permitted to be built nearby, therefore influencing the income-related class characteristics of next-door neighbors, was motivated by the desire to maintain and enhance the value of their own homes.

Many homeowners realize that the constriction on supply within regional submarkets will tend to lift the value of their own homes. I refer in a derogatory way to such motivations for supply-restricting behavior as "rent seeking."[19] With respect to housing, rent seeking occurs when the power of government is used to restrict a factor of production whose value is based on the contribution that factor makes to the production of housing. In housing, of course, that factor is land. By restricting the availability of additional land for development, there is a rise in the value of existing buildings and sites where new development is allowed, whereas the value would be driven down by additional production. For example, if all the producers of rice were able to lobby the government into giving them a monopoly by legislating that no additional acreage can be put into rice production, the price of rice and the value, or rent, of land being used in its production would be higher. Consumers are stuck with paying the higher price of rice. The same is true of housing and urban development.

Urban economist William Fischel of Dartmouth College published *The Homevoter Hypothesis* in 2007.[20] Fischel explained that homeowners were able to assume a dominant role in local land-use politics when the rate of homeownership grew to the point that about two-thirds of all houses were owner occupied. He cites a 1990 survey showing that the median value of the homeowners' equity was eleven times as large as the median value of the sum of all their other assets. For anyone who resides in his or her owned home, that home is a nest egg, usually the most important nest egg. Fischel explains that this motivates homeowners to safeguard their neighborhoods against any suspected value-damaging change, including the possibility that the physical or social character of the neighborhood will change so as to hurt the value of their nest egg.

Fischel points out that homeowners' interest in improving the value of their homes encourages the passage of legislation to provide schools, parks, and other amenities that improve the quality of life. But the same mercenary concerns that bring out the vote for good local schools also motivate homeowners to become tough and effective activists in the fight for low-density, single-use zoning and legislation that limits the scale and increases the costs of new housing within the region where they live.

Fischel has provided valid and important insights into why so many homeowners are NIMBYs who say don't build it—but if you do, not in my backyard. I am less taken with the practicality and long-term benefits of Fischel's suggestion that we buy off the home-owning NIMBYs by insuring their homes against value drops. Instead I will point out that in terms of their political power, American cities are creatures of the state governments. Therefore, in spite of the federal court rulings along the vein of *Euclid* and *Petaluma*, the states could and should forbid the use of zoning to restrict density and force structural and social homogeneity. Homeowner activists lobbying and voting to gain rent seeking and other perceived benefits are increasingly supported by a drumbeat of articles and books with both apt and erroneous descriptions about the evils of suburban development, so-called sprawl.

Politically mandated laws have created the very shift of wealth to land owners that Henry George had prophesized would cheat working men and women out of their rightful share of wealth and income opportunities. But in his 1879 book, *Progress and Poverty*, George predicted that this sad end to the dream that brought immigrants to America would result from the successful collusion of land- and property-owning real estate tycoons. He never thought that the voters of American cities would elect officials and pass referenda that resulted in the inequitable economic conditions he feared. The values of existing homes, and of land permitted to be used as housing sites, increased as public decisions deprived the housing market of the power to induce supply changes in response to demand pressures.

Furthermore, the acceptance of "citizen control" spread to nonresidential markets. Eventually, many urban markets found that barriers to entry had been built around office, industrial, and hotel markets. While these barriers were rarely as high as the barriers built around residential markets, they nevertheless thwarted supply additions enough to affect price and lessen the flexibility of urban business complexes and structures to adapt to changing technological and economic conditions.

If commerce and industry are to remain productive and competitive, they must constantly innovate in response to new technology and changing consumer demands. This requires changes not only in the structures within which businesses operate but also changes to where they locate geographically. Businesses gain efficiencies if they are clustered close to similar businesses, suppliers, and customers. New clusters must be allowed to develop to facilitate continuing commercial and industrial efficiencies. A reformulation of how local authorities make decisions about commercial space as well as about housing is needed to stop the land-use decision-making process from throwing sand into the market-directed wheels of change.

The two-hundred-year period during which the public determinants of urban development and change were sympathetic to competing private real estate investors and developers laid out an informative model. Reading that model and considering why George's pessimistic forecast did not happen during that period can help us avoid the sad future he foresaw. Understanding how the quality, price, and quantity of housing in urban places are altered by neighborhood-changing development or removal would have avoided the expensive failures of slum clearance and other past governmental interference into land-use markets. Similarly, such an understanding will be necessary if future public policy is to beneficially affect housing prices and quality.

It was neither foreseen nor understood that restrictions on suburban development would have the effect of distorting wealth, increasing prices, and decreasing the quality of housing in the United States from the 1950s through the early years of the twenty-first century. The same is true of how urban housing prices and qualities were affected by the slum clearance projects that made up an important part of urban housing policies from the 1930s into the early 1970s. This lack of foresight and understanding stemmed from a tendency to focus on narrow housing segments, such as a single project or a residential neighborhood, while failing to consider how supply-affecting policies ultimately affect housing within an entire region.

Chapter 4 suggests a general model of how housing in neighborhoods changes in physical quality and price over time. The frontier-closing effects of urban renewal tearing down existing housing as well as the constraint of new residential development in older urban places and new suburban cities can be seen more clearly by understanding the functioning and interactions of the linked housing markets of metropolitan regions.

4

Housing Market Structure

Market Functions and Geographic Areas

Markets "Calculate" Prices

In somewhat the same way as computers are programmed with rules for performing specific calculations, laws, social norms, and physical conditions act as the operating rules that govern the choices available to the buyers and sellers in a particular market. In that sense, we may consider that markets "calculate" the price of goods and services from the data inputs of transactions between buyers and sellers.

Understanding the structure of a market and recognizing the conditions affecting the structure provide a picture of how prices are determined in the market and permit us to anticipate the results likely to follow from changes to the market's structure or the conditions affecting it. But before describing the structure of the markets in urban regional housing, I will first review the aspects that make markets good tools for allocating resources in the private sector, the limitations of markets as allocators of public goods, and the boundaries and differences of markets.

In his 1963 book, *The Study of Society*, Alfred Kuhn brilliantly clarified that markets are information systems that convert inherently subjective values and costs into objective money amounts so a decision can be made about the allocation of resources.[1] In real estate markets, the firms that Kuhn refers to are land developers, builders, and property owners deciding whether to invest their own entrepreneurial efforts and their own borrowed financial capital in urban land development and, if so, what and how to build, maintain, or remodel. These relationships are graphically represented in figure 4.1, originated by Kuhn.

By factors of production Kuhn refers to all the materials and supplies—commonly referred to as resources—that humans extract from nature and that

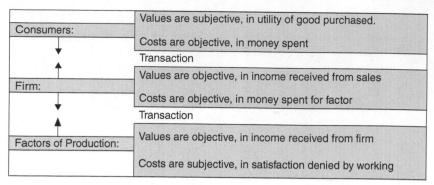

FIGURE 4.1 Functions of Market Information Systems

Source: Kuhn, *The Study of Society*, 567.

are needed to produce goods and services. He includes in factors of production the money paid to workers and managers to obtain their services as well as the interest paid to those who lend the producers the money to pay for the materials and supplies and the workers' salaries.

Kuhn recognized that what each consumer gets in satisfaction for his purchase is a subjective, personal matter. Because the degree of pleasure or pain each of us gets from something is shaped by our individual lifetime of experiences, no third party can assign uniform measures to our reactions to a good or service—that is, how much we may want or not want any particular good or service.

LOOKING AT SUBJECTIVE VALUES. The satisfaction that a couple gets from purchasing or renting the bundle of services that we refer to as a residence or house may not be the same for each person. Each partner may feel differently about the residence or house from day to day. Their changing moods and experiences will affect the satisfaction they get out of it and the surrounding neighborhood, which are affected by the nearby desirable and undesirable places and activities. For example, my wife likes going to the old Tate Museum in London because it has one of the world's great collections of paintings by Joseph Mallord William Turner; Turner's paintings do not stir me, but I like that museum because it has a great restaurant.

LOOKING AT OBJECTIVE COSTS. The dollars the couple spends on rent, utilities, mortgage payments, maintenance, and the like are very objective. That is, the dollars that trade hands at the point of purchase quantify the value put on the good or service in a measure that all people will agree has the same value. For example, when we pay a set amount of dollars for rent, the purchase of a house, or the purchase of a bottle of beer, the amount of dollars spent quantifies the item's cost to us and the other party in the transaction. The amount of money spent provides the universally understood measure of what the good or service we obtained costs and how much spending power we are giving up to obtain it.

The Role of Real Estate Firms

In real estate markets, the roles of the firm usually comprise land developers, builders, investors, and lenders. Each of them—and there are many in the local housing industry—must judge how many dollars consumers are willing and able to pay for alternative housing products built on alternative sites. The managers of the developers, builders, investors, and lenders may gain more emotional satisfaction and social rewards from serving some types of consumers rather than others, or they may gain satisfaction and rewards from paying some costs rather than others. The real estate agent may get more satisfaction out of signing a lease with a friendly young woman than a cranky old man, but each dollar stipulated in the lease and collected as commission are of equal value, whether from the friendly young woman or the cranky old man. Furthermore, there is a tough discipline on individuals and entities who develop, build, and invest. Regardless of the psychic or social satisfaction they get from what they do, they can only stay in business if revenues equal or exceed costs.

As developers and builders shop for vacant land, including possibly obtaining land by razing or rebuilding existing structures, they consider the required outlay of dollars for land. When added to the costs of the labor, materials, entrepreneurial effort, and capital required to develop the site and construct housing, the land cost must be less than the revenue received from the sale or rental of the housing.

Look again at what is represented graphically in figure 4.1: the area between the two parties to a transaction—that is, where the arrow from Consumers would meet the arrow from Firm—is the point of sale where a transaction is concluded. The dollars agreed upon and exchanged at the point of sale quantify the subjective benefits obtained by the buyer and the subjective worth of natural resources, human effort, and waiting received by consumers into objectively measured values and costs.

In the last sentence, I used the term "waiting" rather than "capital," which is the more common term for the cost that must be borne by the firm if the residential product is to be produced. The workers who labored to lay the foundation and build the structure of the home you live in expected to be paid daily or weekly. Likewise, the factories and mills that produced the lumber, materials, components, and fixtures used to construct the home had to be paid on delivery, or at most in thirty to sixty days. But it took many months, or even years, to prepare the site and build the structure that you live in. Thus, even if you paid cash to purchase your home as soon as the builder received the certificate of occupancy that permitted him to sell it to you, that builder had already put out money for many months to people and firms who would not wait for their money.

If you are a renter, your landlord will make payments for years before the rent from the building will equal the purchase price. That is, his waiting time will probably be even longer than that of the laborers and material providers for your building. If ever the expression "time is money" was appropriate, it applies to the costs charged by the lenders and investors who absorb the charges of the many workers and suppliers who will not wait for payment.

Market Structures and Consumer Benefits

Producer Costs and Consumer Benefits

The reality that markets are good information systems does not guarantee that markets will work to give consumers a good deal. Just because markets are good tools does not guarantee that they provide buyers and sellers with level playing fields or the best possible outcome. There is much empirical evidence to refute the oft-stated assertion that all markets are efficient indicators of what is best for consumers. Markets are efficient communicators of information, but that information is merely the reflection of the not necessarily publicly beneficial conditions of the firms and consumers whose actions make up the markets transactions.

As discussed previously, revenues must equal or exceed costs for development to be feasible and for the developing entity to continue in business. But markets only maximize the consumers' benefits if the amount required to put entrepreneurial, capital, and material resources into the product is minimized. When Middle Eastern nations ration the amount of oil they will allow to be pumped out of wells and with pumping costs less than ten dollars a barrel, they structure the market deal so it provides them with revenue considerably over that amount. Likewise, when municipalities restrict the vacant acreage they will allow to be developed, the price of developable land climbs over what sellers of vacant land would otherwise require.

The prices of the outputs of a market depend on its structure. If that structure limits entry to all but a few sellers, and if the sellers are limited by political forces with regard to what they can supply while there are no constraints on buyers, these conditions together constitute a market that economists refer to as monopoly. If the housing market of a region is structured as described here, housing prices will climb beyond the point needed to keep suppliers in the market. Because such monopoly-structured markets hand land and real estate sellers more profit than a competitively structured market would allow, the extra profits are often referred to as excess profits.

Whether a real estate project, such as a housing development, is feasible depends on whether the anticipated market value of finished product—the houses—exceeds all the costs associated with bringing them to the point of sale. If all the cost estimates, particularly the cost of land, when crunched through all the calculations show that the anticipated market value is greater, the project is considered feasible; if not, the project is considered unfeasible. To the individual builder/developer, land is a cost that may well determine if real estate development is feasible, and if so, which among the possible uses of that land will provide the greatest profit. In the jargon of the real estate industry, the use that will provide the greatest profit is referred to as the highest and best use.

The real estate market provides signals that real estate investors read—although they must be able to interpret and infer from what they read—to identify what to do to gain the most profit. What the market is not is a computer software program that uses those signals as input data and then calculates an output suggesting a development that will be priced fairly. Nor is the market a program that provides consumers with information about where and how to get the best quality for their money. Furthermore, the market is not a scientific machine capable of methodically allocating resources into urban neighborhoods that provide the most livable and productive spaces.

Only the competitive scrambling for profits and rents engaged in by the private sector can put a lid on the price of buildings and land. And it's only through competition in the marketplace that pressures are put on land developers and builders to respond to the priorities of space users.

Public Goods and Public Bads

The shared nature of consumer demands for some goods and services makes it unlikely that markets will do a good job of allocating resources for them. Such goods and services are often referred to as public goods. If markets are used to allocate such goods or services, the relevant market structure is referred to as a "natural monopoly" and regulated by a public authority. Public goods include services such as national defense, which are not provided to individuals or separate entities but to all residents of the nation. Most items of widely used infrastructure, such as bridges, tunnels, and roads, fall into the category of public goods. It would be wasteful of resources to restrict bridges, tunnels, and roads to only those who can afford to pay a high enough toll to maximize the profits above what it cost to construct, maintain, and administrate them.

Providing some public goods by private markets would be infeasible. In other cases—for example, the production and distribution of electric power—the recognition that private market allocation would work poorly for such natural monopolies has led to the creation of public regulation of the market for such utilities. However, how much and whether to provide public goods is best treated as a social or political decision rather than as a decision resulting from market allocation.

Disamenities

Laws and regulations are needed to prohibit developments that impose on neighboring properties, such as plants producing dangerous chemicals or slaughterhouses likely to generate noxious odors. Such uses would impose on neighboring property owners discomfort, dangers, and costs associated with seeking to mitigate such discomforts and dangers. As a result, such uses are often referred to as "public bads," or disamenities.

Market signals also have no built-in safety checks that preclude private sector frauds, such as title claims by sellers who actually do not own the property, or deceptions, such as hidden construction flaws. Both are public bads that must be paid for by those who have no control over their costs.

Housing markets are affected by the region in which they are located. The inputs and the structure of a housing market in one region may differ significantly from the inputs and structure of the housing market in another region. No regional differences exist for the capital markets, where prices affect the costs that must be paid by the firms in housing markets. Capital markets are not regional, they are national and international. The interest, or cost of money, charged by lenders will vary only on the basis of perceived differences in risk, not differences in regional locations. However, regions do differ greatly in the size, growth, incomes, and other characteristics of their populations and business entities as well as climate and topography. Nevertheless, the general pattern and working mechanisms of the markets that determine the price and quality of houses in the neighborhoods of all regions are quite similar.

Filtration and Neighborhood Change

In this section, we will look at the general framework of regional markets to see how public policies and consumer demands shape the differences in the structures of markets and how those differences determine the pricing of the outputs of those markets.

The residential stock of urban regions increases in two ways:

- Housing is added in new neighborhoods, extending the borders of urban regions onto sparsely settled, agricultural, and open space at the fringes of existing development.
- Housing is added through the redevelopment of existing neighborhoods.

The price, quality, and type of housing added to the stock is shaped by the builder's forecast of what he can obtain in rent or sale price for the types of housing he is allowed to build, and the costs of constructing and marketing the various development options. A housing unit, once created and sold to someone who occupies it, or a housing development sold to a landlord who rents units, will continue to change in quality and value. The quality changes will be shaped by the personal priorities, financial capabilities, and, most importantly, perceptions of the owner concerning the way changes in quality will affect what buyers or renters are willing and able to pay.

Neighborhood housing demands will change in accordance with the changes in the demographic makeup, tastes, and size of the region's population. Most would-be buyers and renters are willing to consider housing not just in a single neighborhood but also in nearby neighborhoods. Therefore, the prices, quality, and type of housing in different but nearby neighborhoods of urban regions are linked by the actual changes and potential future changes among neighborhoods. What that means is that the demand that applies to each neighborhood is affected by the type, quality, and price of housing and externalities available in the other neighborhoods.

There is always the potential for change in housing quality and price. Whether and how change takes place in any one neighborhood is affected by the state of housing and the available amenities, such as good schools, good roads and transit access, and nearby shopping, and the disamenities, such as the prevalence of crime, dilapidated properties, and pollution, in all the neighborhoods that compete for buyers and renters. The demand for housing in one neighborhood is also affected by the demand for housing in other neighborhoods.

In economic jargon, there is positive cross-elasticity of demand between neighborhoods, which means that to some degree, similar houses in different neighborhoods are substitutable. Therefore, if the price of housing in one neighborhood declines, some of the households in neighborhoods where the "bundle" of housing services is perceived as being similar to those in the neighborhood where prices are declining may consider moving to the more affordable neighborhood. Also, more of the households seeking housing in the urban region who had considered both neighborhoods, say "Park Place" and "Boardwalk," might pick the one that has become less expensive due to the price change. Over time, the filtration process activated by home buyers and sellers tends to move the prices of most of a region's neighborhoods in the same direction, except for those that are significantly changing their position in the ladder of neighborhoods when the housing prices are generally tending to rise or fall.

Figure 4.2 presents a snapshot of market demand for each of seven neighborhoods in a hypothetical urban region. To suggest their relative market demand among the seven neighborhoods, each is identified by a name used in the popular game Monopoly. The little green houses in the Monopoly game are all the same in every neighborhood. What is not the same is what it cost to put one of those little green houses on a particular site. This is true in the fictitious

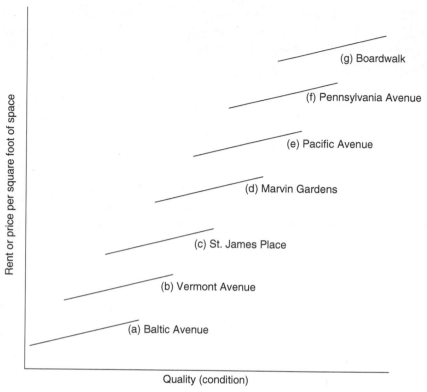

FIGURE 4.2 Prices and Quality of the Residences in a Ladder of the Neighborhoods in an Urban Region

game of Monopoly as well as in the real world. At any one point in time, the price of the land or sites in one neighborhood will be different from the price or value of the land in other neighborhoods. In the real world, these differences influence decisions about what to build, rebuild, renovate, and maintain. Each owner seeking her and his own best interest results in houses in the less expensive neighborhoods that are less spacious and less suitable than the houses in neighborhoods where the price of sites is higher. In the real world, the responses to the demands that pertain to each neighborhood and the costs associated with those responses result in houses on Baltic Avenue that are like sheds compared to the luxury apartments or spacious mansions located on Boardwalk. The same type of economic rationale that makes the proprietor of an upscale restaurant put expensive wines and the finest food offerings on his menu while restaurants catering to diners who must watch their pennies serve hamburgers and beer applies also to the economic decisions about what gets spent on the production, maintenance, replacement, and renovation of houses in a neighborhood.

The shifting of people from one neighborhood to another within a region affects the makeup of both the houses and the residents in urban neighborhoods. That can be seen in the history of New York City from 1845 to 1860, a period of extremely heavy immigration during which the foreign-born population almost tripled to equal about 47 percent of the city's population.[2] As the nineteenth-century immigrants swelled the total population, the rich inhabitants of older downtown areas saw that less-affluent residents were crowding into some of the housing around them.

The wealthy then did what they have long done in America—they sold or rented their older houses to the not-so-well-off and moved farther away from the city's manufacturing core. The novelist Henry James, a much more astute social psychologist than his also-famous philosopher/psychologist brother William, understood this well. In *Washington Square*, written in 1880, the character Arthur Townsend remarks, "At the end of three or four years, we'll move. That's the way to live in New York—to move every three or four years. Then you always get the last thing."[3]

During the late nineteenth century, some wealthy New Yorkers built mansions along Fifth Avenue and its flanking streets while wealthy others converted their country estates into permanent homes. Many of these older houses served a sequence of upper- and then middle-class households. When they were so old that no one wanted to live in them, the houses were torn down, providing sites for tenement houses—low-rental apartment buildings whose facilities and maintenance barely met minimum standards—that could be rented cheaply to the new immigrants but profitably for the owners.[4] Variations of this process of reusing housing have occurred many times in many places.

How each generation experiences these changes shapes more than where and how they will live. It also colors their attitudes about what is proper and, therefore, what private investors should be allowed to build and how landlords should be allowed to operate. The dissatisfactions with what each generation has experienced as well as what they have seen as in their own interests has led to successive changes in public rules and investment behavior. Toward the end of the nineteenth century, the shabby construction and overcrowding of the tenements led to laws that prohibited faulty and inadequate new construction. While these early regulations were weak, continued public outcries inspired by social workers and publications, including Jacob Riis, whose photos became famous for exposing public misconduct, led to tougher laws that, after 1903, prohibited unsafe construction and mandated adequate sanitation.[5]

As you can learn from the lectures available at the Tenement Museum at 108 Orchard Street on Manhattan's Lower East Side, not all of these well-intentioned laws were thought out well enough to benefit the tenement residents. Prior to the laws passed after the turn of the century, the sanitary facilities available to the residents were outhouses at the rear of the buildings.

The new sanitation laws required indoor toilets. To meet this requirement, the bottoms of light shafts were equipped with toilets that vented up to the roof past all the apartments. The result was that the new indoor toilets spread odor and disease, making them both less pleasant and less healthy than the outhouses they replaced. The well-informed guide who took my wife and me on a tour of the historically preserved tenement told us that some of the tenements refurbished with the new indoor toilets were occupied until 1935.

In 1916, New York City went further by passing laws that regulated the type of development that could be built on any site. As time went on, more cities adopted and enforced building codes and zoning regulations that increasingly constrained what could be built as well as, in some cases, what could be occupied. After the second decade of the twentieth century, it was no longer possible in any major American city to build housing without plumbing and basic safety features. Changes to building codes, the economy, and improvements in construction have led to a constant increase in the standards of health, safety, and convenience available to the inhabitants of new homes. The availability of higher standards in new houses leads many to consider older houses without "modern" conveniences and features to be less desirable, if not obsolete.

"Filtration" denotes the way housing growth and development led to the delivery of used housing to those who could not afford or were not willing to pay for new housing.[6] All of the homes my family lived in from 1938 to 2007 were older houses or apartments. We rented or bought those homes between 1938 and 1966. Because of downward filtration, each successive house we purchased cost much less than it would have cost to replace it. The price we paid each time made us feel we obtained a housing bargain. In 2007, my wife and I bought our first new home, a San Francisco condominium in a still "edgy" but gentrifying South of Market neighborhood.

Gentrification refers to the phenomenon of new and existing housing in a neighborhood becoming more expensive—therefore, gentrification can be considered upward filtration. This occurs when the process of neighborhood change responds to demands from households offering to pay more for housing than what was being paid by previous owners or renters. Unlike the static or unchanging position of the neighborhoods in an urban market represented graphically in figure 4.2, downward or upward filtration is likely to take place over time. Depending on the relationship between supply and demand of neighborhoods competing for somewhat similar residents within the urban market area, there is always the potential for both downward and upward filtration with regard to price, and often with regard to quality. Downward price filtration occurs when competition among landlords and would-be sellers in some neighbors causes neighborhoods to move down the ladder, so they are available to less affluent residents. Upward filtration occurs when the demand for higher priced units in some neighborhoods motivates the construction of new neighborhoods or the renovation and densification of older neighborhoods, which attract residents who are willing and able to pay higher prices.

Not only do the neighborhoods in the real world of dynamic real estate markets change their relative position over time but the entire context of neighborhoods within a region also tends to move up—that is, become pricier—when there is more effective demand for housing within a region than allowable additions to supply. Conversely, all housing prices within a region tend to decline when additions to the stock exceed the effective demand. It should be no surprise that when additions to supply exceed demand within the entire region, prices within market-linked neighborhoods tend to decline while the competition for housing tends to keep quality up to attract buyers. Unfortunately, the reverse is also true. When region-wide demand exceeds housing supply, prices tend to increase while a "seller's market" allows quality to decline as sellers expect to attract buyers no matter the decline in quality.

The Filtration Ladder

Housing is one of the most durable of products. According to the 2000 census, the average age of all of America's housing units is 38.5 years. More than 10 million American households live in dwellings that were built more than eighty-two years ago. Just like you and me, as housing grows older it changes. But unlike you and me, the condition of a house or multifamily unit is ultimately dependent not on the passage of time but on how much is spent on its maintenance and renovation.

Pacific Heights and Over-the-Rhine

In the Pacific Heights neighborhood of San Francisco, I have visited Victorian mansions built more than one hundred years ago. They had been brought up to date functionally, equipped with all the most modern plumbing, electrical, heating, ventilation, and sometimes air-conditioning systems. The interiors and exteriors were beautifully painted and the structures reinforced to be solid and earthquake resistant. I have also accompanied my wife as she interviewed the inhabitants of a unit in the Over-the-Rhine district of Cincinnati, built during the same time as much of the luxury housing in San Francisco's Pacific Heights neighborhood. Like many other housing units in that Cincinnati neighborhood in 1964, the unit we visited was dilapidated, the stairs were rickety, the plumbing met the building code only through features such as a bathtub protruding into the living room, the electrical fixtures were worn and barely safe, the paint on the walls and ceilings was peeling, and the floors were sagging.

There were differences that were built into the quality of these dwelling units in the Over-the-Rhine and the Pacific Heights neighborhoods. The mansions of Pacific Heights were built in a neighborhood developed to attract newly rich lumber, mineral, and banking barons of a booming San Francisco. The Over-the-Rhine neighborhood was first settled by Irish immigrants in the late nineteenth century. Many of the multifamily structures that sheltered the immigrants then are still there today on the hills above the now long-filled-in and forgotten Miami and Erie Canal. The German immigrants who came shortly thereafter to that neighborhood called it "Over-the-Rhine," alluding to the canal that then separated the neighborhood from the central business district.

Over time the differences in quality between the mansions in Pacific Heights and the subsistence dwellings in Over-the-Rhine were exacerbated by differences in the demands arising from the neighborhoods in each area. Pacific Heights remained the premier neighborhood of San Francisco, with a social cachet that enabled it to be the principal address of many of the northern California rich. But when the German and Irish residents of Over-the-Rhine became prosperous and could afford more than basic shelter, they moved farther out to new neighborhoods like Mount Auburn and Corryville, and then still farther out to today's suburbs.

As a result, the economic determinants of how much landlords and home-owners in each of these two neighborhoods would spend on maintenance, renovation, and redevelopment were very different. In Pacific Heights, a dollar spent on preserving or improving the quality of a residence would always bring in more than a dollar's worth of rent or resale value because prospective owners and renters had the income and motivation to pay top dollar for housing quality. In 2002, after an economic recession that caused a slight drop in the price of condominium and single-family units in Pacific Heights, the average price of housing in that neighborhood was still $650 per square foot, about twice the average price of units in the San Francisco Bay Region. Since then, prices have risen to more than $1,000 per square foot in 2009.

The houses left behind in the Over-the-Rhine district were, for the most part, multifamily structures. Their rents dropped, making it possible for immigrants living in the hills of northern Kentucky to find homes in what was their first urban environment. Over-the-Rhine housing continued to serve the poor until the late 1960s, when it began to attract some young, more affluent households. During the Depression of the 1930s through the 1950s, the welfare recipients and low-wage migrants from the rural South who lived in Over-the-Rhine could not afford to pay more than a bare minimum for rent. Therefore, it was not surprising that in 1964, when my wife and I did our survey research, we found the housing in physically bad shape. For more than half a century, demand in the neighborhood was such that, if the landlord spent more than the minimum required to keep the structure up to code, those extra dollars would earn him no return in rents or future resale value. Similarly, if owners of housing in Over-the-Rhine were to modernize, they could not expect to recover the costs of modernization when they sold their houses.

In my 1964 Ph.D. dissertation, I predicted that market conditions in the Over-the-Rhine area were about to change. Those who would soon be called "yuppies" (young upwardly mobile urban professionals) sought housing close to the action of neighborhood bars and jazz joints near the center city and the University of Cincinnati. After its long period of decay and hibernation, gentrification was in the cards for the Over-the-Rhine area, just as it was for Cincinnati's now pricey, formerly working class Mount Adams neighborhood. But this future was denied the Over-the-Rhine neighborhood by well-meaning but naïve land-use regulators—they thwarted gentrification, thinking that by freezing economic conditions they were doing the best for the poor households who lived there. Perhaps those who fought the redevelopment of this area thought they were making up for the damage the city had done to the poor by destroying thousands of cheap but physically low-quality housing units in the West End in a vain attempt to create an industrial nirvana they renamed Queensgate.

In 2005 fewer than four thousand people lived in downtown Cincinnati. Many of those who could have afforded to pay for a fixed-up, revitalized Over-the-Rhine home had left the city for Blue Ash or similar other suburbs. Their migration was soon followed by the kind of industries that Cincinnati had hoped to locate in Queensgate.

The economic costs to Cincinnati were many times more than what they could have paid directly to the less affluent residents of Over-the-Rhine to relocate equitably. Cincinnati lost the opportunity to have the private market gentrify a neighborhood that had obsolete housing into a hip environment for well-educated young workers near the downtown offices of major firms such as Proctor and Gamble. The gentrifying developers of the new Over-the-Rhine should have been required to help pay the rents of any dislocated tenants of demolished buildings for a time equal to the years they had been renters in Over-the-Rhine (more on this concept in chapter 8).

Such encouragement of gentrification within the context of a monetary assistance to low income renters and homeowners would have allowed the market-driven dynamics of private urban redevelopment to proceed in this neighborhood and would have kept in balance or even improved the possibilities of housing for poorer residents. What happened in Cincinnati was the worst of urban redevelopment. It removed the housing supply available to the poor in places like the West End while stopping the upward filtration of old neighborhoods that would have helped attract middle- and upper-income households to Cincinnati.

Housing Quality Changes in Neighborhoods

The range of housing quality present within all the neighborhoods of urban markets is typically great. But there are likely to be overlaps in the quality of housing found in neighborhoods close to each other on the array of neighborhoods by price. While the average quality of housing in the more expensive of two adjacent neighborhoods will be higher than the less expensive neighborhood, there will be some houses in the less expensive neighborhood of equal or greater quality than some houses in the more expensive neighborhood of the two. For example, as indicated in figure 4.2, the range of housing quality available in neighborhood (a), or "Baltic Avenue," is generally lower than the range of housing quality found in the next neighborhood on the price scale, (b) "Vermont Avenue." There is overlap on the upper end of the quality scale between two similarly priced neighborhoods. While one can buy a "stripped down" Cadillac for less than the most expensive Chevrolet, a higher proportion of the former brand sold will be loaded with quality features than would the latter. Similarly, while there will be many houses within the Vermont Avenue neighborhood, displayed on figure 4.2, that are of equivalent quality to dwellings in the Baltic Avenue neighborhood, there are some homes in the Vermont neighborhood that are of higher quality than any in the Baltic neighborhood, and the Baltic neighborhood has some units lower in quality than any found in Vermont. Price–quality relationships between the different neighborhood rungs of the housing ladder reflect the investment actions that owners and builders have made over time in response to their perception of the demand for specific housing and associated services. These might include housing size, quality, and special features as well as externalities such as neighborhood amenities, commute times, shopping, and the social and financial status of neighbors. The relevant demands are also affected by the quality of housing in substitutable neighborhoods—that is, by what is available in neighborhoods with similarly desirable attributes.

Unlike the positions of the neighborhoods in the regional housing market shown on a static diagram where they do not change, the positions of neighborhoods on the filtration ladder shown in figure 4.2 do change over time. Such changes in how the housing in a neighborhood is regarded reflect the changes that have taken place over time in a dynamic, demand-driven, and supply-driven process that affects the price and quality of units within a neighborhood as well as potential competition across neighborhoods.

If you were born in urban America more than thirty years ago, chances are that the house or apartment you grew up in is still standing. Perhaps you even know where the house your grandparents grew up in is, and it probably still stands. But even if you can find the house where you grew up, the odds are very high that relative to other neighborhoods, the quality and price of that house as well as others in the same neighborhood have changed significantly since your childhood. The odds are probably much greater that change has happened in what was your grandparents' neighborhood.

Over time, the positions of older neighborhoods will move up or down the rungs on the filtration ladder. As well, more rungs may have to be added to represent newly developed neighborhoods. Downward filtration results when the prices of houses drop in a neighborhood, moving that neighborhood down the ladder where it represents houses affordable to a less-affluent group of residents. Downward filtration may or may not be followed by housing quality decline. If, after the drop in price, the less well-off renters and potential renters are still able to find housing at equivalent prices elsewhere, then the downward prices will not affect downward quality. In other words, if the demand for quality exceeds the cost of maintenance or remodeling, then housing quality tends to improve. If there is a limited supply of housing units in a price range so that the demand for quality is less than the cost of maintaining or improving quality, then physical deterioration and obsolescence will occur among some, many, or all of those units.

Upward filtration, or gentrification, occurs when the price of housing units pushes neighborhoods up to a higher rung of the housing filtration ladder. In this case, the demand for quality is always greater than the cost of providing the quality. In fact, one of the first acts of "the gentry" when they move into a formerly less desirable neighborhood is to start "fixing up" or even replacing the housing units purchased. Upward filtration is always accompanied, at least initially, with quality improvements.

In my own case, when my wife and I moved to a new condominium in San Francisco in late 2007, upward filtration in that supply-constrained city did result in high-quality new housing. But the Bay Area delivered us no housing bargain, in spite of the newspaper headlines about the "housing bubble" bursting that year. There is no way I will ever tell my hard-working relatives how much we paid for our first new housing unit.

How filtration works depends on the relationship between total housing production and total demand in the housing market within a region, including towns or cities within it. The residential areas—that is, the spaces organized as neighborhoods—constitute the interacting housing markets. Downward filtration in housing markets, where competition held prices down in all neighborhoods, made housing for my generation much cheaper than it was in the supply-constrained, upward-filtering market within which my sons rented and bought housing. This is perhaps the only advantage my generation has that I would like to see end.

Expansion: Neighborhood Change and Housing Quality

Urban frontiers everywhere have always been expanded by movements outward from existing places as well as by the more intensive reuse of the land in existing neighborhoods. Such expansions include additions to existing structures, demolitions and reconstructions of entire neighborhoods, and the building-by-building replacement of existing structures with higher density or larger houses.

The Suburban Expansion

From 1947 until recently, the most significant increases in housing took place in the suburbs. The effect of that expansion is very much with us today, even though we are in the midst of a demographic drive toward more housing in central cities and those built-up suburban areas capable of supporting mixed uses. After World War II, advances in transportation technology and investment in infrastructure expanded the boundaries of regional housing markets. Would-be renters and owners were able to expand the areas they considered when deciding where to live. Gasoline was inexpensive, the availability of new highway links were spreading out from the central city, and the attraction of owning a new single-family home with a backyard enticed the young families that were the parents of the baby boom generation. They moved to suburban towns, villages, and the areas of the county that were never made a part of any city, village, or town but remained in the county as "unincorporated areas." It was in these areas where large new neighborhoods were being developed, away from the central cities where young families lived previously.

In the United States, the demand for new houses in the post–World War II suburban expansion was encouraged by the availability of government-backed financing. The mortgage financing system of President Franklin D. Roosevelt's New Deal was greatly expanded by the postwar provisions that Congress passed to provide returning servicemen and servicewomen with low-interest and low-down-payment mortgage insurance, and to pay for their education at colleges or trade schools. Known as the G.I. Bill, these provisions provided veterans with credit they could use to buy new housing and to earn a college degree or technical training.

Networks of new highways built with federal, state, and local assistance made new suburban neighborhoods accessible. Additionally, government grants held down the cost of needed infrastructure such as water and sewer facilities. Bonds and other financing techniques for such infrastructure were facilitated by federal subsidies and financing. These federal aids to the roads, water and drainage systems, and other public infrastructure for development were popular because in the decade and a half after World War II, most Americans believed suburban development and growth were good.

The incomes of baby boomers' parents were rising faster than housing prices, so they could afford new homes in the suburbs that offered them and their young families what was considered a better life than what their parents had during the Great Depression. Housing production in the suburbs, and to a limited extent within the vacant "infill" sites of the central cities, competed with the existing homes of older neighborhoods so that existing home prices declined in real dollar terms. Older neighborhoods that had been near the top of the filtration ladder of the older cities were being upgraded. That became possible because families, such as my own, bought houses in older neighborhoods at prices that left enough from savings and regular income to able to pay for improvements and maintenance. These expenditures on housing quality beyond the primary cost were effectively good investments because our neighborhoods continued to be desirable and, by the 1980s, began to climb in value.

Some Older Neighborhoods Decline in Quality

Not all downward filtration was accompanied by quality improvements or quality stability. Within some older neighborhoods that had been near the bottom of the filtration ladder, housing prices were dropping as owners thought they could not charge their tenants enough to make it worthwhile to improve or even maintain the properties. Because the owners felt that the demand for quality was quite low, they believed that they could keep tenants in the buildings without "throwing good money after bad." As a result, the quality of the housing in the neighborhood dropped as the prices and rents dropped. As the demand for their housing dropped, the owners had to compete primarily based on price, so they cut their costs by putting off maintenance. Such situations can be illustrated in figure 4.3, which shows one of the neighborhoods moving down and to the left as both quality and value per square foot drop.

The economic conditions that existed in many of these neighborhoods, particularly in regions not benefiting from fast economic growth, put the housing and property owners there into the position of either switching to a nonresidential use or allowing the quality of their units to decline as they fought for tenants by dropping prices and rents. Some of the neighborhoods near the bottom of the value and quality scale had nowhere to go but down. They had

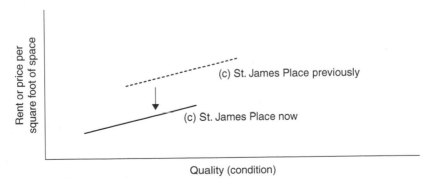

FIGURE 4.3 Price and Quality Decreases of St. James Neighborhood

deteriorated in quality to the point that upgrading them to anything close to the current standards of acceptable quality or condition would be very expensive. Housing in these neighborhoods had been built as working-class dwellings during the nineteenth century. At that time, the theory of Thomas Malthus had led to a belief in "the iron law of wages," which held that the lot of the working class would always be just above subsistence because population growth would put a lid on wages. Since real estate investment decisions are always based on future expectations, this belief led to the cramming of housing that provided not more than the minimum levels of shelter alongside the mills and other workplaces of early industrial America. Some of the slums that were bulldozed during the 1950s by federally financed slum clearance were the remnants of such early workforce neighborhoods.

Whether the housing of the least expensive neighborhoods had begun as simply inexpensive housing or had drifted downward over time toward slum housing, the likelihood that these neighborhoods would be demolished increased as the prosperity of the city or town in which they were located increased. During the nineteenth and early twentieth centuries, low-value housing was usually replaced with commercial and industrial structures; during that era, the value of commercial and industrial uses of land typically exceeded the value of old and deteriorated housing on that land.

Critical Mass for Redevelopment

Regions growing in population and income create the potential for the expansion of the urban frontier through the redevelopment of neighborhoods that had dropped to the bottom rungs of value and quality—in a word, gentrification. But gentrification requires the assemblage of property in big enough chunks for enough of the neighborhood to be redeveloped with new, upscale housing so it can attract a "critical mass" of new, more affluent occupants. Their willingness to move in is encouraged by the belief that the neighborhood is "moving up." The scale of the more expensive, new development must be big enough to prevent demand being drowned out by the spillover of the social image projected by the occupants of the obsolete, deteriorated housing. "Spillover" here refers to the negative, uncomfortable feelings in people who live near obsolete or poorly maintained structures. As a result, successful gentrification often requires the assemblage of multiple ownerships of small properties into one larger property under a single ownership.

I offer the block where I now live, just a few yards from Seventh Street between Market and Mission in the South of Market area (SOMA) in San Francisco, as an example. My sons, now middle-aged men, would have thrown up major objections to my wife and me moving into the area if we had bought a single house next to the homeless shelters and the drug addicts that infested Seventh Street. But we were able to buy a condo in a high-rise built on more than an acre of land with enough units to create its own mini-neighborhood. We also were able to explain to our sons that more buildings similar to ours with the capability of attracting tenants and owners with lifestyles closer to our own would be forthcoming, and soon.

The strongest argument for urban renewal is that it encourages the kind of neighborhood redevelopment that is now happening in San Francisco's SOMA. But the development of SOMA could only be done through the assemblage of land, and that meant invoking eminent domain. Unfortunately, governmentally imposed urban renewal has its pitfalls. One problem is that once the use of eminent domain becomes likely, the process of assemblage is usually further delayed and made more expensive. Consider the motivations of those owners in the neighborhood who, under the threat of condemnation, could not privately redevelop but who would be assured of what amounts to a "golden parachute" if they sit tight. How long the owners of empty units and of units that bring in low rents will hold out rather than sell to redevelopers and "the gentry" is partly determined by their expectations for the future. If they feel that municipal or federal redevelopment agencies will eventually offer them a bonus through condemnation, that prospect will reinforce their tendency to hold and wait.

Here is an irony to consider: between when the publicly backed urban renewal is announced and when that renewal actually begins, the affected neighborhoods begin to deteriorate or worsen. It is the announcement of the new development that intensifies the blighting of the neighborhood because all but the most urgent maintenance and remodeling ceases while the owners wait for the public renewal agency to buy their properties. The advent of public urban renewal virtually eliminates the possibility of private renewal.

Finding Shelter in the Slums

Neighborhoods with the lowest-cost housing have always served both ports of entry and as training grounds for immigrants who initially had neither the language nor concepts needed to succeed economically and take the first step toward upward mobility in the United States. While we are used to such ports of entry being located in the older neighborhoods of the central city, today many have formed in suburban areas and close-in neighborhoods where immigrants are "doubling up"—two or more families living together in a single house or single unit apartment—to lower their housing costs.

Wherever they are located, newcomers not only learn the ropes in their new economic and social environment, they also benefit from available help from neighbors with similar backgrounds. Furthermore, living in such neighborhoods is, for the immigrants, superior to the option of worse overcrowding in the garages and other nooks of more expensive neighborhoods. In the nineteenth century, slum neighborhoods provided shelter and street-corner and front-stoop education to the very poor new urbanites about the way to live and work in the United States. Such education taught them how to assimilate into the American culture and to begin the trek up the scale of price and quality of the housing available in urban neighborhoods.

The availability of inexpensive or cheap housing, even in slum or near-slum conditions, alleviated demand pressures that would make undermaintenance and failure to modernize a more rewarding economic choice than spending money to maintain and upgrade housing in neighborhoods farther up the price and quality ladder. While the quality of housing in the least expensive neighborhoods failed to meet middle-class standards, its availability kept poor people from having to accept overcrowding and increasingly lower-quality and under-maintained housing.

Without low-quality, inexpensive housing, the poor had no option but to pay for housing in neighborhoods where they were not active participants, where they had no voice, and where they were not in the position to bargain for or demand quality maintenance and repair, let alone renovation. The inexpensive housing in slum and near-slum neighborhoods was not recognized as the buffer that it was, keeping quality-destabilizing demand from affecting higher quality neighborhoods. Nor was it recognized by any but a few perceptive social observers that slum neighborhoods played a unique role in serving as "schools" providing social skills for the very poor, social skills that would enable them to enter into urban places.[7]

Ricardian Land Rent and Residual Land Values

Ricardo and the Value of Land "at the Margin"

In 1821 the English economist and businessman David Ricardo was the first to explain that the rent of agricultural land is based on the difference between the value of what can be grown on the most fertile and productive land and the value of what can be grown on the poorest land where cultivation is just barely feasible. He was against tariffs on grain because the resulting higher prices of domestic wheat would result in more land being put into production, which he recognized would cause the cost of land to climb. Therefore, the tariff would, in turn, increase the income of landlords as it raised the rent and value of land, and would take money out of the pockets of the consumers who paid more for the bread they ate. He argued that the landowner did nothing, not a thing, to earn the higher income that the tariff would provide. But because of the tariff the workers had to do more for the same loaf of bread—they had to pay more for it, which meant that had to work more to pay for that same loaf. His argument on behalf of tenant farmers and consumers is quite similar to the argument first made by Henry George on behalf of urban workers and consumers.

When the anticipated cost of growing food exceeds the anticipated revenue that the farmer believes will come from selling the crops or animals raised, farmland generates no rent. Given the market price of what could be grown or raised, it would be economically unfeasible for a farmer, grower, or rancher to work his land. However, if there is a perceived or, better yet, an actual increase in the price of what can best be grown on the land—that is, the potential revenue earned from its highest and best use, so that profit just turns the corner from loss and becomes a possibility—then some land that was formerly considered unfeasible to produce profitable revenue will be put into production. In most cases the land that was formerly unprofitable, just turning the corner onto profitability, will then bear for itself a slight rental value. But more significantly, that land will then increase the rental value of the more fertile or otherwise more cost-effective land that was already in production. The value of agricultural land increases with the widening of the gap between the cost and the market price of what is produced on that land.

Just as agricultural sites that cannot profitably grow crops do not earn rent, there is no obtainable value from urban land when the cost of building for a site's most valuable use exceeds the price that can be collected from the sale or rental of that site. Land value occurs only when the price received for a building on a site exceeds the cost of its development. The rents from such a building can more than pay off the interest and principal on a loan equal to the development costs. Likewise, land value occurs when the revenue from marketing what grows on the land exceeds the total cost of the site's agricultural production.

Residual, or How Much Value Land Can Support

Today's urban land developers and builders often say they are "penciling out what works" when explaining the process they use to estimate what values each of alternative developments of a particular parcel of land can support. But when they get serious enough to calculate what they will actually bid for the land, they use a computer spreadsheet to project four different relevant variables:

1. Estimated costs for building, operating, and selling the project
2. Projected net operating income and/or sale price of the property
3. An estimate of how much of their own money will have to go into the project to supplement whatever amount of money they can borrow
4. The same kind of judgment that the tenant farmer would have to make about the rate of return needed to earn on their own capital to make the risks worth their while

The components of the estimated costs for building, operating, and selling the project include the following costs:

- Extending utilities and otherwise preparing the site for construction
- Administering the planning, obtaining approvals, and financing
- Constructing and furnishing the project

- Advertising and selling or leasing the project
- Interest and fees associated with the money to be invested
- The loan principal that would have to be amortized over time and when the project is sold

The components of projections of net operating income over time and the expected sale price of the property at the time it may be sold include the following cost and revenue estimates:

- Cost of annual maintenance, management, repair, insurance, taxes, and sales expenses
- Annual revenue from rents
- Income from sale of the property at the time it is estimated it will be sold

Estimates of how much of their own money the developers are willing to invest—considered owners' required equity in the investment—are determined by many phone calls over many days; many meetings over many weeks, during which developers extol their own merits; and the promotion of the prospects of the intended development in an effort to minimize the required amount of their own money or equity.

An estimate of the residual value of the land—that is, the amount of land value a proposed project can support—also depends upon the annual percentage return on equity that the sponsor judges necessary to put up his money. This return rate will vary with the risk that the forecast costs and revenues turn out to be wrong, the alternatives available for the use of equity investment, and the competition from other real estate investors. Even with good numerical estimates of the factors that make up each variable, determining the land value nevertheless depends on experience more than on plugging those factors into an equation programmed on a computer—if it were possible to create an equation by which the calculate land residual. It is not possible because there is no simple equation capable of grinding out the residual land value.

The only way to calculate residual land value is indirectly, by trial and error. Fortunately this can be done cheaply and easily with a computer. A value is chosen that is believed to be the resulting land value (trial is where experience comes in), estimates are plugged into calculations that can be done simply on computer, and the result determines the deviation from the trial value. The computer is programmed to calculate the present value of the all the future expected revenues—that is, the sum of the future net cash flows—at the interest rate the investor expects will be the rate of return required to produce those future revenues. The sum of those future cash flows is the residual land value.

When a public agency tries to tear down and redevelop an area, it is possible that the calculations, using an assumed rate of return and cash flow projection, may result in a present value of the project that is significantly negative—it could be negative even if the land value initially assumed in the calculations is what the agency actually paid to buy it from the private owners. When this math shows the land value to be negative, the agency will be forced either to abandon the project or to subsidize it by selling the land for less than its purchase price. Such subsidies are called "land write-downs."

To provide the simplest possible example, ignore the critical issue of time and assume total project costs of $900,000. Assume further that the developer needs to be able to make payments to his investors and lenders equal to 10 percent of the total costs of development. That is, the developer will go ahead if the net operating income from the project each year after completion is equal to or greater than 10 percent of its total development costs. Next, assume that the developer believes the project can earn $100,000 per year after completion. That makes the total value of the project equal to $1 million.

Because all of the development costs except land were assumed to be $900,000, then the residual land value is $100,000, because

$100,000 annual cash flow divided by 0.10 = $1,000,000 total value, and

$1,000,000 total value minus total nonland costs of $900,000 = $100,000

In this example, if the rents or sale prices of the project had increased so that the annual cash flow increased by 50 percent to $150,000 and total project costs remained fixed at $900,000, all of the increase in net earnings flows to the land value. That is, the land could now support a value of $150,000. The amount that could be borrowed on a given return (10 percent in the above example) can also be referred to as its capitalized value. Another way of understanding the residual land value concept is to consider that the residual value of land is equal to its capitalized earnings minus all the other costs associated with producing the development that generates those earnings because land value actually is the residual of capitalized earnings minus costs.

Region-wide Land Values under Downward Price Filtration and Gentrification

Some Neighborhoods Are "Under Water" with Negative Land Values

Figure 4.4 depicts the same array of hypothetical neighborhoods shown in figure 4.2, but with one exception. In figure 4.2, the vertical axis represents the neighborhoods in measures of rent or price per square foot of building space—that is, the area of land the structure of the building sits on. In figure 4.4, the vertical axis represents the neighborhoods in measures of land rents per square foot of dwelling—that is, the area within the structure of the dwelling.

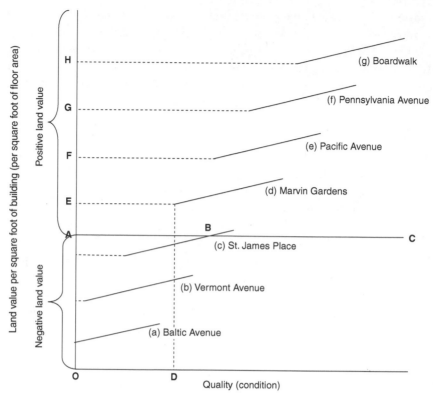

FIGURE 4.4 Land Value and Condition of Neighborhoods

Both figures represent the same neighborhood price–quality relationships in the array while the horizontal axis represents the physical characteristics or quality of the structures. To represent land values per square foot of land or acre would require an adjustment to the chart of neighborhoods to reflect differences in density or building space per square foot of land.

As profit-seeking property owners succeed in constraining the supply of land throughout the region, land prices go up in all neighborhoods. The land prices will go up whether or not the neighborhoods remain in their places relative to one another on the ladder of least to most desirable neighborhoods. Region-wide increases in land value as a result of supply constraint will be particularly great where both economic and population growth are strong.

Conversely, if demand for land in the region drops because the region's clusters of businesses are no longer in line with contemporary technology and trade patterns, the region becomes less desirable as a place to live. The effect of such a drop in demand must be evaluated against land supply constraints. One would tend to offset the other.

The horizontal line AC on figure 4.4 represents the feasibility threshold for new development. Land has no value below line AC because new development is not feasible in any of the locations represented below point B. That is, in the neighborhoods of Vermont Avenue, Baltic Avenue, and all but a small portion of St. James Place, the cost of new residential construction exceeds the market price of new, for-sale housing, and the capitalized value of the net operating rental revenue of new units.

Please remember that in figure 4.2 the vertical axis represents measures of housing price and quality-defining structural characteristics, space, or building. In figure 4.4 the vertical axis represents a measure of rent per square foot of building interior.

It is assumed that figure 4.2 represents a market in which the housing in all neighborhoods can command at least some rent—the key here is housing rent—and therefore the zero or no rent point is at the bottom of the vertical axis. But in figure 4.4, the vertical axis represents land value, not the rent or price per square foot of building. Because the price of housing built on land in the neighborhoods below the line AC cannot pay for the costs of building houses, given the neighborhood's present position in the regional market, the value of the land below AC is negative. Only if the market position of all or a portion of the neighborhood is raised above price level AC through upward filtration will there be any residual land value. That means that if a builder wanted to build new housing in the neighborhoods anywhere represented to the right of the vertical axis and below the AC horizontal line, that builder could not recover his or her construction costs.

Land rent becomes positive above point A. For example, the vertical distance AE represents the value of the land per square foot of building in the area in the Marvin Gardens neighborhood with housing of quality OD. The supportable or residual value of the land is always the difference between the value of the entire real estate, including land, minus the costs of developing the structure(s) placed on the land. A new structure will be feasible only if the land value of the new structure is equal to or greater than its total development cost. Value is only generated if the value of the use is greater than its total cost of development.

Public Subsidies to Rebuild Neighborhoods

Some neighborhoods with zero or negative land value are on the verge of climbing up the ladder of desirability and crossing the threshold of feasibility but are held back by a few existing structures that would have to be razed, remodeled, or rebuilt. As time passes, the prices of land in such areas may drop to the point where investors will acquire and tear down those structures. But in the real estate market some property owners prevail who are stubborn, holding out for higher price or whatever other reasons, which makes it impossible for private parties to combine properties that together would permit development big enough to create enough of a new, positive impact to put the neighborhood on an upward quality and price trajectory.

Without such a forward development push, the neighborhood can be left in an economic limbo of gradually deteriorating quality. The word for this that has become both a descriptive and legal term is "blight." Blight occurs when the private market conditions seem to make it impossible for economically rewarding, quality-improving structured upgrades or new development to take place. If no public actions are taken, it may be many years before new development moves the neighborhood up the ladder of residential value or converts the residences to other uses. Public redevelopment is often seen as the way to shorten that wait and speed up the process of neighborhood change. It is speeded through the use of eminent domain and the demolition of obsolete structures whose continued existence helps maintain the neighborhood in its blighted stagnation.

There is a paradox at work here: Owners who believe that city officials will eventually condemn some of their buildings at fair market value hold onto their older, low-quality units for a longer time, hoping to be paid more money for them. Once the word gets around, true or not, that "the city will eventually condemn the property," the likelihood decreases that owners will initiate remodeling, rebuilding, or selling their properties. In many cities and towns, some owners of low-quality units in physically blighted neighborhoods raise their asking price above their property's reuse potential value. And they wait. They wait because they regard public condemnation as an insurance policy against further losses in value.

Risks and Rewards of Gentrification

In open urban frontiers, where population, incomes, or both, are growing, new neighborhoods will be born, and some existing neighborhoods will change to move up the price and quality ladder as they provide sites for new and usually higher density housing. Whether initiated privately or through public intervention, the positive changes in what were "downscale locations" will eventually move many of those locations higher up the scale of housing prices, rents, and quality. In a word, gentrification will occur in those locations. Because the process of remodeling or redeveloping blighted neighborhoods is expensive, the prices that will be paid by "the gentry" will usually be much higher than what the properties were earning before the gentrification process began.

In terms of figure 4.4, this usually means that gentrification is more likely in neighborhoods such as Baltic Avenue, where land values are significantly negative and the value of structures has dropped to a low value per square foot. The rewards are then potentially high enough to be worth the risks—monetarily and emotionally stressful—assumed by those urban pioneers who could be deemed crazy enough to try to reclaim fallow urban lands.

Young artists, writers, actors, musicians, and dancers may seem out of the mainstream. But whether it is because they cannot afford anything better or because they are "hip," they often see the possibilities of a neighborhood when it is still very inexpensive. They get a bargain during the years that investors are accumulating buildings for subsequent redevelopment and remodeling. But eventually rents and prices will rise, as developers sell to earn their high returns after enduring long periods of waiting and stressful negotiations with previous owners, public agencies, and the neighbors. Over time, they will have created new, desirable developments and amenities and removed the neighborhood's disamenities. The neighborhood will jump up the ladder of desirability, perhaps to somewhere represented above Pacific Avenue in figure 4.2.

However, although homeowners are better off when there is gentrification in their neighborhood, the displaced renters in the same neighborhood are worse off—unless they are compensated. The degree to which uncompensated, displaced households are harmed and the degree of benefit bestowed upon households searching for housing everywhere in the affected region depends on how added housing affects the region-wide balance of housing supply and demand.

Homeowners' Resistance to Change in Their Neighborhood

Some owners of property would not be displaced by replacing their old and deteriorated structures with new housing, and would benefit if gentrification pushes their neighborhood up the ladder of desirability and value, but they just do not see it that way. Some owners do not understand that redevelopment in part of a neighborhood will make the whole neighborhood more desirable, and thereby all housing in the entire neighborhood more valuable. Other owners do understand that proposed redevelopment will enhance the attraction of the whole neighborhood to higher-income households, but they do not want economically and ethnically different households to be part of the social mix of their neighborhood. It is a rare neighborhood that does not have some property owners, as well as renters, who simply resist change of any kind.

Besides outright resistors, the concerns of individual property owners about change near their own residences also must be considered, especially about allowing different types of structures nearby. Apartments or condominiums in previously all-single-family neighborhoods are usually opposed by existing single-family homeowners. Their opposition includes fears that views will be blocked. But more than that are concerns about the social behavior and status of the inhabitants of multifamily buildings. Builders on vacant land in the suburbs know they must build their apartments before they build single-family homes in the same new neighborhood. Once the single-family homeowners are ensconced, they will use their power as voters to try to prohibit high-density housing units.

There is also likely to be strong opposition if the new development of single-family homes is proposed with smaller lots than the size of the lots that existing houses are built on. For neighborhoods with positive land values— that is, where the replacement of existing houses would be feasible without public subsidy—the opposition to developments on smaller lots may well be rational. I remember the joy of a planning director of a midsized town when he announced that he had just bought "the smallest house on the most expensive street in the neighborhood." He knew that while he had not obtained the "most" house for his money, the value of his lot was very likely to ensure the resale value of his property. Where most of the homes in an area are large, that usually has played, and continues to play, a role in establishing the bundle of product-differentiating features that attracted the high-paying buyers initially.

Most homeowners and real estate developers understand that attracting high-paying buyers and renters to the area is the most basic factor underlying the change in market position that enables urban residential neighborhoods to be recreated with better and usually more new dwelling units and other amenity-providing uses. Fears that the economic and social status of those who will be new neighbors may adversely affect the demand for housing in the neighborhood is usually behind the strongest threats felt by existing property owners when new development or redevelopment is proposed.

But although the externality of socially compatible and economically advantaged neighbors weighs heavily in the minds of current residents, the desire to maintain other externalities is also important and more frequently voiced. For example, even if the streets the current residents travel on each day are maintained by general taxes, those residents do not want more neighbors to compete for driving lanes and parking spaces. Vacant lots are often considered as positive externalities that provide views and perhaps informal playgrounds, which would be destroyed by development. Current residents fear that the schools will become crowded if more houses are built.

I will leave it to you to decide whether a valid objection to community growth is what one socially active gentleman told our firm's interviewers. "As we get more people in the community I find it harder to get my picture in the paper." Perhaps he was simply kidding.

5

How Neighborhoods Change, Why Occupants Change Neighborhoods

Trust Lubricates Cooperation

Machinery, factories, equipment, and the financial equity of businesses are all examples of physical capital that produce products that satisfy human wants. The knowledge, values, and relationships that spur production and creativity to satisfy human wants comprise equally important social capital. If social capital is to enable the members of a community to work together for their mutual benefit, there must be trust among the community's members.

That was a major finding of political sociologist Robert D. Putnam's study, published in his 1993 book, *Making Democracy Work*, a summary of his twenty-year-long study of politics and social organization in Italy. In his chapter "Social Capital and Institutional Success," Putnam wrote, "Trust lubricates cooperation."[1] Putnam's foray into the relationship between local community functions found that the "social capital" of intergroup cooperation and a strong civic tradition not only laid the foundation for fair and equitable decision making by the government in a democratic political system but also fostered economic growth. I learned the same thing as a young man when I was elected president of the Corryville Civic Association in 1959.

After my discharge from the Air Force in 1957, I went to work in my family's store, Gruen Apparel, located on Vine Street where it levels off after climbing up from downtown Cincinnati. The Corryville neighborhood had been developed in the nineteenth century to provide homes for working-class, German-speaking families on their first step up the economic ladder in their new country. The advertisements announcing available housing for the new development were written in German. By the time my father opened his store in 1939, most of the German-speaking families had moved on, and their single-family homes and apartments were now occupied by a new group of working-class, white, mainly Catholic households. They had the kind of civic attitudes and personal aspirations that Putnam would have recognized as providing the social capital needed for a well-functioning democracy. My predecessor as president of the civic association was a bus driver for the local transit system—he had a magnetic personality. I was honored that they elected me their new president, even though I was one of the few members who was not a resident of Corryville.

In the late 1950s, urban renewal had come to Corryville in the form of the federally funded General Neighborhood Renewal Plan, or GNRP. One prong of this urban renewal effort was aimed at enhancing the core neighborhood shopping district along Vine, where my family's retail store occupied two adjacent buildings at the center of the block. For virtually all neighborhood retailers, both then and now, the most sought-after component of renewal is parking space—more parking space than there was before renewal—and that was part of the renewal plan. Eventually, the Cincinnati urban renewal agency assembled and purchased the land behind the stores on the main block of Vine Street and converted the vacant land into a public parking lot.

The parking lot was financed by setting up an assessment district that charged an annual tax on the property owners served by the parking spaces. Assessment districts are formed to provide the future revenue needed to pay off bonds sold to finance a capital improvement. They are established when a majority of the property owners in a designated area or district vote to tax themselves to obtain the benefits of the improvement. The proceeds of the tax were used to pay off bonds issued to pay the costs of buying the land and blacktopping the lot with asphalt. At the junction of Vine and Auburn near the main business block, the redevelopment agency added some retail space to replace underutilized and obsolete buildings, which was somewhat helpful to the businesses in the area, or at least did it no harm.

It was much harder to gauge the effect of proposals for beautification and traffic changes through the residential streets and other efforts aimed at arresting the slow decline in the quality of the local residential stock. Both public and private meetings with the urban renewal professionals did little to help me understand how the various GNRP proposals were going to lessen or remove the basic problem faced by the homeowners in the neighborhood. In a nutshell, the problem was that when the risks associated with gauging likely future house values were considered, it was cheaper to sell an existing house in its "as is" condition and buy a new house in the suburbs than to pay the costs of bringing the existing house up to modern standards.

Remodel or Move?

A police officer and his wife were among the families that I had come to know in Corryville. The wife worked in the neighborhood. Their daughter attended a local parochial school. Although they liked the Corryville neighborhood, their house was old and had antiquated kitchen and bathroom fixtures. It was also one bedroom short of providing the "room of their own" that the children of increasingly affluent American families began to consider a necessity. After the officer was promoted to lieutenant, the husband's and wife's combined salaries put them into a financial position where they could afford the options of either remodeling their old house or moving to a new suburban development.

When the couple was in our store, they told me that they were considering whether they should remodel their present home or sell it and move to a new home. I was not surprised that they had looked at model homes in Finnytown, a community in the northwest of Cincinnati where new residential developments were being built on what had formerly been farmland. Several of Gruen Apparel's customers had already moved from Corryville to Finnytown, where they enjoyed new homes and a social and class makeup similar to Corryville at that time. For a year or two after they moved, these customers had continued to drive back into town to purchase clothing at our store. But I noticed that as time passed their visits grew less frequent as they found stores nearer their new homes. As a result, I urged my father to open another store in the Finnytown area. His refusal to do so played a role in my finally deciding to leave the family business, but that is another—although not totally unrelated—story.

The police lieutenant and his wife found that they could borrow the money needed to remodel their house, but given the availability of low-interest G.I. loans, the amount of cash they would have had needed for the remodel was very close to the down payment required for a new house in Finnytown. Furthermore, they noticed that the people of their own age with whom they had grown up, as well as some of the families they had come to know at their church and the school their daughter attended, were selling their houses and moving to the northwest suburbs. They feared that if they sunk their savings into remodeling their house, they might then be unable to afford to move if the fortunes of the neighborhood changed for the worse. As more neighbors with backgrounds similar to their own succumbed to the attraction of a new home in a new neighborhood, a move from Corryville seemed both a prudent economic choice and a more personally satisfying one as well. The move minimized the risks and probably the costs of a real estate investment that represented the family's nest egg. The decision made financial sense. In addition to this economic reason, the decision to move was also motivated by the feeling of comfort and mutual trust that came from living with people whose attitudes and values they understood and shared. The decision made sociological sense.

Mobility, Class Structure, and Neighborhood Cohesion

In 2000 Robert Putnam's *Bowling Alone* was published, a study of the decrease in shared community life, about which Putnam expresses strong disapproval.

He followed up the study with nearly thirty thousand interviews across the United States in an attempt to understand the reasons for the decline in civic engagement. He was not happy with what he learned but had the integrity to report his results.

From the large U.S. survey Putnam found that the decrease in voting, volunteering, and community activities of all types was correlated with the increasing diversity of the populations studied. One of America's strengths as a nation has long been its ability to draw a cooperative workforce and political body from the diverse talents, cultural heritages, perspectives, and economic statuses found in its population. Weaving these diverse threads into a strong economic, social, and political rope works best when the opportunity for economic mobility creates the incentive for all the threads to pull in the same direction. But the strength that this diversity gives the economic, social, and political fiber of the nation should not be taken to suggest that all of the nation's social classes need to be represented within each of its urban neighborhoods. On a neighborhood level, your feelings of comfort and trust may decline if your neighbors are of a different social class and their attitudes and values are clearly associated with class status. Consider the way that young artists like to move to bohemian enclaves when they are young, yet they leave when those neighborhoods no longer fit their aspirations as they become successful and want to move upward.

Unfortunately, even in a mobile society such as the United States, class distinctions at any point in time are often correlated with race and ethnicity. There are examples where racism or prejudice against ethnic or religious groups played a role in why many people moved from older neighborhoods to the suburbs. Labeling all moves as "white flight" misses many of the complex social and economic reasons for those moves.

Our failure to consider those reasons blinds us to many of the factors fueling the current political impetus for neighborhood control of land-use decisions. While white flight is always thought of as reactionary, and while community control is most often thought of as progressive, they are really two sides of the same coin—individuals attempting to find living arrangements appropriate to their desires. The families who moved from Corryville to Finnytown were looking for the best economic and social setting they could find. Like most people contemplating major life choices, families are not going to move where they feel uncomfortable.

Labeling as "racist" people's natural desire for neighbors and neighborhoods that they are comfortable with is not only incendiary, it is condescending and elitist. There is much research to suggest that this understandable desire for "compatible neighbors" is shared among different races and different ethnic groups, especially as it relates to compatibility within the same economic class. This might explain why, in spite of the potential for guilt, many communities that consider themselves progressive fight any change that might cause people of a different social class to move into their neighborhood.

From my experience in Corryville, I came to understand that for those whose economic success enabled them to move up a rung in class, it made social and economic sense to move to a new neighborhood. What I could not understand was how the plans and programs of the GNRP were going to do anything either to arrest the physical and social changes taking place in the neighborhood or to help those who were unable to move to gain refuge from that change. My need to understand these neighborhood social dynamics led me to walk from where I worked in the family store in Corryville to the nearby University of Cincinnati, where I enrolled in graduate school. That walk would eventually lead me to a new career as I continued to fulfill that need to understand. In the years since, the housing and other buildings along that walk have redeveloped to serve the university community, which has expanded into the Corryville neighborhood and has replaced the neighborhood I represented many years ago.

The experience of those who moved to the suburbs reinforced their desire to avoid the kind of social changes that contributed to their decision to leave Corryville. They and those like them also have had experiences that reinforce their economic motivations to avoid the kind of changes that will decrease both the level of public services and the class-related rank of their neighborhood. They have learned the benefits of fighting for those changes that will push their neighborhood up the scale of class desirability and increase access to the public services they want.

Unintended Consequences: The Lessons of Slum Clearance

Although the social role of the slums was rarely understood by the reformers who successfully campaigned for health and safety codes toward the end of the nineteenth century, they sought to improve the quality of housing rather than eliminate slum neighborhoods. The passage of building code ordinances that imposed standards of safety and health did make the older cold-water firetraps illegal. But even when they met minimum health and safety standards, the slums continued to offend the aesthetic and social conscience and the civic pride of affluent Americans. While dwelling codes and zoning were first used to ameliorate conditions such as those found in the slums, Americans came to realize that zoning and similar land-use regulations could be used to preserve and enhance the values of their own properties.

Slum clearance, as it became more complex and broadly applied, came to be known as "urban renewal" in 1949. Nevertheless, the philosophical foundation for slum clearance was based on fiscal, economic, and social theories that claimed that redevelopment was not only good for the economic health of cities, and by extension the nation, but also improved the well-being of those who were cleared from the slums.[2] The best known of fiscal analyses supporting this was presented in a book edited by Mabel Walker in 1938.[3] At the local level, the most effective—although invalid—argument was that slum clearance would save the cities money because it would eliminate the costs of serving those who lived in the slum. Walker compared the municipal revenues received from and the costs of services to slum neighborhoods with the municipal revenues received from and the costs of services to neighborhoods with high-quality housing and environments. Not surprisingly, she found that low-value properties occupied by poor people paid less in taxes and fees than higher valued properties occupied by more affluent households. The average number of police and fire calls was higher in slum neighborhoods than in the more affluent neighborhoods, which also cost local public agencies in the affluent neighborhoods less for welfare and other social services.

None of Walker's findings were surprising. What was surprising was that they were accepted as a rationale for the removal of the slums. No one raised the possibility that tearing down the buildings and moving out the poor would not remove their needs for social services or lower their relative propensity for criminal activity. These issues were not perceived by good people who wanted to believe that the social and economic problems of the poor could be solved by what seemed like a simple reordering of their environment. These ideas were first promoted by sociologists from the University of Chicago and then others (e.g., city planners and architects) who pushed the theory that the physical environment was a strong influence on the development of social attitudes and economic aptitudes. The idea that you could work quick changes on familial and personal attitudes and capabilities by changing the physical environment justified tearing down people's homes "for their own good."

By 1949 the program of slum removal was started on an evolution that over time would broaden to mandate the replacement of "blighted areas" with more valuable economic uses. An area was defined as "blighted" if it appeared that unimpeded market forces would not bring the real estate of the neighborhood up to its "highest and best use." In time, the publicly managed and financed program of urban renewal would become a local tool intended to improve the physical environment and facilitate economic development.

The case for supporting urban renewal at the federal level had been clinched by the macroeconomic arguments that were first suggested by a distinguished group of economists, planners, and architects meeting at the Cranbrook Academy in Michigan during World War II.[4] After it appeared that the United States and its Allies would defeat Germany, Italy, and Japan, the U.S. federal government was concerned with what would happen when U.S. soldiers returned home. They did not want to see a repeat of the veterans' marches for bonuses that occurred after World War I, when returning veterans could not find jobs. The likelihood was high that this could happen again because the United States had been in a long depression when it entered World War II. The economists at the Cranbrook Academy and elsewhere were beginning to accept the idea that the Depression was caused the inability of consumer demand, on its own, without any help from government, to reach levels needed for full employment. There was great concern that once the war ended, the wartime economy would slide back into recession, and soon after to depression, as civilian demands were unable to replace the flow of dollars that the government had poured into the military demands of the war effort.

The economists at Cranbrook believed in Keynesian economics, the ideas of the British economist John Maynard Keynes, who argued that government policies could be used to promote demand, which would alleviate high unemployment. This brain trust of economists, including the most famous American Keynesian economist, Alvin Hansen of Harvard, planned for the postwar years while the war was still in full swing. These economists derived strategies to be put in place once peace came that would accomplish the desirable end—full employment—by maintaining a sufficient flow of federal dollars into the economy. A central element of these strategies was the redevelopment of the urban landscape. The experts who met at Cranbrook urged lawmakers to use federal funding for postwar slum clearance and redevelopment as the way to improve the social and aesthetic health of American cities. This also, not so coincidentally, provided a Keynesian rationale for the massive federal expenditures that their diagnosis suggested would be needed to avoid another depression.

Their strategies won the support of civic leaders and planners across the country, and Congress made it the law of the land in the Housing Act of 1949.[5] This act called for "every American household to be provided a decent home and a suitable living environment." It provided federal funding for the purchase and planning of "blighted" urban property, which would be redeveloped toward higher and better uses. That is, property that seemed not to be moving up the scale of value and quality would be replaced with physically superior and more valuable structures. Postwar legislation provided federally insured loans for new housing in the suburbs, and the Defense Highway Act enabled construction of the vast network of roads linking every major urban place in the country. This legislation, along with the provision of various aids to suburban infrastructure, fueled great increases in new suburban construction through 1970. In addition, the Housing Act of 1949 also financed demolitions of slum neighborhoods.

By 1963 there was already evidence of damage not only to former residents but also to conditions elsewhere in the urban places where slums and other "blighted" neighborhoods were being removed. That year my graduate economics class at the University of Cincinnati was honored with a lecture from Alvin Hansen. I took the opportunity to ask him if he did not think that while urban renewal might have a positive economic effect, any such benefits would be wiped out by the economic results of the act's administration. When he asked why that would be the result, I attempted to explain to Professor Hansen some of the findings of research I was conducting in Cincinnati's Queensgate urban renewal project.

From the relocation records of that project, I drew fifty-one families' records at random and was able to locate where forty-seven of these former slum-dwelling households had moved. In their slum quarters, their average rent payment had been $31.68 per month; in their new quarters they were paying $60.12 per month. The former slum dwellers did not consider themselves better off and were too short of funds to bargain for maintenance or improvements from their landlords. To Professor Hansen, and subsequently in an article, I pointed out that urban renewal's demolition of affordable but poor-quality housing in blighted neighborhoods increased the cost of housing for the poor while it created conditions leading to disinvestment in other neighborhoods.[6] A year later, economist and public policy critic Martin Anderson published his popular exposé, "The Federal Bulldozer," which chronicled the harm being done by federally financed urban renewal to vulnerable residents of inner cities.[7]

Professor Hansen responded to my question by repeating again the benefits of large-scale, pump-priming programs, including Title I, Urban Renewal, but he shrugged off the counterproductive economic effects with the comment, "Of course bad administration can ruin any program." At the time, I was very disappointed because I thought Hansen's response irrelevant and defensive. In retrospect, I have come to think that, while it would have been a herculean task, perhaps some gradual slum-clearing urban renewal could have been administered to avoid disadvantaging the urban poor and unleashing pressures tending to decrease the quality of the neighborhoods to which they moved. Each city or town participating in the program would have had to take care not to demolish more slum housing than necessary to meet the demands for new housing by expected consumers plus the demands for affordable existing housing created by the eviction of former slum residents.

Keeping the older and less desirable housing outside the slums from facing an economic environment that would encourage undermaintenance required a two-pronged attack: First, the stock of new housing that was being created would have to be increased by the number of housing units being destroyed. At the same time, policies to encourage maintenance and enforce code rules would have to be instituted in the neighborhoods that received the former slum dwellers. And second, fairness would have called for compensating the renters who lost their housing to provide the evicted slum dwellers with the dollar power to bargain for quality dwellings in the private market. The property owners whose residential investments were condemned were compensated for the "fair market value" of their property. This compensation often worked like a real estate windfall to pay owners tax-free dollars for property that would otherwise have been very hard to sell at any but a highly discounted price.

The renters who lost their homes were not compensated even though they had to pay twice their previous rents for housing elsewhere. Instead of requiring the former residents of blighted neighborhoods to pay higher rental costs, I believe they should have been paid an annuity equal to the present value of their likely future rent increases. The costs of this annuity should have been paid by the sponsor of the renewal project, whether public or private. The extra dollars paid to renters removed from their neighborhoods would not only have made the urban renewal program more equitable, the annuity would also have minimized the downward drag on maintenance and remodeling investment in the neighborhoods that received the former residents of the demolished property. Additionally, the annuity would have played a role in decreasing the homelessness that has affected many major urban places. But, alas, none of that would be easy to administer.

People Define Neighborhood Boundaries

The boundaries of a location within a neighborhood of a city can be defined by the price per square foot of housing for similar housing in terms of type and size within that location. If you are familiar with the urban place where you live, you probably do not need to go out and do a statistical analysis of prices per square foot of housing to know where the different neighborhoods are and where they stand on the ladder of neighborhoods defined by housing price and quality.

In 1964 I bought and used a statistical technique called factor analysis to analyze massive amounts of data from the 1960 census to identify and define the boundaries of San Francisco's neighborhoods. After spending money and doing all the work, I discovered that the city's experienced residential real estate agents could have easily provided me with the boundaries of the same neighborhoods that I had laboriously located with my statistics. In fact, the San Francisco Board of Realtors had published a map on which all the neighborhood information I sought was clearly drawn and presented. Apparently, everyone but me had seen that map.

The map by San Francisco's Board of Realtors showed more neighborhoods than I have shown on my figure 4.2, which presents the relationship between price/rent and housing quality. Here is the way the neighborhoods on my map could be characterized according to that relationship: The top line ("g") in that figure is representative of neighborhoods such as Presidio Terrace, Pacific Heights, and Nob Hill. Line "f," which is one step down the ladder, describes Sea Cliff, or perhaps the Marina. As we move down the filtration ladder, the lines represent Cow Hollow, Diamond Heights, the Richmond, Sunset, Haight-Ashbury, and, at or near line "a," Hunters Point and Dog Patch. If you are a San Franciscan, please do not send me any hate mail indicating I have put your neighborhood in the wrong place on in the ladder. I could be off, but my purpose is to provide a feel for how to identify the boundaries of a neighborhood within a model that helps us conceptualize the organization of urban housing markets.

For most of us, where we live is our most easily recognizable and widely understood badge of social status. Much more than what car we drive or what we wear, where we live provides a clue to our class status. This is particularly true because we have been told that we are or should be a classless society. When possible, we avoid displaying class symbols that would make us seem ostentatious. But we know that ours is not a classless society—although class mobility, both upward and downward, is still possible within a single generation.

American neighborhoods tend to be homogeneous, not only with respect to price per square foot and quality but also with respect to one obvious component of class in our society—income. We live clustered with neighbors of similar incomes because when we buy or rent a home, most of us are willing to pay close to what we can afford so we can get the dwelling quality and other attributes that come with the neighborhood. In a market system, we use our dollars to get what we want; when it comes to housing, this means we tend to segregate ourselves by class and, to a lesser extent, by age.

Prior to the passage of civil rights legislation and the cultural shifts that took place in the 1950s and 1960s, the neighborhoods in most American cities were segregated by race and by class. When Jim Crow laws were abolished and antidiscrimination laws passed, race-based discrimination was still enforced by the same powerful social bigotry that limited interracial dating and marriage in all but the most liberal American communities. In the 1967 movie *Guess Who's Coming to Dinner*, two natives of very liberal San Francisco, played by Spencer Tracy and Katharine Hepburn, uncomfortably host Sidney Poitier, their daughter's very high-class black suitor. The movie was Hollywood's most popular (albeit hilariously unrepresentative) portrayal of the social trauma that American society was going through in the civil rights era.

By the end of the 1980s, overt race-based segregation was rare, particularly segregation that was enshrined in laws or contracts. But this did not mean racial segregation in neighborhoods had ended. Today's racial segregation in neighborhoods, particularly in the schools, is more likely to be present in liberal northern states than in the historically Jim Crow South. But I do not believe this is because, as the noted French student of American character Alexis de Tocqueville wrote in 1832, "The prejudice of race appears to be stronger in the states that have abolished slavery than those where it still exists." Gary Orfield, a professor of education and social policy and codirector of the Civil Rights Project at Harvard, has noted that "whites and blacks live apart much as they did in the south, and they more often live apart outside the south than inside it."[8] Orfield recognized that segregation today is much more likely to result from responses to housing than by overt racial actions. The census report "Racial and

Ethnic Residential Segregations in the United States: 1980–2000" found that the most segregated metropolitan area is Detroit, followed by Milwaukee, New York City, and Chicago. In these regions, the invisible economic walls that keep out the less affluent also minimize racial integration. The great urban observer and land-use lawyer Richard Babcock explained in his 1969 book, *The Zoning Game*, "Zoning has provided the device for protecting the homogeneous, single-family suburb from the city."[9]

In 2006, when the U.S. Supreme Court was considering whether to allow Seattle, Washington, and Louisville, Kentucky, to use race as a public-school enrollment factor, David Campos, the general counsel for the San Francisco School District, submitted a brief to the Court in support of racial quotas. Campos cited the experience of San Francisco, which had integrated its schools under a 1983 court order that imposed racial quotas. Campos wrote that when race was pulled from the equation as part of a legal settlement in 1999, the San Francisco schools rapidly resegregated. In 2003 the *San Francisco Chronicle* reported, "A single ethnic group exceeded 45 percent of overall enrollment in 49 of the district's 104 schools; in 22 schools, more than 60 percent of students are of one race."[10] San Francisco is an example of the ironic situation that exists in the core area of many cities. If you want your kids to attend a racially integrated school where no one ethnic group makes up more than 33 percent of the student body, you might consider a private Catholic institution such as San Francisco's Sacred Heart Cathedral Preparatory School.[11]

It is clear that where overt segregation is no longer legal or socially acceptable, there still is a high degree of class and economic segregation. Furthermore, it should not be surprising that the social and economic characteristics of current and future residents should enter the psychology of the housing market and affect how and where we choose to buy or rent. When looking to buy or rent, the physical characteristics of dwelling unit quality that are desirable include the comfort of the space of the unit and the lot; the size and layout of the unit; landscaping, plumbing, utilities, and features such as a swimming pool; and the condition of the unit. All those features are affected by the quality of the original building or by remodeling and renovation. That is, the built environment is a product of how much has been spent on the construction of housing with these features, and, over time, by their level of maintenance.

The importance of maintenance was exemplified by the experience of East Germany between the end of World War II and reunification. During that period, more dwelling units were lost through years of undermaintenance than had been destroyed by the combat and invasion of Germany during World War II. Of course, how and why people decide to maintain property has a lot to do with how they imagine themselves in a particular neighborhood and how that neighborhood supports or works against their class aspirations.

You are no doubt thinking that there are many important things about individual homes and neighborhoods that are not related to dwelling unit quality and that are not a product of the original construction and remodeling or preserved through money spent on maintenance. And you are right. There are features outside the house and lot that the owner cannot change without moving. These are the externalities we have defined previously, including characteristics physically linked to the site's geography, such as views and the local climate.

But even more important, we select neighborhoods that, if otherwise acceptable, are close to where we work, recreate, worship, and shop. If we have children, the educational quality, social milieu, and safety of the schools that serve the neighborhood are likely to be critical for social as well as educational reasons. I am not unique in that I was first introduced to the economic tools that I use to earn a livelihood, as well as to the girl I married, while I was in high school. Again, self-imposed class segregation is as important to our housing choices as price.

This reality is so obvious that many of us oversimplify it by assuming that everyone wants the same kind of neighborhood that we want. In an upscale town, I remember well a comment made by the hostess of a lunch at the elegant home of the chairman of the planning commission of which I was a member. During the course of a discussion about the preferences of households likely to move into an affordable housing project, I made the mistake of emphasizing the point that we had to consider their compatibility by saying, "As lovely a house as this is, not everyone would prefer being your neighbor." She cut me short, saying, "Don't be silly, Claude Gruen, everyone wants to live next to my family." She was wrong. Her family's excellent but expensive tastes in what they enjoyed as well as her patronizing attitude toward the less affluent would be a real turn-off to those with the values and incomes of other classes.

While studying a plan to encourage low- and moderate-income housing development in the suburbs around Dayton, Ohio, my firm conducted extensive interviews about neighborhood preferences with a sample of people having high, middle and low incomes. We found that the less well off wanted good housing and services and racial integration but saw economic integration as potentially fraught with problems.[12] One of the women we interviewed summed up what we heard from many low-income respondents: "I think it would be a good idea to find a new section to build a new community. Prefer to see it integrated racially, which would keep balance in schools; since we're here together we might as well learn to live together. Do not prefer income integration because people tend to try to keep up with Joneses when they can't afford it."[13]

The pioneer sociologist and researcher Herbert Gans had a similar finding in his study of Levittown, New York: "People who must watch every penny cannot long be comfortable with more affluent neighbors, particularly when children come home demanding a toy or clothes they have seen next door."[14]

This is perhaps one of the most difficult pills to swallow in a society based on the myth of classlessness, but swallowing it will improve our ability to identify beneficial housing policies.

Housing Prices and Homeownership during the Exodus to the Suburbs

When the federally funded urban renewal program was operating at full throttle, the production of mostly suburban housing by the private sector did act to mitigate the overall price-raising effect of the large-scale removal of low-quality and low-price housing in many of America's metropolitan areas. Between 1950 and 1968, urban renewal removed 404,000 housing units—or about 24 percent of the 1,646,000 housing units removed for all reasons during that period.[15] During the baby boom years of the 1950s and 1960s, housing prices continued to be affordable for the middle class. The middle class was only minimally affected by the demolitions in neighborhoods serving the poorest segments of the population because overall the production of single-family and multifamily units was in excess of population growth.

Between 1950 and 1960, the U.S. population grew by about 19 percent. But even after losing approximately 3.6 percent of the existing stock through urban renewal, the total housing stock increased by 12,293,000 units, or 27 percent.[16] The middle class was increasingly better housed because their incomes rose faster than housing prices. During that period, the availability of housing for the overwhelming majority of people in the workforce enabled economically vibrant urban areas to benefit from an inflow of workers. At least equally important, as will be discussed shortly, these economies benefited from the construction of new and more efficient workplace and retail centers.

However, even in these carefree and prosperous years of private housing production, not all economic classes benefited. Housing demolitions due to urban renewal, as well as the many private demolitions of residences, hurt households on the lower rungs of the income scale and set the stage for much of the homelessness of the late 1980s and 1990s. While middle-class housing improved as the production of new units stayed ahead of housing demand growth, the cost of housing the poor began to rise. The removal of units from the bottom end of the price ladder exceeded the rate at which houses filtered down, so unless the poor were granted government subsidies, they paid more for their housing.

The supply of new neighborhoods was large enough to give the middle class the ability to afford housing halfway up the ladder of neighborhoods sorted by price. They could bargain for quality if they were renters; if they were owners, they could preserve the value of their own units through adequate maintenance. But such was not the case for households on the lower end of the income scale.

TABLE 5.1

Household Size and Homeownership Rates, 1950–1990

	1950	1960	1970	1980	1990
Homeownership rate (%)	55.0	62.0	63.0	64.4	64.2
Average household size (number of people living within same housing unit)	3.37	3.07	3.00	2.56	2.43

Sources: U.S. Census Bureau, Historical Census of Housing, Homeownership; U.S. Census Bureau, Selected Historical Decennial Census, Population & Housing Counts.

Urban renewal often ensured that housing in the neighborhoods they could afford was in short supply. Therefore, most of those who had lower incomes had to accept undermaintenance simply to stay in housing they could barely afford. In time, shifting the poor to neighborhoods where the economics of real estate made maintenance and renovation a poor financial choice became the beginning of new slums.

The differences among those on the various rungs of the income ladder were not shown by statistics of cumulative averages used to compare housing price increases during the period with overall increases in the consumer price index, CPI. Between 1952 and 1970, housing prices grew by 64.4 percent while the CPI for all urban consumers grew by 46.4 percent.[17] But the increase in housing prices during that period was dwarfed by the increase in family income. The result, shown in table 5.1, was that homeownership rates rose as the average number of people living in the same housing unit, referred to as one household by the U.S. Census, declined.[18]

During the decade of the 1970s, housing production continued to be high; more than 19 million new housing units were built during the same time the U.S. population increased by 23.2 million people. Between 1980 and 1990, 13.9 million units were added; during those same ten years, population growth slowed to 22.2 million. In each of these decades, the percentage increase of housing units greatly exceeded the percentage increase of population growth—in other words, the average number of persons per household decreased. Between 1970 and 1980, the population grew by 11.4 percent while the housing stock increased by 28.7 percent. From 1980 to 1990, the population grew by 9.8 percent while the housing stock climbed 15.7 percent.

During the decade of the 1990s, a very different picture began to emerge. The housing stock barely exceeded the growth of population nationwide.

Countrywide, population grew by 13.2 percent while housing stock throughout the country increased 13.3 percent.[19] The reversal of the housing supply-and-demand relationship was particularly extreme in the bicoastal states of New York, Massachusetts, Florida, and California. By the 1990s, many of the cities and towns with strong economies were implementing land-use policies that put large swathes of suburban areas out of bounds for development, prohibited the conversion of obsolete industrial buildings to housing, and restricted heights and densities while increasing the costs and time of the residential development process.

The Wealth Effect

Within the metropolitan regions where local public bodies adopted growth-restraining residential development ordinances, regulations, and procedures, the price of existing houses went up in most, if not all, neighborhoods. These price increases made homeowners feel wealthier because, for most of them, their house was their largest financial asset. Many of those who saw the value of their residential asset increase took advantage of their new wealth by increasing their mortgage debt to extract spendable cash. In time, the loosening of mortgage regulations and supervision to accommodate new home buyers brought increased, but unsustainable, housing demand to these regions.

In regions where all the neighborhoods were pushed up within the map of housing values, there was an increase in the money spent on housing quality improvements. Unlike the wealth effect, which was largely illusory and eventually unsustainable, the effect on housing quality was real. As more neighborhoods entered the value zone within which spending more on maintenance and remodeling paid off in terms of resale value, the existing stock of houses was improved.

Growth Controls Become Popular and Legal

There was a time—a long time, for centuries, actually—when it was possible for residents and property owners to use a person's or group's race, religion, or ethnic background as the basis for keeping them out of their neighborhood because their race, religion, or ethnic background was perceived to cause housing values to drop. Volumes have been written and statistical studies conducted about whether African Americans and other minorities caused the downward shift in the value of housing in neighborhoods they had been allowed to enter.

By the middle of the twentieth century, pioneers in the fight for civil rights mustered the power to force an end to discrimination based on race, religion, and ethnicity. The war on battlefields that led to emancipation from slavery shifted to the courts, law chambers, and the streets of America, where the war was against discrimination. When that war was won, neighborhoods and developers were stripped of their most powerful nonmarket means—race, religion, ethnicity—of barring people they perceived as lowering the social status of their neighborhoods. Nevertheless, that did not alter the tight relationship between the class status and market value of neighborhoods.

The tension created by taking away the ability of incumbent neighbors to boycott those seen as threatening the social status, and possibly the cohesion, of the neighborhood probably accelerated the movement of households from older central city neighborhoods to new suburban communities. Whether they moved to the suburbs or stayed in their old neighborhoods, homeowners began the search for a new tool to provide the same feeling of control they had had over the class of new entrants into their neighborhood. The expanded use of the zoning power that local municipalities had been given in 1926 was the first step toward the new era of local political control over the allocation of land to real estate uses. As the popularity of local control became increasingly evident to politicians at all levels of government, a whole series of new empowerments were requested by local planning bodies and granted by both federal and state courts. The cumulative effect of court-approved planning innovations added the right to control the amount and rate of development to the powers already possessed and used by local bodies to encourage neighborhood class homogeneity. During the two decades that followed civil rights legislation, new procedures and laws evolved that shifted land-use decisions from private to public entities.

The Citizen Participation Process

During the same time that the courts were shifting the right to control the use of land from private land owners to local municipalities, an equally important shift was taking place—the shift from representative democracy to participatory democracy, a new concept in the process of land-use planning. Until the early 1970s, the citizens of local municipalities and counties elected mayors, council people, supervisors, and the like who voted on land-use matters on behalf of their constituents. By the end of the 1970s, elected officials still did the voting on such matters, but with increasingly rare exceptions, they based their votes on their perceptions of what had come out of a "citizen participation process."

Under the citizen participation process, public plans are conceptualized and the proposals of developers are presented to an unelected and rarely representative group of neighborhood and special-interest activists. Such groups of "stakeholders" screen development proposals for the likelihood that these new proposals will attract new entrants of similar or higher social status as the existing residents, and that the status quo of existing services and amenities will be maintained or enhanced. In a series of meetings, often led by a "facilitator" who was a professional city planner, local activists who volunteer for duty as participating citizens are usually asked to envision what they would like to see represented in the plans for new housing in their neighborhood. The facilitator summarizes the inputs—the "visions"—of the volunteer citizens group into a plan, which is then presented to the planning board and councils. While not aimed at preserving the homogeneity of upscale social class, the environmental laws and social concerns that came center stage during the last quarter of the twentieth century expanded the legal basis and rationales used by citizen participation groups to screen development proposals and prepare land-use plans.

The new suburban neighborhoods tended to be geographically larger than the neighborhoods of older urban places. And the communities that encompassed the older neighborhoods were more class homogeneous. By the 1990s, greater restrictions on new development were being imposed on residential construction projects proposed for where there were farmlands, as well as for proposed projects within existing suburban neighborhoods. Successes in stopping "sprawl," combined with restrictions on the vacant land or underutilized buildings referred to as "infill" sites that private developers sought to develop, pushed up the prices of housing in virtually all the neighborhoods of coastal regions where housing demand was growing. This was tantamount to a warfare, but a quiet class warfare that has had the effect of both shutting out the poor from the advantages of homeownership while increasing the gulf between the rich and the poor.

Reducing opportunities for homeownership makes it harder for working households to climb the ladder of social and economic class mobility. Shrinking the middle class, which has long been the glue between the rich and poor, strikes at the health of the American democracy.

"Buyers' Markets" Become "Sellers' Markets"

As prices rose in the regions where the closing of frontiers had created an imbalance between supply and demand, the current homeowners gained in personal net wealth. Neighborhood activists and environmentalists became the new heroes of the urban social set as they slowed growth, saved the status quo, and preserved amenities for those who already enjoyed them. By driving up the value of the existing houses, the activists and environmentalists also created a new standard of value for vacant land that could be expected to be approved for development. Land that was likely to be approved for development was regarded affectionately as "entitlable."

Would-be home buyers who were not already owners were worse off than before, swimming against the tide of rising prices and the undertow of increasingly restricted choices. When the regionwide housing supply grows more slowly than the number of households with the money and desire to buy or rent, consumers of housing pay more and get less. When the housing supply grows faster than the number of those willing to buy or rent, then the consumers of housing pay less and get more. When housing construction moves ahead faster than the growth of demand, housing is more affordable, and landlords, builders, and sellers are listening very carefully to what consumers of housing want. That is what is meant by a "buyers' market" or a "soft market."

As the array of residential neighborhoods represented in figure 4.2 rose, residential land values increased in all neighborhoods. Gentrification became more likely in some of the neighborhoods on the lower rungs of the value ladder, particularly if they had any nearby amenities, such as desirable schools, parks, churches, or cultural/entertainment venues

The building industry also began to change its focus and profitability. Profit margins rose as competition lessened. But the time and capital required to obtain the entitlement of land for development, or redevelopment, weighed against the viability of smaller builders, causing a sudden rush of mergers and the creation of nationwide home construction companies. The priorities of those in the businesses of building housing and developing residential land shifted from catering to consumers of housing to acquiring and obtaining approval for—entitlement—vacant or redevelopable residential sites.

The focus was no longer on providing sites and houses acceptable to prospective buyers. The focus was on satisfying the wishes of those who already lived in or claimed to speak for the neighborhood. Through all this, those people without property and anyone hoping to gain a foothold in the real estate market had no political voice. It is very difficult to gain political traction when you cannot identify who you have to deal with politically, especially those claiming to be merely environmentalists or preservationists, or those who are just making sure that neighborhoods don't fall in value.

Local politics created the kind of long-term sellers' market that the building industry had never been able to impose on the housing market by itself. The sellers' market changed builders' concentration from what the consumer wanted to the public relations battle for entitlement. On tight profit margins, much less attention was paid to building what the consumer wanted than had been the norm in the "good old days when the consumer was king."

Here is a personal recollection from the history of a new builder entering a Texas market in the early 1970s, back during the days when housing supply was growing faster than demand. A former Air Force sergeant retired to his hammock in a small Texas tract home, living what he thought would be an easy life financed by his Air Force pension. Unfortunately for his leisure, his wife wanted more than what that pension could pay for. So she had to continue to work at a demanding job in addition to running the household. After a particularly grueling day, the wife came home from work after stopping to buy the groceries for dinner. She looked out the kitchen window to their small backyard where she saw her husband, flopped as usual in his hammock. Then she did something that changed his life. She marched out into the yard and tipped him out of his hammock. As he lay on the ground, stunned at what she just did, she demanded, "Get a job—tomorrow!"

The next day he started to scout around for what he could do with his Air Force training and some construction skills. He decided to buy some empty lots in a new neighborhood that had recently been opened. Because times were tough for land owners and builders, the lots were not expensive. There were more houses going up than there were new households forming and needing houses in the region. But the former sergeant had a knack for listening to prospective home buyers and giving them what they wanted. He learned to pay attention to things such as which room of the house was important to the buying decision of both the man and the woman buyer. In those days, wives usually deferred to husbands and were reluctant to insist on what they wanted. But the former sergeant noticed that if the kitchen did not have the fixtures that were important to the wife, she would find some reason not related to the kitchen for failing to support the buy decision. He made sure the wife got what she wanted, and he and the buyers could all sleep well at night knowing he delivered a house the buyers could pay for. The former sergeant's company grew to be one of the biggest in Texas.

Wherever demand in excess of supply gives this kind of power to the buyers, consulting firms such as mine are busy conducting surveys and market studies to provide builders and land developers with insight into what housing consumers will pay to obtain. The emphasis of consulting activity, as well as the behavior of building executives, changes when the closing of an urban frontier shifts the regionwide supply-demand relationship in favor of those who are allowed to build. When that happens, consulting firms find their developer clients more interested in impact studies such as cost–benefit analyses and research aimed at legislative bodies in municipalities and at the citizens groups in neighborhoods. The aim of these studies is to convince municipalities and citizens groups that the builders should be given the right to build on vacant land or to give rebirth to old neighborhoods—often in new buildings that will significantly increase residential densities. These studies do not ignore the demand side, but the executive hero is not the man or woman who listens best to housing consumers. Instead, it is the person who presents the most effective argument at zoning hearings and citizens' participation meetings.

The housing consumer is not the only loser when the urban frontier of a region starts to close. Limiting development flexibility and rising land rents also weaken and eventually cripple the economic development of the region. From the perspective of a homeowner or land-owning developer, increases in land rents are increases in wealth. But in time the opposite will prevail. The increasing land rents that follow the closing of a region's urban frontier increase the price of housing, which weakens the housing consumer's choices and the economy of the region.

The term "land rents" does not refer to the "contract rents" we pay when leasing a house or apartment. Instead, land rents refer to the income earned by land in excess of costs—other than the cost of the land—that the use of a particular land site can provide the builder, farmer, or natural resource extractor who uses the land. The economic forces that inscribe the neighborhood-by-neighborhood price–quality ladder ultimately dictate the level of the region's land rents. Like a ship passing through a lock in the Panama Canal, the land rents within all the neighborhoods of a region rise when the prices that can be charged for housing in the region climb faster than all the non-land-related costs associated with the production and maintenance of housing. When this happens, the aims of rent seekers are achieved.

The explanations of the concepts, the related personal narratives, and the graphic representations presented thus far in this book should help you understand how public policies that facilitate or restrain the development of additional houses affect the quality and price of both housing and developable land in neighborhoods of an urban market. The individual builder or individual homeowner cannot meaningfully affect the regionwide balance between the supply and demand for housing. That balance is the ultimate determinant of housing prices. However, both the builder and the homeowner can decide whether to pay the costs associated with building new houses and maintaining or redeveloping existing structures. Price-determining supply and demand balances are like the availability and cost of nearby schools, roads, utilities, police, health care, and many other components of urban infrastructure, in that they are external to the control of the individual home builder or homeowner.

6

The Turn against Expansion and Growth

A New Spirit Constrains Development

The "Indians" who threw tea into Boston Harbor touched off a revolution that gave birth to the United States of America. They were protesting against a government that restricted the supply of a common consumer item—tea. What followed from that protest was a revolution. The government of the new country that emerged from the revolution instituted a bias against interfering in trade and commerce. Its founders erected a fence—of law and habits of thought—between the government and the marketplaces where private parties allocated resources, including land. The government looked over that fence to regulate taxes, provide public services, and be available as a third party to arbitrate private sector disputes.

However, the public services that the government was to provide were strictly limited to those necessary positive externalities like roads and defense that are difficult for the private sector to produce or that tend to be natural monopolies that will not be produced or, if produced, will be priced unfairly. A bridge over a river is an example of such a natural monopoly. The owner of a single, heavily trafficked bridge over a river is in a position to maximize revenues by charging a toll that will exclude many from being able to use the bridge and will earn the owner a return well above the rate of return needed to attract capital to the bridge-building venture. If the bridge is owned by the public, a much lower toll can be charged, equal to the marginal costs of operating the bridge and paying off the costs of building it. At least theoretically, this means that after the costs of building the bridge are recovered, an even lower toll could be charged by the public entity. If this does not happen, it is usually because the public decides to keep the bridge toll above operating costs to raise money for some other public purpose.

The bias against the government stepping over that fence was maintained for almost two hundred years and extended to decisions about the use of land. Throughout those two centuries, land accounted for a small proportion of the total costs associated with creating new housing. As recently as 1964, when I came to California, land typically accounted for between 15 and 20 percent of the total price of single-family "tract" homes. This was the same range I was accustomed to seeing in southern Ohio's new suburban developments. By 2005, when my company was implementing the development of single-family homes at eight to the acre and townhomes at more than fourteen to the acre, the cost of land in northern California accounted for about 43 percent of the price buyers paid for new homes. In the midst of the 2008–2009 housing depression, entitled land—that is, the land that public agencies would allow to be used for housing development—in northern California constitutes about 25 percent of the price builders think they are going to obtain for the single-family tract homes they plan to build.

During the roughly two hundred years when builders and developers decided how many houses they would build on the land they would buy, individual homeowners had little influence over how the land in their regions or even neighborhoods would be used. Today, individual homeowners still do not directly tell builders and developers how much and what, if anything, to build. But that is exactly the power homeowners have as voters who elect the lawmakers and executives who, by controlling the uses of the land, do decide how much housing can be built. Those who were not already homeowners were worse off when local governments started to step over the fence and effectively took over the decisions previously made by developers and builders operating in response to their perception of the signals shown by local housing markets. By consistently allowing less land to be built on for housing than the number of lots that builders and developers would have built on in the absence of regulatory barriers, officials acting on behalf of public agencies and local governments effectively allocated the amount of land used for residential construction.

As most existing homeowners saw it, the shifting of control over how much and which land could be developed for housing benefited them by providing them with a feeling of control and creating the shortage that pushed up the value of their home. As we now know, these increases in home values led to an expansion of the mortgage-providing financial sector and the undermining of the national economy. Less obvious is the damage that housing price increases—induced by publicly created site scarcities—do to the nation's ability to compete in world markets, and to the likelihood that future generations will become homeowners. How elected officials and those who work for them came to create this scarcity is reviewed next.

The Legacy of Euclid v. Ambler

The U.S. Supreme Court's 1926 decision to uphold the right of a village near Cleveland, Ohio, to restrict land to a very narrowly defined use, structural type, and density of development tore a hole in the legal mesh of the fence that had kept government out of the land-use allocating business. But even after that decision— *Village of Euclid v. Ambler Realty Co.*—the habit of respecting private property minimized the degree to which local governments entered the arena where land use is allocated. During four decades or so after that decision, zoning typically stuck to mandating the uses, density, and types of structures that would be allowed once private developers proposed a plan. But during the 1970s, a quiet but very powerful revolution enabled local governments to crimp more fully down the fence that had kept them from directly rationing the supply of land.

More often since the 1970s, local land-use regulators have been intervening in the housing market with a series of measures that reduce the number of residential units allowed to be built, which increases the costs as well as the prices of those residences that are built. Some of these policies are merely expansions of policies that had existed before 1970, such as large-lot zoning, greenbelt laws that make large swaths of open land off limits for development, and development fees that exceed the costs on municipal services likely to be imposed by proposed projects. But other policies would have been illegitimate without the passage of new laws and court rulings, such as the imposition of growth limits or quotas and the outlawing of noncontiguous development.

Perhaps the best example of bad regulatory policy that was sanctioned under *Euclid* but used more extensively in the post-1970 era was the frequent practice of adopting municipal and countywide general plans and zoning that restricted much of the allowable suburban residential developments to large lots while leaving no acreage, or only a small amount, for housing on smaller lots. Without apology or even much of a blink of social consciousness, the result of such policies is to encourage the building of neighborhoods for only the well-to-do while limiting the amount of land that can be used for less expensive homes and apartments.

One effect of large-lot zoning is that the rich pay less than the poor pay per square foot of land area that they buy. Although not the result of any grand conspiracy, this is unfair and antithetical to such democratic values as fairness and equality of opportunity.

Regulations such as these are the tools used in a class conflict fought over land use. The result of the way this struggle has been consistently won by those living in the homes near where new development is anticipated or actually proposed. Political victories won by such "incumbent neighbors" have had profound negative economic and social effects, including increasing the disparity between the rich and poor in the United States. Nevertheless, among all the tensions in America—liberal versus conservative, black versus white, religious versus secular, pro- versus anti-immigration—this disparity is one conflict that barely gets noticed.

Whether the new regulatory powers granted public agencies were motivated by neighborhood activists seeking to keep out the less affluent, or by concerns for the environment, or by preferences for the status quo, among other intentions, the widespread effect of these powers has been closing the urban frontier. The cumulative effect of these supply reductions is powerful.

Inclusionary zoning is the most popular of the contemporary planning policies intended to add some affordable housing. But it provides only a small fraction of what has been aborted by market-stifling policies while creating further dysfunction within the local housing market itself. Inclusionary zoning fails to address the main problem—a housing shortage—and masks a more complex problem—class conflict between homeowners and those who are desperate to buy into the housing market. It is clear that the net result of the closing of urban frontiers by neighborhood activists, along with their environmentalist and antisprawl allies, has had a strongly negative effect on the housing markets of growing American regions, especially in the coastal areas.

Reinventing Obsolete Urban Spaces

A significant aspect of contemporary land-use regulating policies in the United States is a bias against change. This attitude has long affected European countries. Most of us share this bias to some degree. But since the first nomads settled down to farm and trade at one location, urban places could only survive by adapting to changing conditions of production, trade, and consumption. The need for the adaptive reuse of urban spaces is particularly great in the twenty-first century given the speed of change in technology, transportation, resource availability, demography, and environmental conditions, among other factors. Not only should individual commercial, industrial, recreational, and institutional structures adapt to these changes but the way they are clustered should also change to provide the benefits of proximity that we have referred to as agglomeration economies. Buildings become obsolete as technologies and ways of doing business change. The twentieth-century change in manufacturing processes that moved production from multistory to single-story factories also outmoded the clusters of multistoried warehouses and factories alongside the rail lines that were the production-enhancing agglomerations of great industrial cities.

As the pace of change continues, the bustling retail and industrial clusters of a few generations ago may be on their way to becoming the blighted, declining areas of tomorrow. As the strength of their location-based economic advantages wanes, the appearance of lowering land values and rents will be read by astute developers as a message that the time has come for a change in both the structures themselves and their uses. From New York to San Francisco, Chicago to San Antonio, neighborhoods that once housed clusters of manufacturing, warehousing, and meat processing firms, when allowed to change, will be revitalized into thriving mixed-use activity centers. These centers often will have remodeling and design features that preserve reminders of the past, intermixing residences with contemporary retail, recreational, cultural, and commercial land uses. Similarly, changes in the type and location of nonresidential space create opportunities for new development on what had previously been grazing land or other nonurban uses in or near the suburbs.

Yesterday's deteriorating and blighted areas can become tomorrow's business centers or luxury neighborhoods. Such changes are being wrought every day as lands that were contaminated when they served as sites for the mills and factories of earlier generations are redeveloped. In their place will be a new set of businesses and uses that, as before, will see the urban frontier as full of possibility, change, and new functions. Attempts to block such changes in land uses or impose unnecessarily high costs in remediation standards can forestall such new and powerful urban revivals.

But, at least so far, the rigidity being imposed on residential development and redevelopment is much greater than is the rigidity for commercial and industrial uses. Understanding what is happening to thwart the building of enough housing to create a healthy, dynamic, and adaptive balance between demand and supply will provide insight into what is happening on a lesser scale to nonresidential development. There is a feedback relationship between the growth and innovative nature of the economy and change of land uses—each positively impacts the other. Those urban places that do not change will shrivel over time; urban places that grow and adjust will improve aesthetically and enhance the wealth and comfort of those who live, work, and invest in them.

While it may seem as though the solution to the dangerous rigidities that local governments are imposing on land use is simply to eliminate the role of government and go "laissez-faire," this would be throwing the baby out with the bath water. The reality is that the private sector needs the government to play a role in both the regulation of urban development and the creation of the public infrastructure, which government can do more efficiently than private parties can.

We have seen how government has historically played a powerful role in creating and supporting urban environments. Let us now look at the history of how citizens groups have attacked and eroded that support into a full-scale assault against growth. This inward turn against the country's traditions of broad expansion and openness is the story of the last forty years—and an increasingly desperate story.

The Pig in the Parlor

In 1952 Charles E. Wilson, the former president of General Motors and later the secretary of defense, pronounced, "What is good for the country is good for General Motors, and what's good for General Motors is good for the country." "Engine Charley" was surprised to find that what he considered an incontrovertible truth raised a firestorm of protest. Most others of his and earlier generations, and most certainly any businessperson who had grown up in pre-Eisenhower America, would have shared Wilson's belief. Only those most aware of what was then a nascent change in the attitude of the body politic—and ultimately the courts—would not have believed similar statements to be true.

Nowhere was this attitude change that led to outcries against Wilson's perceived arrogance gestating faster than at the local level. The seeds of doubt about the sanctity of private property and the effects of free market capitalism were finding fertile ground in the hearts and minds of those who lived and voted in the fast-growing suburbs of the 1950s. These seeds would grow even stronger in their children, who grew up in the 1950s and came of age in the 1960s.

The attitude shift away from the reverence for private property and away from belief in the primacy of free markets was stronger locally than nationally. But at least in its explicit expression, this shift was as new to city halls as it was to the halls of Congress or the states. Until the 1960s, governmental intervention in the private market primarily protected the value of private property. Laws and regulations were introduced to improve the performance of the private market, not to replace it.

In his exposition of the origins of zoning, land-use attorney Dick Babcock made it clear that the zoning and building codes of an earlier era had not been introduced to usurp markets or to intrude into private property rights. Rather, those early zoning and building codes were represented to the courts and to the public as necessary police actions to protect and enhance ordinary homeowners' property values and to enable the market to operate most beneficially.

New York's 1916 ordinance had the same stated intention when it established boundaries for single-family, commercial, and industrial zones, as well as requirements dealing with physical conditions, such as the size of back yards and maximum fence heights. In *The Zoning Game*, Babcock explained:

> At the start, the concept of zoning was the result of some ingenious legal persuasion by sophisticated and knowledgeable lawyers who believed the courts could be induced to permit municipalities, by an extension of the common law nuisance doctrine, to build a comprehensive land-use regulatory scheme under the aegis of the police power. The United States Supreme Court in 1926 upheld zoning in the landmark case of *Village of Euclid v. Ambler Realty Co.* because that conservative bench regarded the intrusion of industry and apartments into single-family zones as cousin

to a public nuisance, similar to the intrusion of a tuberculosis sanitarium which could be kept out under orthodox common law principles. The Court stated, "A nuisance may be merely a right thing in the wrong place, like a pig in the parlor instead of the barnyard," and, after describing the noxious consequences of allowing an apartment house in a single-family zone, it concluded, "Under these circumstances, apartment houses, which in a different environment would be not only entirely unobjectionable but highly desirable, come very near to being nuisances."[1]

The 1926 Supreme Court heard no evidence concerning the regressive nature of a law that would permit those who could afford large single-family homes to reserve large amounts of land for themselves, thus making it much cheaper for their housing per square foot than the smaller amount of land that would be zoned for small lots and apartments. It would be unfair to criticize the failure of the plaintiff to present evidence concerning this market effect. No one in 1926 could have imagined that by 1970, in an increasing number of municipalities, the regulatory grandchildren of the *Euclid* decision would replace market-driven land-use allocations with planning commissions and city councils bestowing allowances and entitlements.

In many cases, the political pressure to usurp market functions and private property rights is thinly camouflaged as efforts to protect the environment, to minimize traffic congestion, to raise aesthetic standards, or to preserve the public treasury. What they are never portrayed as are ways for the affluent to control and withdraw land from uses that might benefit those citizens who have not yet "economically" made it.

Where the urban frontier closes is where the American dream shuts down and the dynamic nature of geographic, social, and economic mobility—one of America's greatest strengths—withers away. Because these unfortunate consequences often accumulate inadvertently, slowly, and indirectly, the policies, institutions, and individuals that bring them about are rarely held to account by their victims. Politicians and activists may have moved on. Planning boards and staff may say that their scope is limited: "We can't fix the often-unjust national economy." They can wrap themselves in the flags of preserving neighborhoods or preventing sprawl.

Until the decade of the 1970s, there was little in the American experience that prepared us to recognize the gradual encroachment of a regulatory environment that turned the housing market into a struggle between homeowners and the "unpropertied." In the United States, the poor are always dreaming of becoming the rich. It is difficult for the poor to think in negative terms of those they hope to become. After all, "they" are supposedly "us," or those "we" hope to be.

The seismic shift in civic attitudes that changed the way private decisions were made was matched by the way the actions of the great public builders were

judged. The cityscape-changing Roman roads and aqueducts, the grand boulevards of Paris, and the subways, bridges, roadways, elevated transit, and other
publicly financed facilitators of urban growth had been praised, or at least
accepted, by most of the urban citizenry. But by the late 1950s, a new mood of
"we won't take it anymore" was beginning to surface in opposition to big urban
projects that disturbed the status quo.

I have criticized some of the public urban redevelopment that has taken
place, particularly slum clearance projects. But a great deal of good publicly
assisted and private redevelopment has helped cities and towns remain economically vital and attractive to residents who had the option of settling in suburban and rural bedroom communities. Yet by the 1970s, the antichange mood
grew so strong that large-scale intra-urban transportation and public building
projects were stopped.

Robert Moses and the Verrazano-Narrows Bridge

Robert Moses, the once-popular, politically powerful leader of large public work
projects that often demolished portions of existing neighborhoods in metropolitan New York, was viciously criticized. One of Moses's last projects was the
two-and-a-half mile Verrazano-Narrows Bridge (commonly referred to simply
as the "Verrazano Bridge"), which ties the boroughs of Brooklyn and Staten Island
together. It opened in 1964, a few years after Moses had overridden activists in
Brooklyn and Staten Island who fought against the destruction that the roadway
approaches to the bridge would bring to their neighborhoods. Although they
lost the battle, their early attempts to "stop the bulldozers" and preserve their
neighborhoods left them as public heroes. The lessons of their lost battle would
be studied by activists of the future to stop projects in New York, New Orleans,
San Francisco, and many other urban places. In some of these communities,
activists would go beyond stopping proposed projects to tearing down elevated
freeways and other roadways seen as blighting urban views.

Robert Caro's unsympathetic biography of Robert Moses, *The Power Broker*,
depicted Moses as an arrogant despoiler of healthy neighborhoods and pleasant
open space who constructed projects that would impoverish the lives of those
displaced by the projects. In a December 2002 article in *The New Yorker*, Gay
Talese wrote how the biography and other media coverage had affected Moses,
and how the Verrazano Bridge affected the lives of anti-Moses activists thirty-
eight years after its completion. Talese described the perceptions of the man
who had been Moses's personal chauffeur from 1974 to 1980: "He knew that
Moses, deficient in grace even in the best of times, was embittered over the bad
press he had been receiving."[2]

Moses felt reviled by the people whom he had thought would appreciate
projects such as the bridge. The irony is that surviving opponents of the bridge
seem today more resentful over the power that Moses had to change their lives

than they were over the effect his bridge had on their lives. Talese wrote that although many of those who had unsuccessfully fought Moses were dead, those still living "told me that the new locations into which they had been forced to move their businesses or domiciles turned out not as depressing as they had imagined. In general, they said, the buildings they moved into were in better condition than the ones they had surrendered to the wrecking crews. What they lost in sentimental value was irredeemable, and they continued to resent the arbitrary power that Moses had wielded over their lives."[3] But there was no doubt that Moses had improved conditions in the region as a whole without being the "despoiler" of the land, as Caro had claimed.

Talese's article told the story of Henry Amens, a dentist in the Bay Ridge section of Brooklyn who fought Moses because Amens believed he would not be able to relocate close enough to retain the patronage of his patients. Talese also spoke with a mortician, Joseph V. Sessa, who had opposed the bridge in the belief that his business could not survive because construction would disperse twenty-five hundred families in the neighborhood that his business served. In 2002, when Talese went back, he was able to report that Dr. Amens had found a new office close enough to keep his Bay Ridge patients and, at age seventy-seven, still had a thriving dental practice with a new partner—his thirty-four-year-old daughter. It also turned out Mr. Sessa's forecast of his business' demise was wrong. The mortuary had not been destroyed but remained in operation at the same location in 2002. Mr. Sessa died in 1977 at the age of seventy-nine, but the business is still intact and has expanded to include two other mortuaries in Brooklyn, all operated by Mr. Sessa's namesake and grandson.

Most strikingly, the people of Staten Island no longer hate the bridge. Talese wrote poetically that the current residents of Staten Island "cherish it as the high-light of their link to the mammoth mosaic that is Brooklyn and to the waterfront towers of Manhattan, which Truman Capote described as a 'diamond iceberg.'"[4] Many of those who lost their rental apartments to the bridge approaches in Brooklyn moved to Staten Island, where they were able to buy their first single-family homes on tree-shaded streets. Talese quoted a seventy-seven-year-old Staten Islander who retired after nearly fourteen years on the New York State Appellate Court bench. He spoke about the dispossessed high-rise dwellers who had tended to be politically liberal in their old apartment dwellings. "But once they arrived in Staten Island, bought their first home, and got their first tax bill they suddenly became conservative."[5]

Between the completion of the bridge in 1964 and 2002, the population of Staten Island nearly doubled to 443,000, and it is now the home of many of New York's police officers and fire fighters. Like William Shakespeare's Caesar, the good that Moses did by tying together the urban agglomerations of a great region and increasing its local amenities lies buried with his bones while the evil of neighborhood disruption lives after him.

Building a bridge alters the future course of urban life and economics. The same is true of deciding to maintain the status quo. Lack of opportunity to change usually leads to stagnation and a diminishing of possibilities to cause productive changes. Stunting opportunity for change should not be seen as merely preserving status quo. But for us to see this we need once again to accept the civic possibility of growth and embrace of the future. Without the work of Moses, the New York City of today would be poorer in economic and recreational opportunities. In hindsight, there is no doubt that the Verrazano Bridge was an important and beneficial project; and yet, if the bridge had not been built when it was, the spirit of the current times would make its construction today more difficult and highly unlikely.

Widespread Discomfort with Public Redevelopment

Remaking cities through public works that bulldoze stretches of existing neighborhoods is not the only type of redevelopment that has become unpopular in many places. In 2005 the U.S. Supreme Court narrowly upheld the use of eminent domain to take the home of Susette Kelo, a nurse in the Fort Trumbull neighborhood of New London, Connecticut, for an urban renewal project in that town. Voting five to four, the Court approved the taking of her small pink house that the city's redevelopment agency intended to combine with other nearby properties and sell to a private developer to redevelop the area and attract a new research headquarters for Pfizer Pharmaceutical Company. Justice John Paul Stevens wrote the majority Supreme Court decision, which stated that the public taking was appropriate because it promoted economic development, "a traditional and long accepted function of government." Justice Sandra Day O'Connor wrote a strongly worded dissent, which was concurred by Justices Rehnquist, Scalia, and Thomas.

Unlike *Village of Euclid v. Ambler Realty*, which was strengthened by sub-sequent court decisions, the *Kelo* decision left the future of redevelopment cloudy. Much of the criticism and Justice O'Connor's dissent were based on the concern that the effect of the unleashed power of eminent domain often falls on the less affluent citizens while it tends to benefit the more affluent. The discomfort that many feel toward the taking of private property by a public redevelopment agency that acts as an assembler of land for a private redeveloper was highlighted by comments that Justice Stevens made at a Bar Association meeting after June 23, 2005, when the Court handed down the decision he authored in the case of *Kelo v. New London*.

At the Bar Association meeting, Justice Stevens explained that if he had been a legislator, rather than a judge making a legal determination, he would have voted against the plan requiring the taking. He was quoted as saying, "The free play of market forces is more likely to produce acceptable results in the long run than the best-intentioned plans of public officials."

In November of 2009, three and a half years after the Court decision and eleven years after the announcement of the redevelopment plan, Pfizer reversed its decision to build a research headquarters on the site. The pharmaceutical company also announced it was exiting its existing location in the city as it reduced employment and consolidated operations. This scuttled the redevelopment plan, with sole exception of the prospect that the U.S. Coast Guard offices would move into one vacant building in the Fort Trumbull redevelopment area.

In the final chapter of this book, I will suggest a change to the federal and state laws that govern the way values are determined in eminent domain cases, and laws that allow private parties to use such takings under prescribed circumstances. I cannot say whether takings along the line of what I will suggest would have made Ms. Kelo willing to sell her small pink house, but my suggestion would be much fairer than the present procedure. Further, it would broaden opportunities for private, market-directed redevelopment.

Richard Foglesong's Planning the Capitalist City

In 1986 Richard Foglesong, whose perspective was very much influenced by the writings of Karl Marx, critically reviewed the history of planning in the United States.[6] In *Planning the Capitalist City*, Foglesong decried the federal and local support needed to construct and maintain the country's infrastructure as well as the planning approvals that facilitated the accumulation and growth of private land and property from the colonial era through the 1920s. He recognized that land development is an activity fraught with social and political conflict; the creation of the built environment that makes up cities is always a negotiation; and, because it is a negotiation, there is a need for governmental involvement and support.

Foglesong saw as inherently corrupt, or at least against the public interest, public officials' approval of any development based on responses to local land-use markets. To him, developers should never be allowed to call the shots when it comes to allocating resources. He believed the "capitalist city" is badly served by allowing key decisions to be made by private developers—he believed that the market system is inherently weak and less capable of serving the public welfare than centrally planned and implemented development. Although he realized that there is a need to develop and promote land uses and amenities that play a positive role in urban growth, he believed that those developmental decisions should be centrally planned, not left to the uncertainties of free markets.

Foglesong's vision of a powerful central planning authority to direct all urban development has not come about. But the part of his vision that called for putting an end to allowing private, market-responsive developers to call the shots regarding how much and what to build has become a reality.

Foglesong studied how urban building decisions were being made. Looking through his Marxist lens, Foglesong concluded that the capitalist class controlled the planning, the public capital, and the regulatory institutions. He saw in our history that property owners and developers had too long dominated planning commissions, city councils, and other land-use policy makers to insulate planning from popular control. For democracy to prevail, according to Foglesong, these procapitalist institutions must be replaced by citizen groups capable of "overcoming the imbalance between private purposes and social need in the organization of our cities."[7] In 1986 Foglesong urged the federal government, and particularly local jurisdictions, to renounce their historic private property bias and instead put control into the hands of those community activists who spoke out on development issues. He wrote that the time had come to extend "the principle of democratic decision-making to the realm of the built environment."[8]

By the time his book was published, what Foglesong urged for the benefit of the proletarian class was already benefiting the well-to-do capitalist homeowners of major metropolitan areas on both coasts. However, the shift away from the capitalistic system was not the result of a workers' revolution, nor could it have benefited the poor, new immigrants, or others not already among the propertied class. Like a gentle seduction, these changes grew from the general acceptance of new beliefs that had been cleverly, if often unintentionally, sold as an extension rather than a reversal of past principles. The hostility of middle-class Americans, especially in fast-growing coastal cities, to urban change and class mobility found its realization in the readiness of the courts and governmental agencies to erode the basic tenets of property rights—although that hostility was hidden behind the new ideology of citizens' rights. But it is reasonable to ask: Which citizens?

Historically, the willingness of the courts to enforce the rights of property owners to develop in response to market incentives created competitive housing markets. That competition has traditionally raised residential standards much faster than housing costs rose. The erosion of these rights escalated between the late 1950s and 2000, during the years of the United States' greatest suburbanization.

By 2001 the suburbs contained 57,983,000 housing units; another 28,058,000 units were located in exurban lands (beyond the suburbs), which the U.S. Census considers outside the boundaries of metropolitan areas. These two categories of non-central-city locations contained 71 percent of the nation's housing.[9] By 2001 successful campaigns to limit development, which were usually led by recent suburbanites or exurbanites, had succeeded in reducing the amount of vacant land that was allowed for residential construction in the coastal regions that saw great job and population growth during this period. The Foglesongs of the world might applaud these limits on the market without referring to specific circumstances, but any clear depiction of events would have to say that these new policies have been a disaster for adherents of both Karl Marx and Adam Smith.

The Growth-Stopping Tale of Two Cities

I have noted a subtle change in the makeup and perspective of planning commissions and city councils in my daily work as an urban economist whose
clients include local and state agencies. The proportion of developers on these
bodies has declined while the number of neighborhood activists has increased.
The formerly widespread belief that urban growth was progress that would
sooner or later benefit all is now considered wrong-headed or, at least, simply
naïve. Today the prevalent attitude toward growth and change in urban places
is often that growth is bad or, at worst, results in more costs than those costs
would yield in benefits. In city after city and village after village, I sense the
balance of power is shifting from those who wanted to expand the urban frontier
to those who wanted to keep the specter of change from their own neighborhood.
An early experience after the forming of my own economic consulting firm
prepared me for these changes.

Petaluma, California

In 1970 I left my job with a large consulting firm and on the faculty of the
University of California at Berkeley to form a consulting firm specializing in
urban economic and marketing analysis. The other principal in the firm from
its beginning was, and remains, urban sociologist Nina Gruen, my wife and
partner. Among other things, Nina is a specialist in the preparation, administration, and analysis of survey research.

Not long after we opened our office, a planner who was consulting with the
northern California city of Petaluma as it prepared a new general plan asked if
we would conduct a survey of Petaluma citizens. He was interested in having us
ascertain their attitudes toward the planning options facing the city. As a young
firm, we could use the business and we felt that we could do well what he asked
us to do. So we not only agreed to take on the job, we agreed enthusiastically.

But when we met with the planner, our enthusiasm wilted. We discovered
that his interest in the survey and research was based on the desire to substanti-
ate preconceived concepts, not to probe for citizen priorities with respect to
realistic options. One series of questions in particular bothered us to extent that
we withdrew our willingness to undertake the assignment. The questions dealt
with growth. Our would-be client wanted the questions posed in a manner that
represented growth as necessarily having a bad result. Nina told him that we
were not in the business of conducting survey research designed to obtain a
"directed verdict." We took the project off our "lead list" and expected never to
hear any further from Petaluma about their planning effort.

But two years later, Malcolm A. Misuraca, an attorney from Santa Rosa,
California, came to our office and asked if he could question me about what
I thought would result from the development policy that Petaluma had adopted

in June of 1971. Misuraca explained that the planning policy had been adopted in accordance with the wishes of a citizens' committee and the responses to a questionnaire that another consultant had prepared for the City of Petaluma and mailed out to ten thousand residents. The great majority of the respondents who returned the questionnaire filled out with their responses indicated they wanted to limit the growth in the number of future residents. The "Petaluma Plan" limited new housing units to about one-third to one-half of the demand catered to in the 1970–1971 period, or a limit of five hundred housing units per year for all but custom-built homes. In addition, the plan included an "urban extension line" that limited the boundaries of development and resulted in setting a maximum population limit that was significantly below previously predicted and allowed growth. After Misuraca described the situation in detail to me, Nina, and other members of our staff, we felt confident that we could predict the long-run result of the Petaluma Plan, if we could rely on the facts as he presented them to us.

We immediately suspected that the plan was likely to be innocuous because if Petaluma restricted the supply of its buildable land, the supply of land in other communities would have provided sites for growth. But we had already sensed enough of the suburban groundswell against letting in more neighbors to believe that if the Petaluma Plan were allowed, Petaluma would become a leader of a no-growth parade.

Like most California towns, Petaluma had previously held that residential growth was good. In 1962 Petaluma had designed its general plan to encourage high-quality residential construction directed toward a development pattern that was integrated with other land uses, including the expansion of roadways and utilities to efficiently serve the new development. Previously best known for its dairy and poultry production, Petaluma was in the path of growth in the San Francisco Bay Area as workers in Marin and San Francisco Counties sought housing for their families within commuting range of their jobs. By 1970 it was clear that, for at least the next several decades, Petaluma would be under pressure to be a growth center within the San Francisco Bay Area. In 1964, 270 housing units were built in Petaluma; in 1971, 891 units were built. As with most housing booms, Petaluma found itself pressed to satisfy the utility, transportation, and water needs of the new residents.

Petaluma residents who volunteered to be on the citizens' planning participation committee were further concerned when they were told that the city, with a current population of nearly 30,000, could, in conformity with their current general plan, have a population of 77,000 by 1985. At those rates of growth, Petaluma would cease to be a rural community and would become very much a suburb of the greater Bay Area. Committee members and others had been particularly turned off by the rapid building of tract housing on the flat agricultural lands east of the freeway and near the historic Petaluma downtown.

The committee and the planning staff also considered the responses received to the mailed questionnaire that the city had sent out to gauge voter attitudes. Included in that questionnaire were questions such as

It is conceivable that all usable land between Santa Rosa and Novatolo could be urbanized as has happened elsewhere in the Bay Area.

I favor this   I do not favor this

Petaluma has grown from 14,085 in 1960 to 24,870 in 1970. I do not favor control of Petaluma's future growth except in quality.

I favor control of Petaluma's growth and believe an ideal target population would be:

40,000 or less   70,000–100,000

40,000–70,000   100,000 or more

In the world of practical politics, this is called a "push poll"—it's a poll that aims to push unwitting respondents toward a particular candidate or policy position.

It is unlikely that many of those who responded to the survey or who served on the Petaluma citizens' planning committee would have described themselves as working actively to increase the value of their land. It is also unlikely that they construed the problem as a choice between trying to provide *and charge for* the needed changes in infrastructure that large-scale growth requires or increasing the value of their homes by simply limiting the ability of the private sector to respond fully to the demands for more housing.

But the respondents behaved like typical profit-seeking speculators, using needed infrastructure as an excuse for ensuring that the value of their homes increased over time. They simply cut off access to the land for future generations—the same access that had so well served Petaluma's preceding generations.

The citizens' committee, working with the planning staff, summed up their approach to planning and development in a statement of new policy (and ideology). Here's the preamble of that statement: "In order to protect its small-town character and surrounding open space, it shall be the policy of the City to control its future rate and distribution of growth."

The City Council adopted the citizen-recommended development policy as the "Official Statement of Development Policy for the City of Petaluma." The council also passed a series of ordinances that set up a "Petaluma Residential Development Control System" that was implemented with a new general plan, a new environmental design plan, and a new housing element—that is, the portion of the general plan that deals with housing. Like the formation of infantry carrying overlapping shields, the Petaluma City Council's phalanx of planning documents set a limit on the number of houses that could be built each year.

One of the unstated but important purposes of the Petaluma Plan can be gauged by the type of development that was not restricted by any portion of the plan—developments comprising four or fewer custom homes. The plan also established an elaborate set of official procedures revolving around a new "Residential Development Evaluation Board." These elaborate new procedures became known as the "beauty contest." Their stated purpose was to judge the proposed developments that would be included in the annual quota. Each year, any company that wanted to build more than four units would have to submit its plans to the Residential Development Evaluation Board and then woo the board members in the hope that its projects would be included within the five hundred permits for construction allowed that year.

As the perceptive economist R. H. Coase noted in his Nobel Prize speech, ultimately the courts determine who has the right to decide what can be done with land or other resources. The prospective builders in Petaluma knew this and decided to appeal to the courts for the right to build without the imposition of a numerical limit or quota.[10] The builders asked the federal court to confirm the rights that had historically been guaranteed by the Constitution and its predecessors in the evolution of Anglo-Saxon law. The builders stuck to their legal guns, even after learning that in 1972 the highest New York State court had ruled in favor of a similar growth-restricting ordinance in their state.[11] The upper-middle class revolution had begun, and the battlefield stretched across the nation, from Petaluma, California, to Ramapo, New York.

Ramapo, New York

In Rockland County, New York State, the town of Ramapo had adopted a plan designed to protect it and its relatively affluent residents from the market forces that were cut loose when, in 1955, the Tappan Zee Bridge of the New York Thruway crossed the Hudson River. This wonderfully named bridge put Ramapo in the path of suburban New York growth. The boundaries of the town of Ramapo have not changed since the bridge was built, encompassing eighty-nine square miles of land, more than one and three-quarters the size of San Francisco. Because the bridge made the town commuter-accessible, the rate of growth began to climb nearly one thousand residential units per year, and by 1960 its population had reached 35,750.

One of the recent arrivals was a young lawyer from New York, Robert H. Freilich, who moved to Rockland in 1960 to join a small real estate and land-use law firm. He believed that Ramapo was growing much too fast and that attempts to upgrade services and facilities to accommodate the growth were causing taxes to rise. While still a law student, he had read articles that convinced him that the way to keep public costs down was to slow, sequence, and direct the path of growth. That belief would come to be the guiding principle of his professional life.

In 1963, while on the board of directors of the New York Young Democrats, Freilich founded and became president of the Young Democrats of Ramapo. As he revealed in his 1999 book, *From Sprawl to Smart Growth*, Freilich drew on his belief in the efficacy of sequencing and slowing down growth as the keystone in his strategy for changing the political makeup of the Republican-controlled Ramapo City Council.[12] In 1965 he ran for the town board on a campaign to "forge a new constructive program of controlled growth."[13] He lost, but also that year he was platform chairman for a slate of Democratic candidates who promised that if they won, they would appoint Freilich as town attorney to develop a controlled-growth program. Slowing growth was popular enough to elect the first Democratic majority to the Ramapo Town Board since the Civil War. That victory became a clear example of the type of unity that upper-middle-class Republicans and Democrats could show when the issue is the control of land and property values.

Bob Freilich was appointed town attorney and began work on a revised zoning ordinance "to limit development to an amount equal to the availability and capacity of public facilities and services."[14] What became known as the "Ramapo Plan" placed a limit on growth to fit the town's facilities rather than fitting the town's facilities to accommodate market growth. The Ramapo Plan began with a moratorium on development while studies were conducted—studies not to identify how to equitably and efficiently provide for growth, studies not to determine what growth would be allowed, but studies to determine the limit, timing, and location of growth for the next eighteen years. In addition, limiting growth would coincide with the planners' view of how to stop sprawl while minimizing costs to the Town of Ramapo and preserving amenities.

Like the ripples in a pond from the point where a pebble is tossed in, growth was sequenced into a set of geographic bands that emanated from existing development. The further the band from the "center" of the existing development, the more housing units allowed; the closer the band to the center, the fewer housing units allowed. The entitlement procedure was elaborate, requiring a special permit and a demonstration of compliance with a listed set of criteria. Both made very small the likelihood that multifamily housing would be allowed. In other words, as in the original *Euclid* decision, apartments were no better than a "pig in a parlor" under these conditions.

In 1969 Ruth Golden, the owner of one vacant parcel in Ramapo, failed to obtain the required special permit and was denied the right to build. She filed suit against the planning board and the town board in Rockland County Supreme Court, contending that (a) the town did not have the right to regulate the timing of development; (b) the procedure was not in accordance with a comprehensive plan; (c) the procedure was exclusionary in nature; and (d) the town, in failing to allow her to use her property for up to eighteen years, had violated her Fifth Amendment right to fair compensation for her land.

The court held that the ordinance was a valid exercise of zoning powers.[15] When the case was appealed, a majority of the appellate division that reviewed the decision held that the town had "usurped power by regulating population growth in a manner which has not been delegated to it."[16] At that, the town appealed to the final judicial arbiter, the New York Court of Appeals.

In a decision that would reverberate throughout the country and that would launch Bob Freilich on a successful career as the "Johnny Appleseed" of slow growth, the court reversed the appellate decision and ruled that the Ramapo Plan was constitutional.[17] Ramapo continued to operate under the plan until March of 1983, when a Republican town board eliminated it. By that time, Freilich and his firm of planners and lawyers, Freilich, Leitner & Carlisle, had crafted similar plans in jurisdictions all over the United States.

Regional Impacts of Local Plans

Knowing that the Petaluma Plan was very similar to what the top court in the state of New York had upheld as constitutional, Malcolm Misuraca, on behalf of his building industry clients, shied away from state court. In 1973, when Misuraca walked into the San Francisco offices of Gruen Gruen + Associates, he had already filed an action in the United States District Court, Northern District of California. After our initial discussion, Misuraca asked if we could conduct a study of the plan's impact. He explained that after he had reviewed our study, he might call upon me to testify in its support.

As we talked about the planning issues involved, which we came to understand were really a refusal on the part of Petaluma to plan for growth, we realized that the fundamental issue was not what would be the plan's effect on the City of Petaluma but what would be the plan's effect on the region. After a morning of tense discussion in which we learned a lot about the relevant law and Misuraca expanded his knowledge of urban economics, he engaged us to conduct a study. Specifically, our assignment was to study the socioeconomic impact that actions resulting from Petaluma's plan would have on the San Francisco Bay Region if other Bay Area communities adopted plans similar to Petaluma's.

As I would testify in court and write about in an article after the trial's decision, but before the results of the appeal to that decision were handed down, I tried to relate the significance of what was happening in Petaluma to show that this local conflict had at least regional if not national significance. To answer that question, we had to first identify the characteristics that distinguished Petaluma. Identifying those characteristics would permit us to identify similar communities. We then had to consider the role played by these similar communities in the urban development process. Then we could forecast the changes that would be wrought in that development process if communities with Petaluma's characteristics adopted legislation and policies similar to the "Petaluma Plan."[18]

In terms of its role in the development of housing in the Bay Region, the defining characteristic of Petaluma in the 1970s was that it was a "growth center." We came to understand that the urban development process that takes place a specific location over time spreads out to affect the residential markets of the entire region. I wrote about the urban residential development process:

> It is propelled by the forces generated by the desires and resource capabilities of millions of households who exhibit a constantly changing demand for land uses. It moves along a track that guides development to those locations where the cost of providing the public services that must be hooked to the private dwelling unit to make it desirable are relatively low. The track is laid by historic development patterns and public expenditures on bridges, roads, water facilities, sewage treatment plants, and schools. At each period in the urban development process, the track carries development to certain areas where new housing is relatively desirable and cheap to produce. Thus, the track of public-service availability selects certain areas (usually on the fringe of historic development) to serve as sites for a disproportionate share of housing built during that period; while they have a low proportion of the region's existing housing stock at the beginning of the period, a high proportion of the new units added to the stock will be located within their environs.[19]

Our research found that in the two previous decades, a small proportion of towns and cities in the nine-county San Francisco Bay Region had accounted for a large proportion of new housing construction. Between 1950 and 1960, thirty-three cities, whose housing stock made up only 14.2 percent of the region's inventory of residential units in 1950, accounted for 66.9 percent of the new units produced by 1960. In the decade from 1960 to 1969, 54.7 percent of the permits issued for new housing in the San Francisco Bay Area were in twenty-nine municipal jurisdictions that had contained only 17 percent of the area's housing stock in 1960.

In all these places where the majority of housing units in the region were added during the ten years from 1960 to 1969, housing construction added more than 60 percent to the units that had existed in these places in 1960. The Petaluma Plan restricted growth to no more than an annual rate equal to approximately 6 percent of the 8,175 dwelling units that existed in Petaluma in 1969, hardly at or near the rate of the growth of the entire region.

During the decade from 1960 to 1969, 436,351 housing permits had been issued in the Bay Area, of which 238,886 were issued in these twenty-nine growth centers. Including mobile homes and other units for which no permits were issued as well as units completed during the 1960–1969 period for which permits had been issued in the previous decade, the 1970 census reported that 491,000 units had been added to the region's housing stock. The census reported that during this same decade, the number of households added to the Bay Area was 378,000, a 31 percent increase over 1960, while the population of the Bay Region grew by 27 percent in that decade.

The socioeconomic effect of building at a faster rate than population growth, adding 119,000 more housing units than households, resulted in pre–Petaluma Plan bargains for consumers. It also allowed for the removal of obsolete housing, encouraged geographic and social mobility, and enhanced the ability of the region to attract employees and entrepreneurs while minimizing the growth in rural areas outside the immediate region.

Opportunities in Growth Centers

As an economist and as one of those people attracted to the San Francisco Bay Area, I was well aware of the economic opportunities produced by the industrial, service, and trade industries of the area. My family and I moved from Cincinnati to Berkeley, California, in 1964. Although Berkeley was not a growth center, it was close to several East Bay growth centers, including Walnut Creek, Fremont, and Pleasanton; some former Berkeley residents had moved to one of these centers, including the dean of the University of California Business School, where I obtained a teaching position, who had recently moved to a new home in Walnut Creek. I was glad to find a house big enough for our family of five children and, better yet, one I could afford to rent on an instructor's salary supplemented by a little consulting.

In 1966 my wife and I purchased a house built in 1961 in middle-class El Cerrito, close to my teaching job and an easy commute to San Francisco, where I worked for the Arthur D. Little Company. We bought the house from a minister who was moving to accept a pulpit in Phoenix. The minister had bought this house a few years earlier from its first owner and resident, who had moved to Santa Rosa, a growth center just north of Petaluma. Clearly, we were all taking advantage of the fast-growing housing supply that benefited a wide range of consumers and allowed us to move from city to city and state to state to better both our lives and our careers in any way we saw fit.

To forecast the impact that a "Petaluma Plan revolution" (time-related growth caps or similarly imposed growth restraints) would have on the Bay Area in future decades, we calculated the reduction in housing production that would have resulted in past decades if the growth centers of those times had imposed growth caps similar to the 6 percent of the base year housing stock imposed by the Petaluma Plan. We found that in the decade just before the plan was imposed, 25 percent fewer building permits would have been approved, thereby reducing housing construction by 110,291 units. That number of housing units was very close to the number achieved by subtracting the total number of housing units built during the period from the number of households added to the region. In other words, the surplus of housing increase over housing demand increase, which kept prices down, would have been eliminated.

In the previous decade, 1950 to 1959, the results would have been more severe—36 percent fewer permits would have been issued if growth restrictions similar to Petaluma's had been in force.[20] The Bay Region would be a vastly different and less vital region if such plans had been in place prior to 1970.

Testimony in Construction Industry Association of Sonoma County, et al. v. The City of Petaluma

I was called in January 1974 to testify in the United States District Court, Northern District of California, before the Honorable Lloyd H. Burke, District Judge. Under the questioning of the builder's attorney, Malcolm Misuraca, I laid out the conclusions of our impact study for Judge Burke. I showed that the Petaluma Plan would reduce the number of units otherwise likely to be produced in that community in the period from 1973 to 1977 by one-half to three-quarters. I explained the role of growth centers and presented the rationale behind my belief that a regional housing shortfall would be likely to follow a legal ruling that growth restraints similar to those challenged by the plaintiff in this case were constitutional. I estimated that a Bay Area–wide shortfall of 25 percent would be the likely result of giving potential growth centers the right to avoid making the financial policy decisions and planning trade-offs that would be required to maintain the quality of public amenities and infrastructure in the face of normal market growth.

In response to Misuraca's questions about the effect of such a shortfall, I said that

- Prices would rise. The hardest hit households would be those whose incomes would be just enough to enable them to get into the housing most likely to be produced in growth centers on the edge of urban areas such as Petaluma.
- The ability of households to move from within and between urban places would be restrained by the resulting increase in housing prices.
- The regional economy would be harmed by the reduction in labor mobility, and this would reduce the rate of income growth in the region.
- Housing quality improvements through remodeling and the replacement of obsolete units would decrease.
- The long-run effects on the environment would be negative as more and more households sought housing farther and farther from their urban jobs and as municipalities intensified the already evident intracity fight to attract the affluent.

Misuraca framed many of his questions to highlight what these results, particularly the price increases, would have on reducing the options of people who wanted to move. My answers pointed out that price increases and reductions in choice would affect the ability of households to move—that is, to travel between and within jurisdictions.

After a recess, Petaluma's attorney, Robert Anderson, began to cross-examine me. It soon became evident that the thrust of his cross-examination was not to question my underlying findings and theories of how the housing market worked or that less housing would be produced if the court held for the defense. The aim of his cross-examination was to attack the validity of my estimate that 25 percent less housing would be produced in the region if his client's actions withstood the plaintiff's constitutional challenge. At one point in the give and take of cross-examination, I was asked to forecast housing production with and without the imposition of housing limits similar to those of Petaluma in other growth centers of the San Francisco Bay Region. Proudly using my new HP12C handheld calculator, I employed the simple but frequently used statistical estimation technique of regression analysis to project future Bay Area household growth and housing production, with and without the assumption that other suburban growth centers would adopt restrictions similar to the Petaluma growth limits.

During my examination by Mr. Anderson, the argument about the numbers in that projection became rather intense, with Mr. Anderson suggesting that the difference in housing production between the two assumptions would be likely to be much less than the estimate I presented. At this point, the judge held up his hand to stop the cross-examination and asked Mr. Anderson a question along the lines of, "Am I to understand that you agree with the witness that less housing will be produced, but you contend he has overestimated the size of the decrease?"

When Mr. Anderson answered that question to the affirmative, the judge turned to me and asked, "If the plan is affirmed, will the right of some citizens to travel be impeded?" I answered, "Yes, your Honor."

He then asked me, "Is it likely that at least one of these citizens will be seeking to travel across state borders?" I replied, "Yes." I was dismissed. The court had heard enough.

Shortly thereafter Judge Burke ruled orally from the bench, stating, "If the right of just one American citizen to travel is restrained, the constitutional right to travel is violated." He ruled for the plaintiff. The court's written conclusions of law and findings of fact were handed down on April 26, 1974.[21] The defendant appealed the decision to the Ninth Circuit Court of Appeals.

I sat in the audience at the beautiful old federal courthouse at the Ninth Circuit Court of Appeals and heard the appeal to Judge Burke's ruling that Petaluma's approach to retarding growth and "curbing sprawl" was unconstitutional. While listening to the arguments made by the attorney for the City of Petaluma and several supporters, including a lawyer from the State of California's attorney general's office and allied advocates from environmental groups, an old maxim ran through my head. "No one who likes sausages or law should ever see how either is made."

Attorneys for the City of Petaluma argued that the landowners and builders who had filed the lawsuit did not have "standing" to bring the suit. This is a legal argument referring to the general rule that only injured parties have the right to file a lawsuit. The city argued that the harm done by Petaluma's restrictions on residential development would not harm the would-be builders who had filed the lawsuit; only the consumers seeking to find affordable housing so that they could move to California would be harmed. And no consumer group had been listed as a plaintiff on the lawsuit. In addition to the standing argument, the City of Petaluma also stated that the exclusionary ordinances were restricting housing development for rational social and environmental interests of the community and therefore were allowable. They argued that the restrictions were not an unreasonable burden on interstate commerce. The appellate court, whose deliberations struck this observer as looking for a way to overturn the federal district court's decision, picked up on the standing argument. Writing for the Ninth Circuit, Judge Choy's opinion agreed that the plaintiff, Construction Industry Association, did not have standing. But even if they had, the exclusionary plan was still not unconstitutional because it "was rationally related to environmental welfare of city and did not discriminate against interstate commerce."[22]

The significance of this decision, coming as it did on the heels of many others that chewed away at the property rights of individual landowners and builders, was best summed up by a remark that I heard the premier urban lawyer Richard F. Babcock make after he read it and thought about its implications. To put his comment into perspective, one needs to know that Babcock was not only a wise student of the law but also an articulate advocate who loved a good battle and disliked turning down clients who would pay him for litigation or other advocacy. I was with him one day when a younger law partner of his reported that a builder who had proposed a good and potentially profitable project had been turned down by a council who felt the town's character would be better preserved without the proposed development. After the partner related the facts of the matter and told Babcock that the builder wanted to know if they would be willing to file a suit with the city on his behalf, Dick responded, "Yes, we could take the man's money if he insists, but do tell him that he could get the same end result now if he simply cut his own throat." That assessment of where the law stands in most jurisdictions holds true today—as the original ruling stated, development is the "pig in the parlor" and no matter how fine the pig, at the end of the day it's going to get slaughtered.

7

Suburbanization and Sprawl

Charges and Verdicts against Sprawl: An Old Charge Redirected

With the *Ramapo* court victory under his belt, Robert Freilich went on to become a leading hero in the battle against sprawl. He wrote in his book, *From Sprawl to Smart Growth*: "The techniques upheld in *Ramapo* were quickly utilized in other jurisdictions (cities, counties, metropolitan areas, and states) over the next twenty-seven years to expand the role of planning, managing, and channeling growth not in suburban cities and counties on the development fringe and metropolitan areas."[1]

Two universally laudable goals—maintaining the fiscal health of the communities where development takes place and encouraging the intensive use of land for residential development rather than spreading out residences on more land—were always high on the list of Freilich and the other activists in the battle against sprawl. But the techniques they used went much further and often encouraged neither of these goals. Ironically, it was and is possible to further these two goals by simply mandating as a condition of approval that added development pay for the additional public infrastructure and the service demands the added infrastructure would induce, and by implementing zoning to discourage low-density housing development. Instead, a broad set of techniques for planning, management, and growth were incorporated into the planning maps and ordinances of communities to disallow development in a wide swath of territories that bordered existing urban development.

The leaders of these efforts added a long list of other bad things about the sprawl they were stopping. As time went on, their speeches and writings created a new and popular mythology in which antigrowth activists are folk heroes and developers despoil the land by building too much and in the wrong places. This was the stuff of what made it so easy, on a cultural level, for the popular author

Robert Caro to characterize Robert Moses, the powerful New York public works director, as a super villain. By the time that Caro's biography of Moses came out, the ideology that builders were bad and development was at best a sometimes necessary evil was already in place.

However, it is important to understand the roots of this mythology, and that much of it revolves around money, taxes, and the possibility of personal financial gain by shutting down development. In the early days of the movement to restrict residential development, the reason given for turning down attempts to build housing was that to allow development would cost the public more to serve the additional housing than the housing would contribute to the public treasury. That is, the fiscal argument that residential development did not "pay its own way" was often the weapon used to stop developers in their tracks. Then, as the environmental movement became more powerful, other charges against residential growth would be added by urban activists who gathered supporters under "stop growth" and "prevent sprawl" banners. But the charge of public fiscal imprudence would continue to be an effective, explicit antigrowth weapon, just as it had worked in the 1930s to rally supporters to the cause of slum clearance.

Introduction of the No-Build Alternative

The Case of the Palo Alto Foothills

Lawrence Livingston Jr., a widely respected MIT-trained city planning consultant, was one of the first to use the fiscal weapon against residential growth. Among the many plans his firm completed for California jurisdictions between 1953 and 1980 was a project to determine the fate of 7,500 acres of undeveloped land in the foothills of Palo Alto, California. In 1959, ten years before the City of Palo Alto asked Livingston to conduct a planning study, Palo Alto had annexed the land from the County of Santa Clara with the clear and stated intent of allowing the land to be developed, primarily for housing. To facilitate the development, Palo Alto built water mains and sewers on more than half the land and purchased 2,500 acres on which to build a park. In 1969, before Livingston's firm began work on the study for Palo Alto, a part of the development containing single-family homes, townhouses, apartments, and a shopping center had been proposed for 500 acres of land near Atascadero Road. Palo Alto put that proposed project on hold pending the Livingston study. Because every phase of the work would be followed by lengthy and often heated debate, "The Palo Alto Foothills Study" that Livingston led was not completed for nine years, in 1978.

The elderly Livingston described that study in his sometimes brutally candid "Confessions of a City Planner," a piece he wrote for the *San Francisco Sunday Examiner & Chronicle* after his retirement in 1980. He was careful to lay out all the options open to Palo Alto. "Our study examined twenty alternative residential patterns from the standpoint of their effects on the biotic communities, potential fire hazards, visual impact, geological impact, hydrologic impact, social effects, and net costs to the local taxpayers."[2]

While not called for in his contract, Livingston decided to add another alternative—the option of no development. The choice of leaving the land unchanged by development was an option that previous planning studies had rarely considered. Instead, it had been generally accepted that the purpose of a plan was to decide upon and describe the development that would change the existing landscape. At the time, his inclusion of a "no project" case among the alternatives was an innovation in the planning process. (The reader should know that Livingston worked with me and my firm on many projects. We regarded him as a professional and a friend, and found Larry usually to be ahead of the planning curve.)

In 1970 the State of California enacted the California Environmental Quality Act (CEQA), which called out new procedures "as a system of checks and balances for land-use development and management decisions in California."[3] A variant of this act has been enacted by many states. In California this act mandated the preparation of an environmental impact report (EIR) by all 59 counties and 470 incorporated cities before the state would approve any proposed land-use development or management projects that could impact the environment. The National Environmental Policy Act of 1969 (NEPA) required the preparation of an environmental impact statement (EIS) for projects proposed on federal lands or projects proposed by federal agencies or any projects that are or will be federally financed. Both state EIRs and federally mandated EISs are required to evaluate proposed land-use changes such as those Livingston conceived for the foothills of Palo Alto.

Today, land development decisions must consider the possibility of leaving the land undisturbed, no matter what has been proposed or previously contemplated. Of course, the mere inclusion of "no change" or "no build" leads to the absurd but implicit NIMBY idea that for many projects, "you just know that if a project isn't built here, it'll have to be built somewhere else." The myopic view of the "no build" alternative takes the easy way out and washes the hands of city planners of the questions where to build, when to build, or whether to build.

At both state and federal levels, the law requiring that "no change" must be considered and evaluated in proposals for real estate and infrastructure development was motivated by a desire to protect the environment. I most certainly do not argue against protecting some aspects of virtually all environments, or against protecting all aspects of some environments. But in practice, the required process for preparing and reviewing a project's effects on its environment has made approval much easier for those who favor the preservation of virtually all of an existing environment, harder for those who wish to change some aspects of an existing environment, and virtually impossible for those who want to change all of an existing environment. As was the case in the Palo Alto foothills, when preserving all of an attractive existing environment also benefits the financial interests of incumbent voters, the chances of building on or otherwise altering the status quo are slim.

Legislation mandating the preparation and consideration of environmental impact reports has done more than create a new industry of environmental specialists and advocates. It has altered the political reality of planning and zoning by highlighting the likely environmental consequences of proposed policies, plans, and projects. It has also provided an effective tool that those who wish to stop or radically reduce any proposed land-use change are tempted to use without necessarily revealing the real reasons for their opposition. And it provides particularly good ideological cover for assaults against housing development.

Certainly, it makes sense to project the impacts of proposed development. Development projects may help shape the area for decades to come. And there are valid concerns about a project's environmental impact that sometimes justify serious modifications or even outright denial of the project. But as was true in the path-breaking decision by the Palo Alto City Council when the foothill plan was before them, the contents of the thick environmental reports, much discussed during the deliberations, are not what determine the decision to go ahead with or halt a project.

The fiscal impact report that Livingston had commissioned from a subcontractor revealed something that aroused interest about the effect that increasing the residential population of Palo Alto would have on the balance between who paid for and who received city services. The study revealed that the existing residents were in effect being heavily subsidized by industrial and retail taxpayers who shelled out significantly more in taxes to the local treasury than they received in services from the city.

Palo Alto had two immensely profitable groups of taxpayers. The Stanford Industrial Park, built and owned by Stanford University, was the premier site for the high-tech firms of what came to be known as Silicon Valley. In addition to this home of prosperous and expanding companies and the smaller developments suitable for research and development activities in structures called "flex tech" that grew up around it, Palo Alto benefited from the retail sales tax dollars generated by the huge Stanford Shopping Center, which attracted shoppers from the well-to-do communities of both Santa Clara and San Mateo counties. The study commissioned by the Livingston firm made clear to the city fathers that if Palo Alto restricted residential development, the current residents would not have to share the dollars brought into the community by either the employees who commuted to Palo Alto or the customers who shopped there and did not receive residential services. The point was that neither group received residential services from Palo Alto while adding considerable dollars to its tax base.[4]

The determining criteria that Palo Alto used to decide among the twenty alternatives of development and the one no-change option offered by Livingston's planning effort were not to be found among the study's listed evaluation variables—biotic (the ecosystem of living organisms), fire, visual, geological, hydrological, and social. Instead, the city council's decision to select the option of leaving the entire area undeveloped—that is, they chose Livingston's "no build" alternative by zoning the 7,500 acres permanent open space—was based on the study's finding concerning the net costs of development to the local taxpayers. Livingston remembered in his 1980 article:

> Although it was not included in the original work program, I decided that we should compare the results of a policy excluding all development from the hill area with the twenty other alternatives. Our calculations assumed that if the land were to remain in open space it would be necessary for the city to purchase it at fair market value and to repay with interest the taxes levied for the water and sewer lines that had been installed but not used. In addition to the obvious environmental advantages of barring development, our study found that this alternative would cost the taxpayers less over a twenty-year period than any of the developments, despite the high cost of purchasing the land and repaying the taxes.[5]

Except for the site of the planned development that had been proposed for the five hundred acres along Atascadero Road, the Palo Alto City Council managed to bar all development without paying for any of the land—an acquisition not quite on the level of the Louisiana Purchase but a real estate coup nonetheless. The legal decision on an inverse condemnation suit filed by the potential developers of that acreage required Palo Alto to pay $7.5 million for the five hundred acres. This judicial result was almost certainly achieved only because of a damning transcript involving a very articulately aggressive city councilperson. In the course of a public council meeting, he threatened the developer with zoning the land for open space, making the property worthless unless the developer sold the land cheaply to Palo Alto. The judge who heard the case found that threat evidenced an egregious and overt use of public power, providing a basis for the finding that the five hundred acres were being taken without a legitimate public purpose. On that basis the court awarded the developer $7.5 million.

In terms of wealth potential, Palo Alto got a hell of a deal, even on the five hundred acres for which the city had to compensate the owner. In 2003, given what has happened to residential values as a result of this and similar zoning actions, if Palo Alto's planning regulations were to allow residential development at the mid-range density of twelve units per acre, the residual land value of the five hundred acres would be between $261 million ($12 per square foot) and $392 million ($18 per square foot).

The real estate deal that Palo Alto's residential property owners got from their council was the increase in the value of their properties, which became inevitable once the foothills and similar vacant lands were regulated out of bounds for development. The windfall of this regulatory act, in conjunction with similar subsequent actions of San Francisco Bay Area governments from Petaluma to San Jose, brought Palo Alto's residential property owners the 1970 equivalent of hitting the mother lode. The California gold rush may have been declared ended in 1849—but not yet in Palo Alto.

Palo Alto's Historical Growth

In 1959, when the land in the adjoining foothills was annexed, most of Palo Alto's voters and council leaders had a prodevelopment mindset. This belief in growth had been such a part of the American psyche that John Kenneth Galbraith referred to it as "the conventional wisdom" in his 1958 book, *The Affluent Society*.[6] Few Americans at that time considered that a desire for economic growth was a problem, although Galbraith defined our preoccupation with production as a "problem."[7] Most believed that housing production and the availability of housing to consumers at competitive prices and quality was a good thing. From that perspective, the conditions in the Palo Alto real estate market made perfect sense for Palo Alto to annex the foothill lands to continue adding to the supply of housing and retail land uses.

By the mid 1960s, the 9,127 acres that then lay within the boundaries of Palo Alto had been pretty well built out. It was not necessary to be farsighted to see that it was time to begin development on the annexed lands in the foothills to maintain a competitive housing market that could provide for those who worked in or near Palo Alto. In 1970, the population of Palo Alto was about 59,000, living in 21,352 dwelling units. Palo Alto's housing supply had grown by 3,707 units, or 21 percent, since 1960, but during the five years between 1965 and 1970, about 80 percent of the additions were units in multifamily structures.

As Palo Alto entered the 1970s and the city council zoned the 7,500 acres of vacant foothill land as permanent open space, the resulting shortage of vacant land and growing demand encouraged the building of multifamily housing through the conversion of existing larger single-family homes, the removal of some single-family homes, and the construction of new apartment buildings on the small amount of remaining vacant sites.[8] By 1970, the U.S. Census reported that in Palo Alto, single-family vacancies were less than 1 percent while vacancies in multifamily units stood at 2.7 percent. If the rules of development had allowed builders access to the adjoining vacant land in the foothills, land developers and builders would have responded as they had in the past. The increase in residential prices and rents triggered by the high demand, as indicated by the low vacancy, would have set off a surge of development in Palo

Alto. New residences would be built until, and usually beyond, the point where prices and rents would level off or even decline.

Unless mitigated by actions that would offset the supply-reducing effect of taking the vacant land in the foothills of the lands potentially available to developers and builders, the effect of the council's dedicating the foothills to open space should have been obvious to anyone who noticed what had been happening to employment in the town that was giving birth to the Silicon Valley economy. Since 1959, employment in Palo Alto had already been growing at a much faster rate than housing construction was growing, and employment was predicted to accelerate. According to the economics of supply and demand in real estate, it was apparent that only the addition of more vacant land, or a massive rezoning from single family to multifamily housing, could hope to forestall a significant shortfall of housing supply. No massive rezoning was then or is now politically acceptable in Palo Alto. In 1959, the only politically acceptable choice was annexing 7,500 acres, which would have increased the size of the city by 82 percent. With 2,500 acres taken out for parkland, the remaining vacant acreage would have increased the amount of land available for development by 54 percent.

This would have been enough additional housing for Palo Alto to play an important role in forestalling the housing shortfall that would come to plague the region. Although local decisions shape how the overall regional market will play itself out, a key aspect of the housing market is that it is regional. The decision regarding Palo Alto's foothills is not the sole reason for the Bay Area housing shortage, but it provided a good example of how the local municipalities that should have been key players in keeping the supply of housing equal to or greater than the growth of housing demand took themselves out of the game.

The Palo Alto City Council's decision to reverse course and stop any growth from occurring in the annexed foothills had a chilling effect on local housing production. Nevertheless, Palo Alto encouraged economic development policies that facilitated continued growth in employment and retail trade as well as the demand and need for housing. It is a textbook case of how to make a potential housing shortage worse by spurring on all the conditions for local growth but not the growth of housing.

Palo Alto commissioned my firm to identify a strategy for revitalizing the city's historic downtown, which had been its retail and commercial center until the development of the newer Stanford Shopping Center and Industrial Park. We did our job. Today the Palo Alto downtown is a vibrant and profitable location for stores and offices that bring more tax dollars into the city than they cost in services. More tax revenue than cost in services might be referred to as the "Palo Alto way."

In the decade between 1960 and 1970, the housing supply in Palo Alto had grown by 21 percent, or nearly 2 percent per year. Despite rising demand, housing growth dropped to about half that rate after 1970. Employment growth was particularly strong because Palo Alto was the birthplace of technological innovations such as those by the founders of Hewlett Packard and the electronic and information scientists at Stanford University. Palo Alto did zone large amounts of land for commercial and industrial use in the 1950s. The availability of that land facilitated the booming growth of employment in Silicon Valley.

Employment growth had increased by 70 percent from 1960 to 1970; by 1973 employment was estimated at 65,000 jobs.[9] In 2003 there were 104,920 people employed in the City of Palo Alto, an increase of 61 percent over the thirty-year period, or an annual growth rate of about 1.6 percent per year. In 1970 there were 21,353 housing units in Palo Alto; by 2003 the housing supply had grown only 22 percent in the thirty-three years since 1970, or at an annual rate of 0.6 percent per year. In 1970 the median value of owner-occupied housing in Palo Alto was $33,022.[10] Using the Bureau of Labor Statistics all urban consumer price index for the United States, the 1970 median home value was $121,190 in 2003 dollars. But if you shopped for a home in Palo Alto in 2003, you would have found the median price to be $950,000.[11] The numbers can get knotty, but the concept is easy: job growth plus halting residential development equals housing shortage and housing price increases.

When I first obtained these data, I e-mailed a question about the increase in construction costs from 1970 to 2003 to Leland Saylor Associates, a premier firm that has been providing cost estimates for San Francisco area builders and developers since before 1970. They e-mailed back that, when adjusted upward for the effect of inflation on the value of the dollar, construction costs for the kind of houses that were being built in Palo Alto in 1970 had gone up less than half of the 683 percent increase in housing prices, and that "most of the increase must have come from an increase in land value."

A few days later, I got a call from my old friend Leland Saylor, who had seen the e-mail that one of the engineers had sent to me in response to my question. Leland seemed a little upset with me and started to lecture me on why my question was simpleminded. He said I should have remembered that before 1970, builders were building production houses to get sales volume up by delivering a product that middle-class households could afford. To be specific, Lee pointed out that "while in the sixties Palo Alto was known for bargain-priced, simple, well-designed and priced 'Eichlers,' today only custom houses with spare-no-expense finishes and features are being built—the land is just too expensive for production homes." By "Eichlers," Lee was referring to the simple but attractive homes built in the 1960s by a builder whose name became associated with homes affordable to middle-income households.[12] These modern, minimalist tract homes were so well designed that today the City of Palo Alto seeks to preserve them by refusing owners' requests to "scrap" them and use the lots for new and much larger luxury houses. Try to buy one of these architectural gems and see what it will cost you.

Of course, Leland was right. Over time, the increased scarcity of entitled land, that is, sites the land-use regulators approve for development, has done in the San Francisco Bay Area and other U.S. coastal communities just as Henry George had feared. The price of land gets pushed up so that its capitalized value becomes a larger and much more expensive component of the total cost of housing. As a result, the price of housing in each competing neighborhood rises much more quickly than the price of other goods and services.

A Community of the Wealthy

Affluent homeowners in communities such as Palo Alto were able to maintain their position or skip up to neighborhoods with more desirable locations, more commodious and expensive housing as their businesses prospered, as their professional employees were paid well, and as the fiscal strength of the jurisdiction facilitated the maintenance of good schools and other public amenities. By shutting down the growth in housing but revving up everything else, Palo Alto not only annexed the foothills but without justification claimed for itself much of the shared resources of the entire region.

The effect of increasing land values raised housing prices, effectively preventing all but the well-to-do from becoming Palo Alto's new residents. The high housing prices also affected the average household size and incomes of those who were able to move into Palo Alto and the region in general. Between 1970 and 2003, the housing shortage and resulting price increase caused a drop in the average number of persons per household in Palo Alto so that the total population remained unchanged in thirty years—actually, it declined slightly from 59,000 in 1970 to 58,598 in 2003.[13] During those three decades, the entire area was in the midst of an economic and population boom. The 1970 census reported that the median household income in Palo Alto in 1969 was $15,000. Using the change in the consumer price index between 1969 and 2000 and applicable data from the 2000 census, that $15,000 is equivalent to $52,000 household income in Palo Alto for the year 2000. But the median household income in Palo Alto from the 2000 census data was $90,377. Palo Alto had gone from a community of the moderately well off, with $52,000 average household income, to one of the very wealthy, with $90,377 average household income.

When dollars earned in 1969 are adjusted for inflation to reflect what the dollar was worth in 1999, per capita income in Palo Alto was $5,259 in 1969. By 1999, per capita income in Palo Alto had climbed to $56,257. Similarly, household incomes climbed to relatively greater wealth. Constricting the opportunities for residential development pushed up the value of land, enriching those with a stake in the existing supply of land while simultaneously raising the income requirements for new residents who wanted to move to the area. The roads to Palo Alto slowed not with the cars of its residents but with the cars of increasing numbers of commuters who could not afford to live near their jobs.

Perhaps unwittingly, Palo Alto pioneered the political attitude of shutting down housing to create local wealth that became prevalent in most communities of the San Francisco Bay Area. From there it spread east into the rest of the United States, just as the spirit of *Ramapo* appeared first in Greater New York and then moved westward. For the most part, this ideological contagion has not yet spread throughout the mountain states, the Midwest, and the South—although we see it in some resort and retirement communities. But the spirit of shutting down housing to create wealth has been felt nationally and has played a role in the ever-increasing divide between the rich, the poor, and the middle class in most of our major coastal cities.

In Palo Alto today there is concern about the obvious shortage of affordable housing. But that shortage is not seen as the legacy of more than thirty years of competition-throttling land-use decisions. Rather than altering the land-use policies that have effectively shut down the city, that concern is expressed in inclusionary zoning and the support of specific projects with housing priced at below the market. These policies are at best too little and often further restrictive of the long-run supply even when they benefit a few lucky recipients of public subsidy or regulatory pricing.

It is a peculiar way for communities to feel good about themselves—adopt policies to make sure no poor or middle-class person could afford to buy property in your community and then give a little bit away in a lottery. That's right—a lottery! When subsidies or inclusionary zoning are used to artificially lower the price of some houses, the number of qualifying low- and moderate-income households who seek them is so great that the houses are often distributed via a lottery. Despite all the good intentions, it is still class warfare, and the obvious display of concern makes it no less damaging.

The Fiscal Argument

A major reason given for the emotionally fueled spread of growth-constraining policies has been the popular appeal of the fiscal argument, the very argument that Livingston's study used to shut down the foothills development. The belief that growth restrictions would result in lower taxes and more services for current residents has motivated community after community to "manage growth" by restricting what would otherwise have been built, even in the many situations where that belief is not justified.

Larry Livingston came to recognize that the results of the fiscal study for planning Palo Alto were being widely cited as a generalization that applied to all communities. Ten years later, after his study had concluded that no growth was best for Palo Alto property owners in 1970, he realized and pointed out that the situation in Palo Alto was unique. In his 1980 "Confessions of a City Planner," he decried the widespread misuse of that study's results by "no-growthers" in many places. Livingston wrote: "Unfortunately many zealots hastily concluded what is true in Palo Alto must be true anywhere. They overlooked the fact that residential development in Palo Alto is unusually costly to tax payers because of the city's lavish public service program and the excellent school system. *This situation is acceptable to the voters [in Palo Alto] because, as homeowners, they pay only one-third of all property taxes, and business and industry pays the rest.*"[14]

In his "Confessions," Livingston went on to mention cities where he had found the proportion of service costs to tax revenue from businesses to be lower than that ratio in Palo Alto. The financial health of these cities would not have been improved by zoning vacant lands out of bounds for housing and other development. He wrote further: "Studies we subsequently made in Santa Rosa and Santa Cruz, where the level of public services was significantly lower, indicated that residential development came close to breaking even in terms of tax yield versus service costs."[15]

Livingston was right that it would be incorrect to apply to other cities the conclusion he found in the Palo Alto of 1970, as well as incorrect to apply to Palo Alto or anywhere at other points in time. He could have gone further and indicated how Palo Alto's tax structure and development mix received so much revenue from sales taxes that all then-current Palo Alto residents were being subsidized. These taxes were collected from customers residing outside Palo Alto, and from the property and business taxes of the large-scale business parks and office centers that were built around Stanford University.

The reason Palo Alto's citizens of that era paid little in local taxes but enjoyed a very high level of all public services is that they benefited from the cash that came into the Palo Alto treasury from the businesses located in their town. By keeping out new residents, the Palo Alto Council was restricting access to the rich business subsidy to the current residents and voters. By the time California voters passed Proposition 13 in 1978, which reduced the real estate tax rate on all properties and limited annual escalations except when properties were sold, there was even less of an incentive to develop housing in the foothills.

Proposition 13 Changes California's Tax Revenues

Proposition 13 froze property taxes except for a maximum increase of 2 percent per year for all California properties, until the properties changed ownership. This law, versions of which have also eviscerated the property tax laws in other states, is virtually a poster child for unintended and misunderstood consequences. Sold to the public as a means for putting a lid on spending, it has hobbled one of the most stable (for governments and taxpayers), transparent, fair, and equitable forms of taxation available to urban places. It rewarded the affluent, mature members of society at the expense of its less well-off and younger members. By shifting taxation away from property to sales and income, Proposition 13 has made public revenues less stable and predictable and has further encouraged antidevelopment sentiments.

The officials of local municipalities where property taxes have been limited by laws such as Proposition 13 tend to prefer nonresidential development to residential development. The activities that take place within retail, commercial, and industrial facilities generate business tax, sales tax, and other non-property-based revenues for local public treasuries. Proposition 13 has increased the fiscal pressures on the managers of California's cities while simultaneously encouraging them to favor only the development of expensive housing and nonresidential uses within their jurisdictions. Avoiding such unfair taxation schemes is indicated among the recommendations in the final chapter of this book.

A Reappraisal of Sprawl

Even before the Palo Alto Foothills study, there were studies of municipal service costs, such as the one conducted for the Department of Commerce by William L. C. Wheaton and Morton J. Schussheim, which had found great differences between locations but no systematic evidence to support the belief that density was more fiscally beneficial.[16] Both Wheaton and Schussheim were widely acclaimed planning teachers and scholars. Wheaton was one of my mentors and my boss when he was dean of the College of Environmental Design at the University of California at Berkeley.

Since the 1970s, when the debate over growth and sprawl began to heat up, hundreds of studies have sought to reach definitive conclusions about the balance between the costs and revenues that flow into and out of local public treasuries from different types of residential development. Few have recognized the truth of Livingston's 1980 insight that it is not correct to generalize about net local public costs of residential development—there are other factors, many different factors that need to be evaluated. Nevertheless, we continue to see an outpouring of studies, most of which purport to show that suburban residential development, or sprawl, costs the public treasury more than it contributes. Very often such studies are followed by a rebuttal poking holes in the assumptions, methodology, or data affecting the conclusion that suburban development is always bad for the fiscal health of municipalities.

The first one of those studies is still often cited as a landmark work and used as a font of truth by opponents of the development of vacant, previously undeveloped land in the suburbs frequently referred to as "greenfields." This study was commissioned by the President's Council on Environmental Quality and prepared by the Real Estate Research Corporation (RERC). Published in 1974 and titled "The Costs of Sprawl," it concluded that providing public services to housing developments built on previously undeveloped areas would cost more than providing public services to denser development in already built-up areas.[17]

In 1977 Alan Altshuler, a nationally respected planner and frequent commentator on land-use matters, effectively rebutted these conclusions in a "Review of the Costs of Sprawl," citing cost omissions, the use of theoretical prototypical models that compared high densities with unrealistically low densities, and a confusion between costs and inequitable taxation and exaction policies.[18] Exactions are the payments required of developers by public bodies as a condition of development approvals.

In 2002 Robert Burchell, David Listokin, and Anthony Downs, three distinguished urban scholars and longtime opponents of "sprawl," worked with graduate associate Catherine Galley to conclude that the use of urban limit lines and measures aimed at directing regional growth to central cities would "save government, developers, homebuyers, and citizens $250 billion over the next 25 years, or $10,000 a dwelling unit." Their *Wharton Real Estate Review* article stated that this estimate was based on "the pooled results of findings from studies conducted in New Jersey, Michigan, South Carolina, Florida, and the Delaware Estuary."[19] But the model they used to come up with their conclusion did not consider the effect that locking out residential development would have on the price of land within existing urban areas that would be needed to site future housing. The experiences with growth restriction in the United States since 1970 provide ample evidence that closing down the suburbs would increase the price of sites for new homes by many times the $10,000 per unit "savings" estimated in the study.

Models and studies that leave out the effect that land values have on housing prices when seeking to tell the economics of residential growth limitations are about as meaningful as telling the story of *Hamlet* without the Danish prince. Two factors invalidate generalizations about the fiscal effect of suburban development:

- The costs of repairing and adding to public infrastructure and operating public services such as police, fire, schooling, and the like, are rarely less costly in older, built-up communities than in newer suburban communities; and if these costs are less, it is because of superior management, not any inherent advantage of development in older or central cities.
- If new development causes infrastructure or operating costs that exceed operating costs for infrastructure already functioning in existing residential development, then local public agencies have the right and duty to impose fees and exactions on developers that will cover these excess costs, at least to the extent they are being paid by the present residents. The legal requirement for such fees is that the local government must show a connection, or nexus, between the proposed new development and the potential costs associated with it, which then can be amortized or offset with a fee or exaction. This alone should trump the fiscal argument against growth.

Throughout the United States, the local taxes and fees charged to nonresidential land uses commonly exceed the costs that such land users pay for all the municipal services they receive. That is, like the situation in Palo Alto of the 1970s, nonresidential land uses subsidize residential land uses. Not surprisingly, because only the residents vote, this situation creates a bias in favor of high-tax-paying nonresidential uses. One result of this bias is that most communities zone enough land for nonresidential uses to keep land prices for such uses competitive. This is particularly the case in California and other states where restrictions have been placed on the use of the property tax. The fear that housing will not be able to carry its share of the local tax burden has added a fiscal argument to support the always-present desires of homeowners to increase their property values by limiting supply.

In the states with sales taxes, a portion of which is allocated to local governments, battles for retail developments are fought with weapons that usually include various forms of subsidy and aggressive promotional efforts. For years I have noted that if I come to the offices of the city manager or town administrator with questions on behalf of a retail chain or developer (other than Wal-Mart), I rarely have trouble gaining an audience and may even be taken to lunch. But when representing a residential developer, I often am kept waiting in the outer office, waiting for some time, before anyone will see me.

Balancing Costs and Revenues of New Development

Taxation policies that cause local agencies to push hard for economic development while treating residential development as distasteful but necessary are difficult to alter. They are difficult to alter politically because most communities are fighting to keep the advantages they gain from high-paying, nonresidential users. This has created a tax system in which it is beneficial for property owners to oppose new housing developments, therefore benefiting the individual interests of property owners over the collective needs of the region and the country.[20]

It would be desirable to eliminate tax policies that are slanted against residential development, such as the apportioning of state-imposed sales tax to municipalities on the basis of where the sale took place rather than on the basis of population. However, that does not mean municipalities should look to the acceptance of retail developments because residential developments fail to pay their own way. Municipalities need to consider that if unbiased studies show that a proposed residential development would burden the local treasury, then impact fees can be imposed to cover the gap between what the new development would pay at prevailing property tax rates and the cost the new residents would impose on the community. Such fees have long been common. The requirement that new residential development pay the costs of extending utility and transportation lines over vacant, undeveloped areas is frequently made a condition of approval for leapfrog development. Usually the agreements include provisions that call for repayment for the costs of building infrastructure over the vacant area by any subsequent builders who fill in that area with construction.

The best time for a city to estimate both capital and operating cost fees, and to take constructive action if such costs are not likely to be covered by future development, is when the city or county prepares its plans (such as for capital facilities, zoning, etc.) that will guide as well as facilitate anticipated growth. Our firm has frequently conducted fair taxing and fiscal impact studies as part of the general planning process, as well as economic impact studies for private developers, builders, and associations. The goal of these studies is to assess the fairness of fees that public land-use officials charge the sponsors of development to be paid before developments are allowed to proceed.

Sometimes both the private developer and the city accept our studies and recommendations as to how fees and exactions should be assessed. But not infrequently, there is considerable debate and negotiation before the parties can agree on the dual questions of what public expenses will result from the anticipated or proposed development and how many dollars are required to offset the costs of the anticipated development that will not be covered by the taxes and exactions on future residents and businesses.

When developers disagree with our study and recommendations, it is usually either because they feel we have underestimated the direct and the indirect taxes their buyers will contribute to the public coffers, or it is because they feel that we have overestimated the costs associated with paying for the infrastructure additions or public services their development will require. When planners, city staff, or representatives of various city services disagree, it is usually for reasons contrary to the ones just given for disagreements by developers.

City service agencies typically provide data for the studies, and not infrequently those agencies have a vested interest in setting high fees or exactions, just as developers want to avoid or minimize those kinds of fees and costs. It is not unusual that the business manager of the local school district may argue that the project will generate more students for the local school system than our surveys or other data on projected enrollment elsewhere have suggested. On the other side of that same coin, the developer will argue that we have overestimated the number of students who will attend local schools from the proposed new homes. The only fair solution is objective, well-constructed surveys and data based on truly comparable situations, which can be used by public officials, or if necessary, courtroom judges or professional arbitrators, to resolve alternative views concerning costs and revenues.

In our experience, the most contentious issue that arises in the course of fee- and tax-setting studies has to do with standards of service. When we interview the police department in the course of our research, they usually tell us how many sworn peace officers per one thousand population *should* be on the payroll; often it takes some prodding for us to obtain the data needed to calculate how may peace offers per one thousand population actually *are* on the staff. Unless the municipality has simultaneously increased the taxes or fees throughout the community to be able to hire more police officers, it is the actual, not the wishful, figure that should go into the cost side of the net cost–revenue calculation for the project. Similarly, if traffic, which is usually a high-priority concern, is currently at a given level on the streets to which the new drivers will be added, the traffic costs allocated in the study should be the costs of streets and signals needed to keep traffic flowing at that same level, not to reduce congestion to an arbitrarily lower level.

It is not surprising or unreasonable that extreme disputes about fees or taxes on builders sometimes go to court. But from the perspective of both parties, such litigation is expensive and time consuming. Furthermore, time lost through litigation often subjects projects to market risks; most developers know it will be difficult for them to recover the full financial cost of delays even if the court should rule in their favor. Most developers also know that their chances of obtaining development approval on current or future projects are not enhanced if they take a hard-nosed, litigation-aggressive attitude on these kinds of disputes. If the right questions are asked, both the public authorities and savvy developers are motivated to get the kind of objective answers that will lead to the imposition of fair and equitable fees and exactions that avoid saddling the community with new developments that drain the local treasury and lower the quality of public services.

Municipalities add staff and bulk up the capital facilities budget during periods of rapid growth. If development fees have been set correctly, the revenues that come in during these periods cover these costs. A fiscal surplus usually results if the fees and exactions are set high enough, along with the taxes from expanding retail and other business whose growth is usually estimated conservatively when the fees are set. Nevertheless, communities are often reluctant to take the fiscally wise but politically difficult step of scaling down staffs and capital budgets after growth has slowed or stopped. We advise suburban communities that are experiencing rapid planned growth that, in addition to their standard two-year budget setting process, they also need to prepare a ten-year, department-by-department cost and revenue forecast. The process of preparing such forecasts facilitates planning to employ a public resource base that is appropriate and reasonably efficient in the years after the growth spurt is over. Accomplishing such "right sizing" is often more difficult than fee- and exaction-setting to ensure that development growth will not burden the fiscal resources of the urbanizing suburban or rural community.

Planning urban development is not easy. It requires an orchestration of many different elements—the fiscal element is only one. Other elements include the local, regional, and national economic factors that influence and are influenced by development in urban markets, where virtually everything affects everything else, as well as engineering, architectural, and, of course, environmental factors. All of these elements of the urban mosaic must be scored toward realistically achievable goals that enhance the cultural, recreational, economic, and functional viability of the built urban environment.

Before discussing this goal further and suggesting the tools and materials for reaching it, we take a side road to consider, "What's wrong with sprawl?" The rationale for this deviation is that in recent years, much of what has been written about planning has focused on how to eliminate sprawl.

What Is Wrong with Sprawl?

During the last half of the twentieth century, most of the open urban frontier was located at the edge of existing communities and around small, formerly agricultural communities. This is where vacant land was most accessible for new development. During the 1950s and 1960s, the economic and political barriers to development in the suburbs were much lower than barriers that impeded changing development in already built-up cities and towns. But since the 1960s, suburban development has been increasingly criticized as "sprawl." That disparaging term has led to the measurement of much of planning and regulation to provide the basis of determining whether a proposed suburban development will tend not to sprawl or be a good alternative to sprawl.

Many people find it difficult to realize is that sprawl is neither a well-defined nor a completely negative condition. Nevertheless, the term has been used to lock up suburban development with the same type of supply-restricting regulatory handcuffs that have frozen much of what needs to change in built-up places. This is unfortunate because it is coming at a time when much of suburban as well as center-city development is ready for needed change and augmentation.

The recent publication of *Sprawl: A Compact History* by Robert Bruegmann of the University of Illinois at Chicago considers the charges against sprawl from a historic and planning perspective. Bruegmann found most of the charges either just plain wrong or the result of bad planning decisions that are not inherent or unique to suburban development. Some of the most frequently made assertions about what is bad about sprawl, which I will discuss from an economic and social viewpoint, include the following:

- Sprawl is financially inferior to close-in development and costs the local public entities that provide services to residents more than those residents pay in taxes and fees.
- Sprawl destroys critical natural environment and species.
- Sprawl destroys open space.
- Sprawl exacerbates traffic congestion.
- Sprawl hurts the viability and demographic diversity of central cities.

- Sprawl wastes land.
- Sprawl endangers the food supply.
- Sprawl destroys the historic character of rural areas.
- Sprawl is ugly to behold.

This list excludes some interesting but, I believe, absurd charges levied against sprawl, such as that sprawl causes obesity because the suburban lifestyle discourages exercise and encourages gorging on fast food.

The charge that developments in the suburbs are more likely to be a drag on public treasuries than developments in central cities just does not hold up. Given that replacing obsolete and worn infrastructure is likely to be more expensive in older cities than building new infrastructure on vacant land in the suburbs, the likelihood that new development will not pay for its public costs is probably greater for development within the core of older urban centers, often called "infill" development. But as is true of many of the other accusations leveled against sprawl, the incidence of developments burdening public treasuries is much more a result of prevailing planning and regulatory policies than it is of location.

Most of us will agree that development in the suburbs, and the farther out rural areas referred to as exurbia, has the potential for destroying natural visual and ecologically important resources and open space. But avoiding the removal of such features by banning suburban development projects is throwing the baby out with the bath water. The environmental analyses now required by both state and federal statutes serve as powerful microscopes to prevent developers from hiding or disguising any damage their proposed developments would inflict on the natural environment. Local government, backed by state and federal laws, clearly has both the authority and responsibility to require as a condition for approval of a new development the mitigation of any damage it would do to the natural environment. What actually happens in most such cases is that the regulatory body uses its ability to deny or hold up the proposed project as leverage to make the developer replace any expected damage to environmental elements on more than a one-for-one basis.

However, what happens in cases where there is no argument that privately owned open space contains any environmentally or historically significant features? The public has the right to buy such noncritical open space at its fair market value—which should be similar to the assessed value that has been used to calculate the annual property taxes. To keep such property in "open space" because allowing development would encourage "sprawl" would constitute a taking, wherever the property is located.

Sprawl and Traffic Congestion

Studies on the effect of land-use patterns on traffic congestion are far from clear. The current wisdom is that shifting population to urban centers from suburban areas will decrease the use of the auto and reduce traffic congestion. But a study reported in the March 2008 *Annals of Regional Science* by Yoram Shiftan of Israel's Technion, using Portland, Oregon, as a case study, concluded that moving twenty-five thousand households (4.2 percent of the population) from the suburbs to the central city would increase trips between suburb and city. Shiftan estimated that the net effect of the move would result in an overall increase in vehicle miles driven by 1.4 percent.[21] To the degree that land-use patterns worsen congestion, they tend to lengthen the distance between work, shopping, and recreational destinations and the homes of the urban population. Thus, mixed-use developments that include a diverse mix of urban residential neighborhoods within walking, biking, or convenient transit distance tend to reduce congestion.

Building residential uses that use land more intensively by putting more dwellings on less land, thus increasing housing density, and by including shopping, work, and other nonresidential uses within the same development (that is, compact mixed-use development) may help reduce congestion. If what is meant by sprawl is the spread-out, excessively large lot, single-family development, then I would agree that sprawl is worse than compact mixed-use development. My reason for accepting this generalization about what is bad about sprawl defined in that way rests only partially on the possibility that dense residential development near stores, workplaces, and entertainment may make it easier and less costly to provide efficient, traffic-serving infrastructure. Development that is denser than what is legislated by a great many local zoning ordinances would permit more equitable, consumer-satisfying market responses to residential demands.

But even if it could be possible to wave a magic wand to compact and diversify the uses of all development, traffic congestion would nevertheless continue unless expenditures on the operation and capital of transportation infrastructure were greatly increased. These increased expenditures should be used to maintain existing roads, bridges, tracks and air traffic systems, add to these systems, and adapt available but unused technological improvements. One example of the latter is electronic guides that would permit roadways to carry more vehicles faster and more safely as they, in effect, allow vehicles to be "self driven," or on auto-pilot, while occupants could converse face to face or on electronic devices without the need to keep their eyes on the road. The current capacity of transportation linkages is woefully below what is required to reduce congestion significantly in economically vital urban places. Focusing on alleviating traffic snarls and delays by changing land-use patterns hypothesizes a solution that will take generations to test while simultaneously diverting attention from the increases and improvements in transportation infrastructure needed to decrease congestion levels.

Sprawl and Agricultural Land

During the successful campaign for a proposition to place an urban limit line across the greenfields of eastern Alameda County, California, the bumper stickers of the antisprawl folks in nearby Berkeley read, "Cows not Condos." In some form or other, the myth that allowing suburban development will choke our food supply is almost always implied or stated as a reason for why residential construction should not be allowed on vacant land, farms, or ranches near existing suburban or rural municipalities. That suburban development will endanger the food supply is a myth that has grown out of irrationality into powerful antisprawl emotions.

Agricultural productivity has consistently decreased the real costs of growing food over the last two centuries. Nevertheless, when oil prices increased farming costs at the same time that the federally subsidized ethanol program caused a sudden increase in demand for corn, the productivity of agriculture continued—and still continues—to increase. Neither higher fuel cost nor the spurt of biofuel demand is likely to change the direction of long-run agricultural trends. A study of U.S agriculture over the last two centuries concluded: "The general picture, common to U.S. agriculture and to trends in world agriculture, is that over the last century world agricultural production grew faster than demand. As a result, real world prices of agricultural products declined roughly by a factor of two."[22] Although a great deal of the advance in agricultural productivity has resulted from the invention and use of labor-saving technology, the rise in per-acre yields has also played a key role in making food cheaper to produce.

Most relevant to the charge that suburban development must be stopped to ensure the food supply in the West is not that land is in short supply—it is water that is in short supply. Agricultural land values are driven up when water is available or when the land is perceived as having valuable nonagricultural uses in the future. Even without likely further improvements in hydroponics, genetically modified seeds, and irrigation technology, recent studies by the Oxford Institute of Ageing at Oxford University and by other demographers agree that the world's population will grow more slowly than agricultural output. Rather than trying to preserve every inch of land that is in agricultural use today, it would make more sense to allow the reuse of agricultural land for residences built at high densities on small lots near places where people go to shop, work, and recreate.

In 1990 my firm, which usually does urban development analyses, was asked to study Stanislaus County in the agricultural heartland of California's rich Central Valley. The purpose of that study was to determine whether Stanislaus Country could allow the conversion of agricultural land to accommodate a population increase of 3 percent per year for twenty years without damaging its agricultural economy. Our interviews and examination of studies by the local farm bureau employees suggested that to allow farmland to be "chewed up" by urban development would wreck the sustainability of the local agricultural economy.

One university professor with considerable experience in agricultural economics and who had often consulted with our firm on other studies informed us that he would not consider working with us and risk alienating colleagues who held strong views about farm preservation. But when we interviewed farmers, a very different picture emerged. Again and again we were told that because of the statewide system of irrigation they could easily move their farms to other locations where water would be available. What would be needed was the establishment of buffer zones between farmlands and urban development. The buffer zones were needed for two reasons: to protect agricultural activities from urban encroachment and to provide a boundary-identity for existing and new communities. We found that there was more than enough land to provide adequate space for efficient agricultural activities and all the likely levels of urban development within the county.[23]

Given the critical need to preserve water as a resource for agriculture, wildlife, industrial, and human use, a rise in the price of agricultural land actually may have beneficial results. Increasing the price of farmland encourages the more intensive use of land, including so-called drip irrigation that conserves water by delivering it directly to plants through tubes rather than open furrows or ditches. This permits more food to be produced not only with less land but also with less water. An example is artichoke production in Monterey County, California, which grows all the artichokes in the United States. In an article titled "More with Less" (*San Francisco Examiner*, May 14, 2000), Hugo Tottino, the co-owner of Ocean Mist Farms, a 3,600-acre artichoke farm, was quoted: "We're planting different (closer) spacings, we know how to use fertilizer better, we're using drip (irrigation) to use water better." Tottino's father had started growing artichokes on nearly 14,000 acres in 1923.

The billions of dollars in agricultural subsidies paid by both American and European governments to keep farms in business and to keep acreage out of production would not be needed if there were a real shortage of land for farms, ranches, and orchards. One sad result of the high production that is induced by the subsidies is that exports from that output compete favorably in global markets to the disadvantage of farmers in undeveloped countries. The rationale for these subsidies is both political and emotional. Legislators from farm areas want to keep subsidies flowing to the people who elected them. The subsidies also have the emotional appeal of supporting the small family farmers whose lifestyles pique our nostalgic memories of archetypical American pioneers.

Farm subsidies do help some families continue to live on the farm. But the subsidies also support lifestyles that most voters would consider less worthy of subsidy from public funds. Here is one example of what I mean. In 2002 the majority stockholder in a large brokerage farm put his 1,600-acre duck-hunting tract up for sale. The advertisement for the sale mentioned that the property included a "duck plucking" room. The land sits near a state wildlife preserve so that "unstressed" ducks fly over the property, which makes it a duck hunter's paradise. But the land is also within the Western Canal Water District, which means it has access to a lot of water at very little cost, which enables the land to be used for rice farming. Here is the kicker. That farming operation makes the land eligible for federal farm subsidies. Therefore, not only did the owner get to enjoy hunting, he also collected more than $730,000 in subsidies between 1996 and 2001, according to the *San Francisco Chronicle* of August 25, 2002.

The historical and cultural reverence held for farming and ranching raises issues well beyond the irrational claims by activists and their successes in erecting land preservation green belts. But closing the urban frontiers to keep farmland at low cost does little to deal with the nation's or the world's agricultural issues, it just creates the illusion of social engagement. This illusory quality of the activists' arguments against development is what is ultimately so dangerous—they do not describe the reality of the world, but they seek to control policy based on those illusions.

Included among the objections alluding to sprawl is that "sprawl wastes land." The rationale behind this differs from the notion that suburban land is needed more for farms than for housing. The objection is based on the high use of land per household in suburban residential development—or, looking at the other side of that, the low density of much suburban housing.

Sprawl and Residential Density

We have already discussed the lack of compactness as a possible contributor to the transportation problems of contemporary society, and have accepted that this is an evil of sprawl—if we accept that sprawl is defined as low density, single-use development. Jonathan Levine of the University of Michigan defines urban sprawl as the "low-density car-dependent development that characterizes most U.S. metropolitan areas."[24] To his definition of low density I would add "single-use" because isolated residential development far from the frequent destinations of its residents probably has the effect of making it more difficult to provide cost-effective, pollution-minimizing, traveler-satisfying transportation options. But there is no "probably" about the charge that this type of low-density or large-lot residential development has frequently been mandated by local planning and zoning legislation since and including the landmark *Village of Euclid* ordinance.[25]

The thrust of Levine's findings in *Zoned Out* is that the failure of much suburban development to use land efficiently is not a market failure—rather, it's a planning failure. Lot sizes in many communities developed since the first quarter of the twentieth century are bigger than what would have resulted from the competitive interplay of supply and demand in the market. Levine says they are bigger because local zoning typically favors large lots. Planners do that to bias the developments in their jurisdiction toward people who enjoy the higher end of income distribution. Large-lot zoning seeks to create and maintain neighborhoods at the upper end of the ladder of price-sorted neighborhoods graphically represented in figure 4.2 and figure 4.4. By biasing developments toward larger houses, they raise the total value of houses and lots.

The result of this is that the less affluent have to pay more per square foot of land than the rich have to pay per square foot of land. When we zone land so that building lots are large, we not only waste land, we also program the information system we call markets to charge less for the square foot of land sold to the wealthy than the square foot of land sold to those with moderate incomes. Such market programming that misallocates land is often referred to as "overzoning." In many cases, the publicly mandated misallocation is so great that the per-square-foot cost of half-acre and larger lots is less than the per-square-foot cost of small lots with twelve or more dwelling units to the acre.

Consider, for example, that a rich man pays $1,000,000 for five acres of land upon which to put his mansion. Five acres is 217,800 square feet, so the cost to the rich man for the land is $4.59 per square foot. At twelve units to the acre, a small lot for a new tract home priced at $200,000 to serve a young, modest-income family would require 3,630 square feet of land. Assuming that land costs equal 30 percent of the sales price of such a tract home, the required lot would cost $60,000, or $15.62 per square foot. That is more than three and one-half times what the rich man paid for his home site.

Levine also quotes Robert Cervero of the University of California at Berkeley, who correctly assigns one important cause of long commutes from home to work to the prevalence of large-lot zoning. "When developers are prevented from building housing near employment centers that are targeted at the local workforce, as recently happened in Pleasanton, California and Hunt Valley, Maryland, there are, I believe, grounds for some degree of policy intervention—to correct planning, not market failure."[26]

There are many examples of mixed-use developments being stopped by local regulations that, to use Levine's term, "zoned out" such options. Fortunately, many planners and civic leaders today are encouraging mixed-use developments as the benefits of such developments are increasingly understood and as the consumer demand to live near the places they want to visit intensifies. The final chapter of this book suggests the kind of changes that can and should be made to zoning ordinances to remove the "bad" of large-lot zoning that applies to sprawl without depriving those who want, and are willing to pay for, the per-square-foot value on such housing sites that result from competitive markets.

Sprawl and Aesthetics

I repeat here the last two bad results from my list of prevalent objections to suburban development:

- Sprawl destroys the historic character of rural areas.
- Sprawl is ugly.

Either objection is more the result of a failure to use appropriately the planning skills and authorities that exist at the local level of government. Neither results because development is taking place on the suburban or exurban edge of existing urban places. Often all or a part of the historic character of places can be enhanced and used as a positive branding, demand-inducing attraction for development additions and renovations that increase the economic returns to be earned from additional investment in development.

I do not feel particularly well qualified to write on the subject of the aesthetics of urban place making. But I do feel that turning down development that fits the definition of ugly in the eyes of local land-use regulators certainly falls within the rights of protecting the community from negative externalities. Nevertheless, time will change the character of some rural places, and some new development will be ugly. But minimizing this is more likely to be a matter of how we plan and regulate than where we allow development.

After considering the arguments I have presented so far, I hope you will agree that much is to be gained by reopening urban frontiers, both within the older central cities and at the suburban edges of major metropolitan areas. Chapter 8 lays out some general approaches and specific operating policies aimed at using the planning and regulatory powers of local government to invigorate competitive development markets, the better to serve the interests of housing consumers and strengthen the local economies that are the country's entrants into global economic competition.

8

Urban Policies for the New Economy

Equipping America to Thrive in the New Economy

President Barack Obama's chief of staff, Rahm Emanuel, is reported to have said, "A crisis is too good an opportunity to miss." I suspect he was talking about how the economic and financial crises that ushered in the current recession should be remedied with alterations in national, rather than urban, policies. But what is implied in what Emanuel said applies even more so to urban America, because America cannot retain its position as one of the world's strongest economies if its metropolitan production centers do not update and strengthen their agglomeration economies. These changes must be done during the same time that the world deals with the destabilization and hardships of the recession that started in late 2007. The world economies that have been reshaping themselves since the advent of globalization will emerge from the school of hardships imposed by the recession into an entirely new world economic order—referred to here as the new economy.

Correcting those flaws that pertain to the United States will be necessary for the United States to thrive in the twenty-first century economy. It is particularly and critically important to correct the flaws that limit the productivity and social cohesion of the cities, towns, villages, and counties of the urban regions that are home to most of the country's economy. Here are some of the already discernable changes to which local, state, and national policies and cultures must adapt to enable the United States to prosper in the emerging global economy:

- The use of the U.S. dollar as the reserve currency of the world can only be expected to continue if the United States makes significant progress in reducing its negative balance of trade.

- The concept that capital markets can be expected to self-regulate for the public benefit is dying, if not already dead. This reality must be realized in regulations of capital markets that reinstitute the safeguards erected following the Great Depression and add rules to protect against the dangers of new financial instruments and the opacity of electronic records and transactions.
- American consumers will save more than they have in the past.
- Americans will no longer believe that housing values will always escalate. As a result, houses will be bought as homes, not as investments.
- To survive and prosper, American business will have to compete with cost-effective products and services developed and marketed in response to consumer tastes, rather than rely on financial engineering.
- Public awareness of global warming and the market and legal costs associated with environmental regulations will require the use of alternatives to high carbon-releasing fuels, and energy-saving vehicles, equipment, and buildings.
- In the next twenty years, the population of the United States will increase by about 27 million people. The two largest age brackets in the population will be "Generation Y," born between 1970 and 1995, and the "Baby Boomers," born between 1946 and 1964. The high propensity within these generations to seek new housing adjacent to services, entertainment, shopping, and workplaces will create strong demand for housing in mixed-used clusters that facilitates lifestyles that conserve energy.

America's urban places cannot help the United States meet the challenges of the twenty-first-century economy—not with local regulations that prevent the replacement and updating of municipal infrastructure, patterns of development, and structures that were built in response to the demands of the nineteenth and early twentieth centuries. The U.S. economy that emerges from the recession will need the support of enhanced agglomeration economies in the metropolitan areas that provide its workplaces. Without metropolitan regions attuned to the needs of a growing new economy, the nation's gross domestic product growth will be weak and shallow.

The recession and chaos of the credit crunch have left the United States with the advantage of more affordable housing. The haircut given to housing values was bad news to individual homeowners and their lenders. But it is good news to the nation's future economy and citizens. The metropolitan areas of the United States that lead the country's economic resurgence will be those that maintain the advantage of more affordable housing. These regions will also facilitate and encourage the replacement of obsolete building with an adequate supply of mixed-use clusters of development.

If urban development policies along the lines of the thirteen changes subsequently spelled out in this chapter are put in place now to meet the challenges of the new economy, we will look back on the current recession as showing us the path to a new and prosperous economy. Otherwise, America's race to stay in the vanguard of the world's economy will be severely handicapped.

Rebalancing Urban Land Use Policies Is a Trigovernmental Job

By law in the United States, each of the fifty states creates the counties, cities, towns, and villages within it. As a result, the powers of those local governments are granted by the states. The U.S. Constitution and the way it has been interpreted by the courts usually gives the federal government the upper hand when there is conflict between laws passed by Congress and laws promulgated from state capitols. The federal government's ability to expand and contract the money supply is unique. Only the federal government has power to fund projects and programs directly by expanding borrowings, even when the treasury's net flow from taxes and related revenues is negative. Washington can also use its financial muscle in tandem with legislative actions to encourage the scale and direction of many locally administered projects and programs within the fifty states.

One of the first questions that comes up when local officials and municipal staffs consider construction projects or the expansion of service-providing programs is, "Will the feds pay all or a part of the costs?" A "no" answer to that question is commonly enough to quash proposed local programs and projects. A "yes" or "maybe" galvanizes local officials, planners, and lobbyists into action. Rules governing the actions of the nation's financial organizations, which play a large part in fashioning the rules that determine the borrowing capacity of local municipalities and citizens, are also largely dictated from Washington. State legislatures, and in some cases the federal legislature, will have to pass new laws to implement some of the thirteen recommended actions discussed at length in the following pages of this chapter.

Local citizens will have to support the changes in the allocation of suggested taxes; but the laws required to implement those changes—in taxes and the allocation of those taxes—will have to be passed by state legislatures. Changes to the way taxes and other funds are collected and allocated are unlikely to happen without local voter support, but the changes will have to be implemented at the state and federal levels.

Neither community hesitancy to accept the risks associated with change nor the inertia of preservation can be overcome without the incentive of additional funding for desired improvements. Such funding can only come from the decision by the executive and legislative branches at both state and national levels to give funding priority to those local communities that allow both the supply of residential development to outpace the growth of residential demand and the conversion of outmoded workplaces and the infrastructure that serves them to enhance the productive and innovating power of their occupants.

In other words, new state codes will have to authorize changes in local taxation and planning rules. Local communities are unlikely to implement many of these changes or the way they spend their public works dollars without financial incentives from both federal and state governments.

Suggested Changes for a Strengthened Economy

The following recommended changes are not suggested as once-and-for-all cure-alls to the urban development policy missteps that I have cataloged in the preceding chapters. But these changes will provide opportunities for a better life for urban residents and a strengthened economy for our nation. Nevertheless, once effected, these changes will require regular evaluation and, determined by that evaluation, further improvements and additions to achieve the original goals.

1. Plan and Zone to Add More Development Than Would Be Required by Estimated Likely Demand Growth

Community planners and their legislative and executive bosses should begin their planning for all land use by first estimating the future needs and demands of households, businesses, and institutions. Plans, zoning, and regulations should be directed toward the goal of meeting those needs and demands at locations where development is likely to be feasible. In all cases, meeting the demands of future households requires the addition of supply in excess of forecast housing needs. Unless housing prices are to be driven up and the economic pressures for undermaintenance encouraged, the supply of housing must be increased enough to replace existing houses removed from the stock. And here is why there must be addition in excess of forecast: There must be sufficient housing vacancies or slack between demand and supply to maintain competitive conditions in the region's housing markets.

The term "housing needs" here, and as used in the California State Planning Code, refers to the total amount of housing required to provide an adequate supply of homes to all the citizens of the area, including those who cannot afford to purchase or to rent homes at prevailing market prices. "Demand" is the number of households with the income and willingness to purchase or to rent housing at the prevailing or likely future market price. Demand with these characteristics is commonly referred to as "effective demand."

The practice of using forecasts of housing need and demand as the basic criteria for planning and zoning is nothing new. It was once religiously followed by virtually all planning agencies everywhere. It remains as a mandate on the law books of many states. But today that practice is honored in the breach rather than in the observance. The reason for this regression in local planning practices is that planning for future needs has become unpopular with local voters who strive to maintain the status quo and who do not want to see more households move into their community. For this same reason, lawsuits to enforce the state laws, seeking to force local authorities to zone enough land to allow builders to supply enough housing units to meet forecast housing needs and demands, are rarely brought before the courts.

I have served as an expert witness on two lawsuits in which builders or public advocacy groups turned to the courts to enforce compliance with the law requiring the land use planning and regulations of municipalities to provide for enough housing to meet future needs and demands. Both cases were filed after outrageously offensive land-use planning actions deprived builders of the opportunity to respond to housing demand, in contravention of what is mandated in Section 65583 of the California Government Code, the California code that requires the housing element of each municipality's general plan to provide its "fair share of housing," a term that in essence describes the planning objective I am recommending here.

I was engaged in 1987 by the attorney representing a builder whose permission to build 110 units on 404 acres of vacant land had been effectively rescinded by voters—voters who passed a referendum rezoning the site as open space. The builder filed a suit against the town of Moraga, California. My testimony in court stated that the failure of Moraga to allow residential construction under conditions exemplified by the zoning change from residential to open space of the plaintiff builder's property would significantly harm traffic conditions, the welfare of citizens seeking housing, and the regional economies. The court ruled against the builder and upheld the rezoning. My personal, and perhaps biased, opinion is that elected judges in local courts hesitate to overrule decisions made at the ballot box by the same electorate who put them on the bench.

In 1991 I conducted research and submitted evidence concerning the economic and social effect of a municipality failing to follow the kind of planning and zoning recommended in these pages and required in the California Code. This lawsuit was filed by a public interest group against the aptly named City of Industry, California. As I testified, the planning and zoning in Industry had created a huge imbalance between local jobs and housing. In 1989, more than 60,000 workers were employed in Industry. Between 1970 and 1989, the city's population had declined from 712 residents in 1970 to a total population of only 371 in 1989. In this case, the court ruled for the group that hired my firm, and ordered the city to open up more lands for residential development.

On June 24, 2009, California Attorney General Edmund G. (Jerry) Brown Jr., a former California governor and Oakland mayor, sued the City of Pleasanton, California, in an effort to enforce compliance with the State of California law. Brown sued the city as an intervener in a case filed on October 17, 2006, in the Superior Court of the State of California, County of Alameda, by plaintiffs Urban Habitat Program and Sandra De Gregorio. Central to the complaints by the attorney general and the initial plaintiffs was a 1996 voter-approved referendum in

Pleasanton that had placed a permanent cap of 29,000 total housing units within the city. By the time the attorney general entered the case in 2009, Pleasanton was updating its General Plan to encourage the creation of 45,000 additional jobs in Pleasanton by 2025. In 2009, there were about 27,000 housing units; thus, given the cap, only 2,000 additional units could be added in the future. The attorney general asked the court to raise the cap to allow 3,277 new housing units to be built between 2007 and 2014. That amount had been determined by the State Department of Planning as Pleasanton's "fair share" of regional housing requirements.

The state planning agency's determination that Pleasanton should add 3,277 new units between 2007 and 2014 seems like a very mild prescription to cure the housing shortage. Even if the number of housing units suggested by the State Department of Planning were built, it would not add enough to the supply to keep future housing prices from once again escalating. In 2009 Pleasanton had more than 58,000 jobs. A 2005 study by the Association of Bay Area Governments found that 79 percent of the 58,000 employees in Pleasanton lived outside the city. Some of those workers' commutes took more than two hours each way.

Attorney General Brown may not have moved very quickly to the judiciary for help in forcing Pleasanton to plan and zone for an adequate housing supply. But for a 2010 gubernatorial hopeful, stepping into the courtroom when he did took political courage. And he seems to have won. As we go to press, Superior Court Judge Frank Roesch has just ruled against the city.

Courts rarely intervene to force city planning agencies to adequately balance between land for jobs and land for housing. Although favorable to such a balance, the scenario being played out in Pleasanton, California, cannot be taken as a basis that the courts can be expected in the future to enforce the kind of planning recommended in these pages. The courts are more likely to follow public sentiment rather than lead it when it comes to requiring municipalities to identify and zone sufficient land to exceed, or even equal, likely future residential demands. However, compliance is likely to be achieved without court action in most jurisdictions if the planning and zoning changes, financial incentives, and state and federal funding support included in the following recommendations are accepted. Once most local governments do adopt planning that opens the urban frontiers to competition so that the results of such competition are seen in terms of lower housing prices with no decline in housing quality, the odds of getting the courts to discipline those municipalities that do not comply will be much greater.

2. Include Sufficient Zoning for Mixed Uses

Zoning must always enforce plans that prevent the development of incompatible adjoining uses. Single-use zoning that segregates housing by tenure or by type from other uses is archaic—it is a remnant of the past. On the grounds of encouraging environmentally desirable and time-saving travel modes and patterns, mixed-use projects near transit stations and other major transport links should be planned and authorized by zoning. Clustered developments, including those near transit stations, often referred to as "transit-oriented developments" or TODs, have proven to be well received by residential and nonresidential buyers and renters. They constitute a type of sustainable development that can be built at high densities and heights, maximizing the use of land and encouraging the conservation of energy and time in travel from home to and from work or other places.

3. Mandate Default Maximum Densities for Zoning in Urban Regions

The suburban development in metropolitan areas usually called sprawl is validly charged with using excessive amounts of land, spreading out development thereby increasing vehicle miles driven, increasing the required distances of utility lines, and increasing the distances from public service facilities, such as fire stations. Restricting development in the suburbs wastes much more useable land than the low-density development encouraged by large-lot zoning. But suburban development in urban regions need not be either/or; the low-density development that is the hallmark of what is bad about sprawl can be cured by changing the rules of planning and zoning. The most important change would be to zone land for development of no fewer than twelve or fourteen units or lots per acre. Before readers who want to live on larger lots sit down to write me nasty letters, allow me to jump ahead and say that the zoning change called for here—a call for maximum zoning density as the default or starting point for all zoning—would not preclude the purchase and combining of several lots to build on a larger site. For example, if land were zoned twelve units to the acre, developments of one-half acre lots would be legal but would require the builder to buy six lots.

The elimination of zoning that requires residences to be built on large lots not only encourages the more efficient use of land and utilities, it also eliminates the inequities of providing land bargains to the affluent. As explained in chapter 6, houses built for the affluent tend to be bigger and have more expensive features than the houses of middle-income households. Large-lot zoning gives the rich a bargain in land. The public requirement that land can only be sold as large lots depresses the price of land per square foot.

4. Encourage the Feasibility of Developing Passed-Over Vacant or Underutilized Land

Little is gained by disallowing development to skip over land held by owners who do not want to develop the land or who are asking a higher price for their land than the price of land farther out from existing development. When "urban limit lines" or "growth boundaries" shown on the zoning map and reflected in the zoning ordinances cut off development outward of such vacant land, the result is to benefit the owners who sit on their land until land prices increase.

When planning regulations set up zones within which vacant land must be developed before allowing development beyond the boundary mapped in the general plan of the jurisdiction, those who promulgate those regulations hand a monopoly to land owners on the "developable side" of the boundary—this is effectively the growth-limiting boundary. Land skipped over because its owner has put a high "reservation price"—that is, a high minimum acceptable sale price—on the site tends to discourage other land owners from putting such a high reservation price on their land. A high reservation price also provides infill sites when feasible development density or perceived value of the site increases.

To ensure that the economies of development encourage subsequent development of passed-over sites, the following planning and municipal capital budgeting practices should be followed:

- Utility pipes, lines, and facilities such as sewage plants built to serve the development beyond the passed-over site should be sized with sufficient capacity to serve subsequent development on the passed-over site.
- Roadway, drainage, or transit rights-of-way purchased to serve the farther out development should be wide enough to serve passed-over sites so that those sites can subsequently be developed with adequate utility services without the extra costs and interruptions that would be occasioned by the need to resize existing pipes, drainage systems, and the like in the lands outward from the passed-over sites.
- As a condition of approval for the development of the land beyond the boundary and considered originally undevelopable, an agreement between that developer and the local public agency that grants approval should require the reimbursement, with interest, to the developer of the land within that boundary for the "excess costs of the oversizing." Keep in mind that the original developer will be required to build utility pipes, roadways, and so forth, larger than needed to create the sites within the boundary originally considered undevelopable. For that "oversizing" the original developer will have to pay "excess costs." Those costs should be paid by the later developer of the passed-over land as a condition of approval for the development of that land. Similarly, to the extent that the earlier developer was charged for all or a portion of the right-of-way purchased, reimbursement must be made by the later developer of the passed-over land at the time that land is to be developed.
- Approvals of septic sewage treatment or other substandard utilities for passed-over or vacant land should only be granted as temporary, without the granting of any long-term rights for the use of such facilities.

None of these four suggested practices is original. They have all been successfully implemented in the past. They are among many techniques for solving the problems of sprawl, but such techniques have fallen into disuse in recent decades. This may be partially because some of these techniques have been forgotten. It could also be that the antisprawl mood has conditioned many people to think only in terms of stopping suburban development rather than effectively dealing with sprawl.

5. The Costs of Public Services That Would Be Induced by a New Development Should Be Charged to That New Development

An environmental impact analysis must be prepared and considered before development can be approved in most states and for all federal projects. If it looks as if the development could cause significant damage to the environment, it must be reconfigured to avoid or mitigate possible impacts on the environment.

Such an analysis should be no different with regard to the fiscal impact of proposed development projects that local land-use authorities must evaluate for approval. An example of mitigating both the environmental impact and the fiscal impact is the approval process for the Santa Clara, California, mixed-use project called Rivermark. This award-winning community was completed in 2007 and included more than 1 million square feet of research and development office space, three thousand homes, and a shopping center with 165,000 square feet of retail stores. An environmental impact report was completed and carefully considered by the Santa Clara Planning Commission and City Council when this proposed mixed-use project came before them. In addition to considering the environmental effects, the traffic, aesthetic, and fiscal effects were also considered. Plan changes were made to align the development with the design preferences, open space requirements, and historic preservation interests of the city. As a condition of approval, all negative environmental effects of the project had to be mitigated, such as the ones discussed next.

The history of mitigating one of those environmental impacts sticks in my mind. The development demolished and replaced the aged structures of what had been California's first institution for the mentally ill. One of that site's areas had been farmed by the patients as a method of therapy. Pesticides used during farming had added arsenic to the arsenic that naturally occurs in the soil. The cumulative level of arsenic was above the level allowed in land to be used for housing sites. The developer was required to pay the costs of removing several inches of topsoil and trucking it to a hazardous material disposal facility.

The environmental impact report had also noted that burrowing owls were thriving in the arsenic-laden soil. I was the consultant who represented the state in the implementation of this development. Under an agreement we had negotiated that gave the state a base price and a percentage of development profits in return for the land, I was not to happy to be told there was another environmental mitigation demanded by the city council. Even though the burrowing owls were not an endangered species, the city council ruled their protection to be a condition of project approval. We engaged a biologist, who informed us when and how the owls could be safely moved to land suitable as a new habitat. It occurred to me that perhaps rather than take the several inches of soil to a hazardous waste disposal site, we could spread the soil on the land purchased as a new home for the owls. I called the California Department of Fish and Game, which had been charged with monitoring our moving the owls, and asked if we could move the arsenic-containing soil along with the owls to their new home. Their response was short but definite: "You're not funny, Claude." Perhaps not; the owls are now living well in a rural site without the arsenic-laden soil of their previous home.

Preparing a fiscal impact report that identifies any negative effects that the project would have on the quality of public services is usually easier than identifying the environmental effects of proposed developments. Once identified, the fiscal impacts are also easier to mitigate with the payment of money to increase the capacity of service-providing agencies and facilities so the predevelopment levels of service can be maintained. Fiscal impacts mitigated as a condition for the approval of the Rivermark development included roadway improvements, an off-site pedestrian bridge, and the provision of land and funds for the construction of schools and a fire station. These payments for infrastructure improvements ensured that the use of the new facility by workers, residents, and shoppers would not worsen the fiscal burden or lessen the quality of infrastructure and other services available to the preexisting community. In fact, the taxes contributed by the project will lessen the load carried by the public treasury to maintain levels of service that existed throughout the community while the 360-acre site was used as a state facility.

Our firm has done hundreds of fiscal impact analyses for local governments to measure the costs and revenues likely to result from the construction and use of new developments. Although the developers often pay for such analyses, the estimates can and should be sufficiently transparent so that planners and managers representing the community can and should check out the validity of the estimates. My own experience suggests that, more often than not, projects are charged with more than their fair share of fiscal costs—this is particularly the case for residential projects. Elected and managing officials of most jurisdictions know they must assure their current voters that new entrants into the community will not cause their taxes to go up or their services to go down. In most cases, the screening of nonresidential projects for their impact on fiscal solvency and maintenance of existing standards within the community is less stringent. This is because commercial and industrial development is assumed to enhance the job base and fiscal health of the community.

For the most part, fiscal impact analysis is not rocket science. It boils down to the detailed work of identifying the municipal, county, or special district capital and operating costs likely to stem from the increased need for facilities and services that will be induced by the users of the proposed project to be developed. Estimating the revenues likely to come from that project is largely a matter of totaling up the taxes and user fees likely to be paid by the residents and shoppers at the retail stores that will be available within the project. Nevertheless, fiscal impact analyses are often controversial because project proponents emphasize the revenue elements of the analysis and opponents emphasize the costs to government.

The way to maintain fairness is to make all calculations based on the existing level of services in the community, rather than the ideal level of services. For example, if the community is currently served by six sworn peace officers per thousand residents, then that level of service should be assumed when estimating the costs likely to be induced by the proposed project. Even if the chief of police firmly believes and expounds that the community should have eight sworn officers per thousand residents, to charge the new development for the cost of the extra police officers would be unjust, unless the existing community is also prepared to raise their payments for such added personnel and services. Likewise, it is not reasonable to assume that the new community will require less police services unless it can be shown that the makeup of the individuals who will populate the proposed development is such that they will require less police service. As another example, if the new project will be an active adult community, it should be required to pay more than the average cost per household for police services because the future residents are more likely to call for emergency paramedic care than would younger households with children.

I will not expound on the nuances of fiscal impact analysis. But as a matter of public policy, there is no more need or justification to ignore the effects that a new development will have on public treasury expenditures and receipts for capital and operating costs than it would be to ignore the likely environmental effects of a new project. Putting such policies in place will help the community budget and tax sufficiently to deliver needed public services and infrastructure efficiently and adequately.

6. Repair and Expand America's Infrastructure

Improve all your infrastructure, particularly the transportation and communication links between your urban places, and between your farming and resource-rich rural areas and your cities: this is the advice that economic advisors from international organizations and the United States give emerging nations seeking to advance up the economic development ladder. Often the advice is proffered along with financial assistance. It is good advice, supported by the experience of ancient empires such as China and Rome, and by the more recent history of the modern states that have prospered most in mercantile, industrial, and electronic revolutions.

Qin Shi Huang-di, the first emperor of China, tied that country together with more than four thousand miles of roads, which allowed commerce and troops to move easily within the empire and to and from the capital. During his reign, canals, cleverly designed irrigation systems, standardized weapon components, and granaries were built. The invention and dissemination of a uniform script enabled the populations of the far-flung empire, with their many different dialects, to communicate among each other. In addition to a metropolitan capitol, the emperor also built rammed-earth protective bulwarks that subsequently were updated to become the Great Wall of China.

It is not clear who first said, "All roads lead to Rome." But at the time of the Qin Dynasty, they did. The glory that was Rome was built on the foundation of Etruscan engineering accomplishments. Their structures were laid out and built in conformity with the three criteria we still apply to architecture and engineering today: functionality, aesthetics, and safety. The remains of the roads, aqueducts, and other structures attest to the Romans' ability to stretch the technology of their times to build the infrastructure that enabled the farmers, traders, and artisans of the empire's cites to thrive. Historians disagree about when the decline of Rome started, but there is agreement that the "barbarians" could not have conquered Rome until after its economic strength withered. The economy of the Roman Empire stagnated and then declined because its cities, which had magnified the strength of the original agricultural economy, were weakened by corruption and overtaxation. Taxes were collected by local agents who were compensated with a portion of what they collected. As the empire aged, its demands on those agents rose to where they were required to collect more than the local economies could give them without cutting into their productive muscle. In time, the flow of taxes—or tribute—simply became too small to sustain Rome's administrative, military, and social requirements.

America's economic history also supports the thesis that economic growth is engendered by improvements in transportation, communication, and other benefits that increase incomes, satisfaction, and productivity—improvements that neither individuals nor business entities pay for fully in any market transactions. I have referred to these public works, nonmarketed activities, and services as the positive externalities available in urban places. Surges in Roman trade and commerce accompanied the upgrading of harbors; likewise, the industrialization of America followed the development of the railroads.

Today the United States again needs the impetus that the modernization and expansion of its infrastructure will bring. But merely providing the infrastructure will not ensure the subsequent surge of economic productivity and growth. The federal government, as well as state governments, will have to provide the bulk of the funds needed to update and expand both intra- and interurban infrastructure. This will have to be done with sensitive "carrot and stick" planning and funding allocation that prods and helps urban places gain full benefit from the infrastructure by allowing the land within their jurisdictions to be built on, and their obsolete structures adaptively reused or redeveloped, partially as payback for the financing of needed infrastructure and other public externalities. Priority for federal and state funding of infrastructure improvements for local municipalities should be tied to the degree localities encourage competitive increases in housing supply and the replacement of obsolete nonresidential land uses.

But encouraging the "locals" to cooperate and facilitate private and public development within their jurisdictions will take more than the pull of dollars and the push of laws. Federal and state infrastructure planning and funding guidelines must be sensitive to the psychological and economic effects of alternative construction and location decisions. Driven primarily by engineering and cost-saving considerations, many of the plans for the federally funded roadways through long-established neighborhoods near the centers of great cities stirred up a hornet's nest of citizen opposition that came to be called "freeway revolts." The following discussion of the traffic jam cites examples of such revolts against well-intentioned roadways that tore through and sealed off existing positive social and physical amenities.

As is true of other types of infrastructure, America's highways and roads are in desperate need of updating and expansion. But this must be done with planning and guidelines that carefully tune the infrastructure to the unique development opportunities and cultures of each of the urban places that will be served by infrastructure that is being considered.

By considering all types of infrastructure, the American Society of Civil Engineers (ASCE) described in a 2005 report the degree to which America's infrastructure has deteriorated. The ASCE graded America's infrastructure with a "D" and estimated that $1.6 trillion was needed to bring the country's infrastructure up to acceptable levels. A summary of the grades handed out by the ASCE for various types of infrastructure is shown in table 8.1.

The scale and persistence of underinvestment in infrastructure has made many people give up on the idea of ever catching up with the shortfall of the capital needed to provide the public with adequate transport, energy, communication, and utility linkages. The picture with regard to judicial, penal, and administrative facilities is also discouraging. With the exception of communication linkages (e.g., fiber optic cables), the rate at which technological innovations have been adapted by public infrastructure tends to be slower than the pace of change in the technologies employed by private industry and consumers. What is needed is a massive investment in infrastructure construction employing the best available technology to increase its productivity.

THE TRAFFIC JAM. Many urban residents want and need relief for both interurban and intraurban automobile traffic congestion. It is likely that many who support restrictions on density, heights, and land for housing would compromise their positions to allow more housing if they believed that traffic

TABLE 8.1
The State of America's Infrastructure (ASCE)

	Grade	
	2001	2005
Aviation/aerospace	D	D+
Bridges	C	C
Dams	D	D+
Drinking water	D	D−
Energy	D+	D
Hazardous waste	D+	D
Navigable waterways	D+	D−
Public parks and recreation	−	C−
Rail	−	C−
Roads	D+	D
Solid waste	C+	C+
Transit	C−	D+
Wastewater	D	D−
America's infrastructure GPA	−	D

Source: RREEF Research Paper, "Opportunities in Private Infrastructure Investments in the US" (September 2006), 3.

Note: Total investment needs = $1.6 trillion. Each category was evaluated based on condition and performance,capacity versus need, and funding versus need.

congestion would be reduced in return for the compromises. But our thinking on traffic has become so fogged with fallacious reasoning that it has led to two erroneous but related conclusions: adding to roadway capacity will add still more cars than the added capacity can handle, and the battle to relieve congestion can never be won without ruining our cities.

These beliefs did not come out of the ether but grew from the seeds planted by an antiauto elite. These seeds were nurtured and fertilized by highway design that took no cognizance of unique urban development opportunities or neighborhood sensitivities, and that failed to adapt new technology to roadway design.

Lovers of cities were conditioned to turn their thoughts against cars in the city by the writings of the highly respected planning and architectural critic Lewis Mumford. In his 1963 book, *The Highway and the City*, Mumford made clear what he though about the impact of President Dwight Eisenhower's 1957 highway program: "When the American people, through their Congress, voted a little while ago [1957] for a twenty-six-billion-dollar highway program, the most charitable thing to assume about this action is that they hadn't the faintest notion of what they were doing. Within the next fifteen years they will doubtless find out; but by that time it will be too late to correct all the damage to our cities and our countryside, not least to the efficient organization of industry and transportation, that this ill-conceived and preposterously unbalanced program will have wrought."[1] His criticism of the auto was clear and succinct: "In short, the American has sacrificed his life as a whole to the motorcar, like someone, demented with passion, wrecks his home in order to lavish his income on a capricious mistress who promises delights he can only occasionally enjoy."[2]

But not everything Mumford wrote was hostile to the car. Read carefully, Mumford asked not for an end to roadway construction in and around cities. He argued that cities should be served with a variety of transportation options, giving citizens a choice as to which form of transport they may want to use. He argued for rail and roadway routes and junctions at locations where they will be likely to enhance development and recreational opportunities. Even more vigorously, he decried roadways and elevated freeways that cut off urban areas from scenic and historic points of interest or that split unique neighborhoods.

Unfortunately, too few transportation engineers seem to have read the constructive suggestions made by Mumford and other urbanites. Whether by substituting a cost-minimizing model of highway planning for cost–benefit analyses, by conducting cost–benefit analyses that failed to vector in the benefits of putting roads where they induced development improvements, or by reckoning the costs of destroying existing clusters, the type of highways that served rural areas were thrust into cities. By the mid-1960s, enough of the highway construction that Mumford and others had criticized was on the ground to incite what came to be called "freeway revolts."

Many planned freeway and expressway projects in United States and Canadian cities were stopped as a result of these revolts. In some cases, they were torn down after construction, as citizen groups railed against roadways that tore through neighborhoods and walled off cities from historic waterfronts. In the United States, successful revolts were mounted in Baltimore, Boston, Cleveland, Los Angeles, Memphis, Milwaukee, Minneapolis, New Orleans, San Francisco, Seattle, Philadelphia, Phoenix, Portland, and Washington, D.C.

One of the longest and best publicized of these successful outcries against poorly thought-out roadways through urban core areas was the battle against the construction of the Vieux Carré Riverfront Expressway in New Orleans.[3]

An elevated roadway along the route of the proposed expressway had been suggested by Robert Moses in 1946. With the blessing of the Louisiana Highway Department and the New Orleans City Council, who saw such a roadway as relieving congestion within the historic French Quarter, the roadway was designated as part of the federal highway system in 1964. At the time of its designation, it was estimated to cost $29 million, with 90 percent of these costs to be borne by the federal government. As early as 1965, the then-mayor of New Orleans, Victor H. Schiro, asked for a tunnel option, which was quickly rejected due to the high costs and difficulties associated with building under the groundwater conditions that exist in New Orleans. By 1966 New Orleans newspaper articles in support of an ground-level roadway presented estimates that switching from an elevated to ground-level roadway would cost $12.4 million more than the $31.2 million the proposed elevated expressway would cost.

Opposition to the proposed expressway was able to have the route designated as historic in the National Historic Preservation Act of 1966. In 1969 the federal government withdrew its funding of the proposed expressway. By then, the antiexpressway campaign, waged in what was called the "Second Battle of New Orleans," had encouraged urban activists in other cities to fight against roadways that they saw harming views and neighborhood cohesion.

In San Francisco, opposition to proposed freeways started early. In 1959, the San Francisco Board of Supervisors cancelled plans for seven of the ten freeways that were planned for the city. Strong, well-written articles by the *San Francisco Chronicle*'s outspoken architectural critic, Allan Temko, helped keep alive opposition to the elevated freeways that were built. The Embarcadero Freeway was closed and torn down after the Loma Prieta earthquake in 1989, and other freeway segments were demolished in the following decade. Some of these roadways in San Francisco and other cities have been replaced with surface improvements to streets, often in conjunction with the introduction of light rail transit. But much more needs to be done in San Francisco and elsewhere to reduce—if not eliminate—congestion while improving access to destinations within the urban areas.

Most of us have unpleasant and memories of time sitting in a car or bus that seemed to be crawling, if not parked, on streets that once facilitated rapid urban traffic. Stop-and-go traffic, with its wasteful idling and acceleration, generates far more air pollution—and uses more energy—than less congested driving. The 2005 ASCE report estimated Americans spent 3.5 billion hours stuck in traffic that year. The same report estimated that poor road conditions cost U.S. motorists $54 billion a year in repairs, operating costs, and lost productivity.

Today in many communities, the cry that "building more roads will only bring out more cars" has become the standard reaction to proposals for more highways. The result is that funds collected from gasoline taxes originally imposed to pay for expanded roadways are diverted to fill in the deficits of general funds at both the state and local level. In the voting booth, expenditures on transit are much more popular than roadways, and therefore those roads that are proposed are bundled with transit projects. The most obvious are interurban railways.

When doing a feasibility study for a parking garage in downtown San Francisco during the 1960s, I gained my initial insight into the paradoxical nature of anticar attitudes in a society that nevertheless clings to the automobile. One step in our research aimed at forecasting the occupancy of a proposed garage at alternative rates. Our research team conducted interviews in the office buildings around the site of the proposed garage. My wife, Nina, was in charge of designing the questionnaire and analyzing the completed survey. The survey was being conducted around the same time the citizens of the San Francisco Bay Area were voting on a proposal to build the Bay Area Rapid Transit system, known as BART. The BART project was approved by well over 50 percent of the voters just a few days before Nina completed her analysis. The parking survey suggested that the project was feasible because more than 50 percent of the office workers surveyed answered "yes" to the question that asked whether they would drive to work and pay enough for a space in the garage to make its development possible.

When I read Nina's report, I should have known not to question the results of her work, but I was young. So I walked into her office and told her that the results of her survey were questionable because "people would not vote to tax themselves in order to build BART if they intended to keep driving their cars to destinations well served by BART." Instead of arguing with me, Nina suggested that we resurvey a sample of those who had responded to the question I was skeptical of and ask them how they voted on the BART issue. We did as Nina suggested. Much to my surprise, we found that virtually all the people who said they would continue to drive to work every day also said they had voted for BART. When questioned further, it became clear that they had voted for BART because they expected other drivers would use BART, and they expected there would be less congestion on the roads and freeways they planned to continue to use.

Support for transit, or virtually anything but roadways, has become more intense with the increasing awareness of the threats posed by air pollution and increasing dependence by the United States and Europe on foreign oil. The contradictory behavior of the body politic and interurban American travelers continues.

In his book *Sprawl: A Compact History*, Robert Bruegmann suggests that the earlier generation of highway engineers and public officials set up the public for disappointment by promising that the expansion of the highway system would reduce congestion. He wrote: "This led many people to conclude that congestion in fast-growing places proved the failure of highway-building. It would probably have been more useful to consider congestion in these regions more a testimony to an economy so vibrant and quality of life so high that people continue to move in and to drive, despite the obvious problems."[4]

Bruegmann suggests that a more rational debate might have occurred if the discussion had focused less on congestion and more on mobility. He also points out that, like zoning and density, our attitudes toward the automobile have been partially the result of the objection of upper-class intellectuals to the increasing use of public roadways by the class of people who previously could not afford automobiles. He argues that the attitudes of those who are most stridently against roadway expansions are similar to those expressed by the duke of Wellington in the nineteenth century, when he opposed railroad construction because trains "only encouraged the common people to move about needlessly."[5]

Today, few concerned people would express their antagonism to the common man so blatantly, but their attitudes toward the emerging middle class are strikingly similar to the duke's. The intellectual elite who were captivated by the architectural beauty and social milieu of the nineteenth and early twentieth century tended to place primary emphasis on preserving the physical and social structures of the recent past. They forgot, or never thought, that the function and role of all urban structures is to serve and better the lives of the people who live and work in urban places.

Clearly, to improve traffic conditions with roadways and to improve transit will take some compromises from those of us who like things just as they are today, or even the way we remember them. To obtain those compromises from urban citizens, transit and roadway builders must do more than present plans that minimize disruptions of good development and enhance desired development opportunities. In particular, roadways proposed for the future must include innovations that make use of the personal transportation option of automobiles much safer, faster, and more convenient.

Merely going back now to resurface and extend the existing highway system would repair the past while missing the opportunity for the future. What is needed now is not more of the same old freeways and expressways that we have built in the past but a new system of transport linkages that provides the mobility people want and will use while mitigating the very real problems of air pollution and energy use created by the cars we love to drive. Just as the development of containerization, which revolutionized the ocean-borne transport of goods, required the development of a whole system of ports, ships, backup areas, gantries, and other equipment that had not previously been known in the shipping industry, a new system of personal vehicles, roads, and supporting equipment must be created.

When I refer to cars that are much less polluting, faster, and safer, I am not envisioning a more gasoline-efficient version of the engine-powered speed that can be seen in NASCAR events. Our goals should be to use electric, hybrid, or completely non-carbon-using vehicles that use electronic guidelines for safety and to increase the capacity of the roadways by speeding up traffic throughput.

7. Using Taxation to Encourage Environmental and Congestion Improvements

As much as possible, infrastructure improvements should be paid for by those who benefit from them in a manner that encourages private behavior that benefits society. I present, in the following, alternative ways of delivering the bill for the cost of roadway improvements as an example of the way to pay for the maintenance and improvements in urban infrastructure while simultaneously encouraging a shift to less environmentally harming vehicles.

IMPOSE GAS TAXES TO SET A MOTIVATING FLOOR UNDER THE COST OF GASOLINE. The taxing powers of states, and particularly the national government, can encourage or discourage actions more subtly, but no less powerfully, than the force of police powers. Improvements to the transportation networks that serve traffic to and within urban areas should be paid for with a tax on automobile gasoline. Such a tax will make funds for improvements available quickly and will increase the beneficial effects of all transportation improvements.

The Environmental Protection Agency estimates that transportation generated 27.9 percent of U.S. greenhouse gas emissions in 2007. A significant portion of that is contributed by emissions from privately owned cars and will be greatly reduced when we switch to electric or some other less polluting power source for cars, such as improved hybrids, natural gas, or hydrogen. Whereas some of us want to do the right thing and buy nonpolluting cars for the good of society, most Americans will only switch when the "eco-cars" can outperform the gas guzzlers or when the price of gasoline is over $3.50 a gallon and is more likely to go up than down in the future. As summarized so well in the April 27, 2009, issue of *The New Yorker* magazine: "The American market for pricey enviro-cars is fickle, as Toyota has painfully learned." When the price of gasoline was over $3.00 a gallon and consumers thought it was going higher, auto dealers were able to sell above "manufacturer suggested prices" all the hybrid cars the Toyota factory could deliver. But when the price of gasoline fell, the customers for the hybrid stayed away and the dealers' showrooms and lots were crowded with cars.

It is going to take more time than would be good for the Earth to wait until the auto industry produces eco-cars that can compete in performance and price with big cars operating with the muscle of gasoline and diesel powered engines. That's why a gas tax should be instituted now to keep prices above $3.50 and pay for a twenty-first-century roadway that could contain electronic guides that permit roadways to carry more vehicles faster and safer as they are in effect "self-driven" while occupants can converse face to face and on cell phones without needing to keep their eyes on the road.

TOLL ROADS. Toll roads have been used as a funding mechanism for the construction of roads, bridges, tunnels, locks, and other modes of transportation since shortly after the founding of the republic. In recent years, the use of electronic fee collection has reduced the costs of collecting tolls and decreased the time formerly spent waiting to pay at the tollbooths. These improvements in toll-collecting technology have tended to further improve the results of using tolls to pay for infrastructure. The vast majority of tolls have charged the users of roadways less than the benefits the payers receive. That is, in the language of economics, the tolls have provided a "consumer surplus" in giving the users more than they paid for.

The most recent study to report these results was conducted by the Bureau of Business Research at the University of Texas at Austin, and dealt with the tolls charged for pedestrian, car, and truck traffic across bridges between El Paso, Texas, and Ciudad Juárez, Mexico. The bridges serve and facilitate growth in international trade and tourism between the neighboring countries. The University of Texas study found that rates are less than what users would be willing to pay, and that raising the rates would not significantly decrease the use of the bridges.[6]

If roadways, garages, and any types of infrastructure are initially funded by private investors and then paid for by tolls or user fees, it will be critical to avoid handing these monopolies—and that is what these infrastructures are—to private equity organizations. Infrastructure tends to be a natural monopoly because second or third competitors providing the same route or service are unlikely to appear, which is why the price charged to users must be regulated. Private investors who fund infrastructure such as a toll road require agreements that include noncompete clauses that prohibit additions to competing traffic-handling facilities. Such agreements must be resisted. Any such restrictions that are agreed to should include sunset provisions that limit the life of the agreements. The lessons learned on how to regulate public utilities and "natural monopolies" wisely must be relearned and applied to the new generation of privately funded public infrastructure of all types.

OPPORTUNITIES FOR INDUCED LAND-VALUE CAPTURE. Roadway planning and transit right-of-way planning should be alert for possibilities to locate where existing development will be made more profitable and likely to expand, and to create options for feasible new development clusters. Both types of induced benefits—increasing profitability and expanding options for new developments—should be included in the cost–benefit calculations of alternative route, junction, and station locations. When opportunities for the creation of new development are identified on vacant or underutilized sites, such sites should be purchased with the rights-of-way for selected alternatives. Subsequently, when the infrastructure is completed or progressed sufficiently that the opportunities created are easily understood, the sites can be sold to help pay the costs of the infrastructure investment. Although purchasing lands along the rights-of-way of planned roads and then subsequently reselling those lands is unlikely to pay for all the land and construction, income from the sale can nevertheless carry some of the cost burden.

It will be possible in some cases to include enough land in the condemnation process (the "take") to be resold as sites that take advantage of the access created by the new road to build high-density mixed-use projects. The resale of such sites will help defray the cost of the new roadways and transit lines whereas the occupants of the developments will tend to take fewer and shorter trips by car and therefore release less carbon into the atmosphere.

8. Take the Burden of Social Housing off the Backs of Market Housing Producers

The term "housing needs" denotes the requirement of shelter for households with the financial ability to purchase or rent adequate housing at market prices—and it also denotes those households whose incomes do not enable them to rent or buy adequate housing in the prevailing market. The Europeans use "social housing" to describe additions to the housing stock made available at below-market pricing so as to alleviate the needs of those who cannot find adequate housing that they can afford in the private market. Examples of such social housing in the United States include public housing, usually paid for by federal funds and built and operated by local public agencies. Social housing also includes the housing built with a host of differing federal programs that provide subsidies to private builders in return for agreements to rent or sell the newly constructed or renovated housing at prices geared to the incomes of tenants and buyers rather than at prevailing prices in the private housing markets.

The funding for such social housing might be referred to as direct funding because it comes from the public coffers that are filled with taxpayers' money and government debt. But an increasingly large amount of social housing and its funding are now being provided by private builders as local ordinances require them to sell or rent a portion of the housing they construct at prices determined by the incomes of future occupants. These local ordinances are termed "inclusionary zoning" because they spell out what proportion of new units built in designated areas must be set aside for sale or rental to households whose incomes fall below specified limits. Some local ordinances permit developers to pay cash into public coffers, such as those of the local redevelopment agency that will build the social housing, rather than include so-called affordable units within the project being developed privately. Social housing is also created by rent control ordinances that set limits to what can be charged and that forbid the eviction of tenants in rent-controlled units.

Forcing the creation of social housing by inclusionary zoning or rent control limits the amount of housing supplied. In the case of rent control, losses to the housing stock occur as landlords withdraw units from the stock and as units are rented as second or third homes by people who would not remain as tenants if they had to pay market rents. As I write this, I am reminded of a friend, a professor at a school in New Jersey, who used to argue with me about the merits of rent control whenever we met at planning or real estate conferences and social events. Once, when I called to tell him that my wife and I were going to be in New York and suggested he and his wife meet us for dinner if he had business in New York, he told me something that had never been mentioned in our debates on rent control. He said, "When you're in New York, why don't you stay at the rent-controlled apartment I keep there? We rarely use it."

Much has been written, too, about the harm done by rent control to the available quantity and quality of housing. Rent control provides a windfall to the tenants who inhabit rent-controlled apartments. But over time there is a rarely noticed, very significant drain on the availability and quality of housing to those who are not privileged by the protection of rent control. There is a constant political battle between those few who enjoy its protection and the many who neither enjoy its protection nor understand the way it harms them.

Inclusionary zoning, the new short-term palliative to the problem of insufficient affordable housing, started as a court-sanctioned attempt to stop communities from using their planning and zoning authority to exclude renters and middle-income home buyers. It has evolved into a popular tool to force the production of new, below-market housing. Unfortunately, the net effect of such a forced mix of profitably priced and unprofitably priced housing is to reduce the total supply of added market-rate housing while providing bargains to only a lucky few low- and moderate-income households.

Whether developers are required to create the below-market units that are added to the pool of social housing as a part of their development, or whether they are required to make cash payments in lieu of adding such units to their development, the net effect is to reduce the profitability of the development. Because developers are rarely the most popular of entrepreneurs, that may seem OK to many. But unfortunately, it only seems OK. Reduced profitability is actually the opposite of what should occur when a product, particularly a very durable product such as housing, is in short supply. By burdening housing builders with the need to include unprofitable units in the mix of what they build, or pay a high fee for not building those units, we ensure a continuation of the shortage. Building insufficient quantities of housing will continue to be profitable. That profitability would be extinguished by the increases in supply that would result from the pile-on of builders going after the extra big profits they could make in the absence of inclusionary zoning requirements while the housing shortages prevail.

During the recession that started in late 2007, major builders stopped adding to the supply even if they have the land and the permits to build. Stalled projects include high-rise developments such as the second tower of the One Rincon Hill project, whose spokesman, Oz Ericson, was quoted in the July 24–25, 2009, *San Francisco Business Times* as saying the project is doing "just fine" in the market but that construction in the second tower cannot go on because the inclusionary zoning fees make it infeasible.

Inclusionary zoning does benefit the households lucky enough to get into the required below-market units, who are able to enjoy new housing while paying about 30 percent of their income. But the same process that produces this bargain for them holds down the total production of housing, so that most households in the moderate and lower income brackets of the community must pay more than 50 percent of their income for older housing. Young, middle-income families without parents who can subsidize them must move out of the community to find housing.

In time, the undermaintenance encouraged by rent control is also induced by inclusionary zoning. Whether you live in a single family house, an apartment in a multifamily structure, or a condominium, you or your landlord have to pay the costs of maintaining the space you live in, the common areas, and whatever yard exists. Neither those costs nor the costs of replacing worn-out equipment and fixtures are negligible; those costs tend to increase over time. Unless the incomes of the occupants of the inclusionary units also increase, they will find themselves strapped to pay the condominium fees and assessments or the increases in rents needed to fund the rising costs of maintenance and replacement. In San Francisco, some households who move into the affordable units of condominiums have come back to the city asking for subsidies to help them pay assessments. For buyers of condominiums and single-family affordable units provided under inclusionary zoning, resale restrictions intended to keep the lucky new owners from "flipping" their properties for a profit lessen the incentive for such buyers to stretch for the higher homeowners' dues, assessments, or out-of-pocket costs for residential maintenance and replacement.

A shortage of affordable housing in a region can only be solved if the production of market-priced housing in that region adds more housing units than are demanded. When the demands of those who can afford to buy or rent new market-priced housing are satisfied and there remains even the slightest over-supply of market-priced housing, prices begin to drop. But if the barriers to new housing production prevent the supply of new units from surpassing increases in demand, then prices of existing units will never decrease. Since about 1970, this is exactly what we have seen happen in the urban places of the United States, the urban places that provide the United States with the production and innovating capability to compete in global market places. The recession that started in 2007 has created an opportunity to undo the increasing shortage of affordable housing. The biggest and first step forward to solving that problem would be to stop the use of inclusionary zoning.

The support for local laws requiring the inclusion of below-market rate housing whenever new housing projects are considered is usually strongest within two groups of proponents. There are the "no growth" or "slow growth" proponents who, for economic reasons, do not want to see the supply of housing increased in their neighborhoods and beyond. From the social perspective, they do not feel comfortable ignoring the hardships of low- and moderate-income households that have to cope with steadily rising rents and home prices, especially if those households are anywhere within view. These proponents support inclusionary zoning while continuing to oppose planning and zoning that encourages development because this permits them to feel good while putting one more stake in the heart of housing production.

The other group of proponents quietly supports inclusionary zoning ordinances. This group comprises the builders who have recently started production of luxury housing projects that are saddled with inclusionary zoning requirements and the owners of housing units in expensive projects whose builders have already had their profit margins cut by carrying the burden of below-market units. By supporting the continuation of more onerous inclusionary requirements, these entrepreneurs, landlords, and homeowners are increasing the likelihood that competition will not stop their properties from escalating in value.

On the one hand, these two groups may see themselves as winners when inclusionary zoning and rent control are imposed. On the other hand, all current and potential future residents of the community are losers when such measures are passed and strengthened.

Both the federal government and the states have long funded a broad variety of subsidy programs to create housing available to low- and moderate-income households. Those programs do not detract from the incentives that private investors, developers, and builders have for building housing to serve those who can afford to buy new dwelling units. Furthermore, experiments with housing vouchers to provide funds to lower-income households so they can select housing from what is available in the market offer freedom of choice to the recipients, without stunting the motivation of private housing suppliers. There is no reason why these forms of socially conscious housing augmentation should not continue. In contrast, inclusionary zoning thwarts the filtration process that can provide affordable housing over time. It is not a coincidence that the same communities that enact increasingly more onerous inclusionary zoning requirements rarely see declines in the prices of existing homes throughout the community but do note the gentrification of neighborhoods in proximity to desirable amenities.

9. Vest Tenants of Redeveloped Properties with Rent Differential Subsidies

Whether their properties are taken by the eminent domain powers of condemnation or by private purchase, the owners of obsolete structures and underutilized lands do receive compensation. While tenants in buildings taken by public bodies often receive relocation assistance, they are stuck with having to pay higher rents if equivalently priced units are not available. To provide them with equal protection, tenants should be offered the difference between what they have to pay for available units of equivalent quality when they move. Assistance should be continued for the same number of years going forward as the number of years they had been tenants in the structures demolished in the redevelopment process.

10. Distribute a Portion of Sales Tax Revenue on the Basis of Population Rather Than Point of Sale

In 1978 the voters of California passed Proposition 13, which froze the value of property to the value assessed that year, allowing for increases of only 2 percent per year until the property changes hands. This proposition also limited the tax rate to 1 percent of the property's assessed valuation, unless 60 percent of local voters approved higher tax rates to yield revenue for special purposes, such as raising the school district budget, improving street lighting, or other projects for which the voters are willing to raise their property taxes. Since then, Oregon and Massachusetts have passed somewhat similar restrictions on the use of property tax.

The restriction on property tax is unfair because it discriminates between current and future property owners. But for that same reason, such restrictions have remained immensely popular among homeowners. In my own experience, my family lived for forty-one years in a large, single-family house on a quiet street in the middle-class town of El Cerrito, California, located between Berkeley and Richmond. Because my wife and I owned the house in 1978, the assessed valuation increased only 2 percent per year during times that housing prices were escalating about 7 percent per year. In 2006 one of my sons and his family moved eight houses up the street into a pleasant but slightly smaller house than where he had lived as a child. His property taxes at that time were four times what I was paying on a much larger house. That much disparity in taxes seems an excessive reward for getting older without moving.

The crippling of the property tax has made it difficult for cities in California to maintain high levels of public services and facilities. They have tried to replace the lost taxes with new fees and by attracting sales-tax-producing businesses, such as retail stores and auto dealers to their jurisdictions. The sales taxes received from these businesses rarely pass the test of paying for public services in an amount proportionate to the benefits received. Nor does the property tax paid meet the test of equity. Not only is the sales tax less equitable than the property tax when measured by the relationship between payment made and benefits received, the attempts to get businesses to locate within municipal borders engenders "beggar thy neighbor"—when one benefits at the expense of another or others—fighting between municipalities. Builders of shopping centers and auto malls whose customers pay sales taxes, hotels whose guests pay transient occupancy taxes, and businesses of all types that collect sales taxes are courted and often subsidized. Housing developments are discouraged because municipalities fear they will not "pay their way."

The 2009 financial woes of the State of California and many of its municipalities make it possible that the citizenry and those who represent them will rethink the taxation policies of the state. The removal, or at least lessening, of the restrictions placed on the property tax would be one step out of the financial morass that bedevils California and its cities. A further step forward would be to distribute at least a substantial part of the sales tax collected to municipalities based on population, rather than back into the municipality where the tax is collected. Crippling the property tax and allowing the sales tax to serve as an incentive for putting a premium on the attraction of tax-paying businesses over housing should be discouraged in all states of the union.

11. A Private Alternative to Public Urban Redevelopment

Defining residential and commercial blight by physical criteria alone adds little to our understanding of the fundamental causes of blight. A more useful definition recognizes that there are economic conditions that tend to make undermaintenance of real estate a preferable policy for owners of the affected properties. Defining blight as existing when market conditions will not support maintenance and upgrading recognizes the underlying causes of those physical deficiencies. In real estate jargon, the definition of blight is market conditions that will not allow properties to be brought to their highest and best use.

Real estate economics are determined by the costs of the options for improvement, the income offered by the real estate, and the priority-based demands of potential buyers or renters of the bundle of services offered by the real estate. The makeup of the pool of relevant or potential buyers and renters will vary by the submarket areas we call neighborhoods. The boundaries of neighborhoods are defined by the similarity of the demanders that shop for homes, commercial spaces, or investment properties within those boundaries. Therefore, for redevelopment in a blighted area to be successful, improvements must take place in an area big enough to differentiate it positively from the preexisting neighborhood and to attract higher-paying renters and buyers. In essence, a new neighborhood or submarket area must be created with a higher position on the filtration ladder of neighborhood, as was discussed in chapter 4.

In addition to carving out a large enough area to differentiate its properties in the marketplace, a new neighborhood's scale of activity needs to be big enough to allow the upgrading of some elements of the infrastructure. The needed infrastructure improvements can be a little as moving overhead wires underground or as major as rerouting streets, rebuilding drainage and sewers, and creating new parks and other public spaces.

The scale of the land area required to make redevelopment successful in the housing market and in the improvement of public infrastructure almost always requires control over more than a single owner's properties. As a result, successful redevelopment has most frequently been carried out by public entities with the power of eminent domain and with the ability to allocate public funds to infrastructure improvements.

Perhaps the best of these examples comes from the redevelopment of Paris by Baron Haussmann. He was appointed by Napoleon III in 1853 to modernize a city with narrow, congested, filthy streets and an inadequate sewer system into the modern city with broad tree-lined boulevards and monumental public spaces we enjoy today. Haussmann's redevelopment did more than inspire many of the redevelopment planners and czars that followed him in cities around the world. During his time, Parisians criticized him for the public costs of modernization and the social changes that occurred as the physical changes in the city encouraged economic growth. The public outcry against his redevelopment led Napoleon III to fire Haussmann in 1870.

American urban renewal projects are often criticized for the same two reasons that stirred the Parisians of the nineteenth century. Even one of the justices who voted for the majority indicated discomfort with the Supreme Court's five-to-four decision that the Connecticut town of New London had the right to confiscate Susette Kelo's property in order to turn it and other assembled real estate over to a private redeveloper. But in spite of furor and the discomfort of many Americans with the process of eminent domain as it is practiced by municipal redevelopment agencies, the courts are unlikely to reinterpret past decisions to disallow its use to assemble land that is subsequently turned over to private developers. I refer here to state as well as federal courts.

For example, in May of 2009 a New York Appeals Court dismissed objections to the transfer of property acquired by the use of eminent domain by the New York State Urban Development Corp. to the Forest City Ratner Company. That firm is planning to build housing and an arena in the Brooklyn Atlantic Yards project. In their ruling, the New York four-judge panel wrote: "Any incidental profit that may inure to Forest City from the remediation of the blighted project site does not undercut the public purpose of the condemnation of the substandard land."[7]

I cite that quote from the New York justices because it echoes an aspect of the use of eminent domain by public bodies that, while critical, is rarely discussed. Redevelopers of blighted areas do not just make a profit by selling or renting the new space they build. By their branding—that is, by moving the area up the filtration ladder of neighborhoods—they increase land values over what they were when the area was blighted. But under eminent domain laws, the deposed owner of a condemned property is compensated by being paid the price of the land in its "as is" condition. Because governments were first granted the power of eminent domain for public purposes, both state and federal laws specifically disallow the condemnation valuation to include any value increase that might be bestowed on the property by the project for which it is condemned. Appraisers and juries in condemnation lawsuits are always instructed that the value they place on the property can never include the benefit impact of the project for which it is to be taken. When the New London Redevelopment Agency compensated Susette Kelo, they paid her the "fair market value" of her house as it sat within a blighted neighborhood. That is, they followed the law, which states that the condemnee is never to get the value that will be created by the impact of the project. I suggest the law be altered in two ways: First, private parties who have acquired 80 percent of the properties within a blighted project area will be granted the power of eminent domain to acquire the remaining 20 percent of the property under the condition described next. Second, upon taking title, the private redeveloper will pay the owner of taken property the fair market value of the property in its "as is" condition. When the project or a significant portion of it is completed, the project's developer must make an additional payment to the former owner equal to the difference between the original fair market value of the condemned property and the proportionate share of the property's value after the project has been completed and is 90 percent occupied. This payment of the difference between the original compensation and the value of the property taken, after the new project has been marketed, could be paid in cash or in a share of the project ownership.

I do not know whether Ms. Kelo or the eight former property owners in the Forest City Ratner case would have been satisfied if they had been able to share in the profits of the project to be built on their land. But giving them a proportionate share of the profit made from the use of land they had possessed seems fairer than simply paying them what the property was worth in the blighted neighborhood.

The recommended change could enable adjacent property owners to understand the benefit of combining the lands they own into a parcel large enough to provide a good site for a project that will make their share of its profits greater than the market value they or their heirs could hope to obtain by selling the property they own. For developers, the benefit of this combined package of land could be that their plans are not frustrated by one or two stubborn "holdouts."

Providing private competitors to redevelopment agencies would have the beneficial effect of competition between them, at least in some cases. The competition would motivate both public and private redevelopers to improve their performance in whatever ways will better satisfy property owners, contractors, approval agencies, voters, and such. One likely result of such competition would be to speed up the time between the initial acquisition of the property and project completion. Public redevelopment agency members, their executives, and staff may be motivated by a desire to provide public service and a desire to improve urban places. Private redevelopment agencies are motivated by having their own money tied up in a project, or as they say on the street, having some "skin in the game"—a sharp prod to moving quickly on the path to completing projects, once up-front studies, planning, and some initial acquisition have taken place. That prod is dull for bureaucratic public agencies whose payrolls will be funded as long as they still have projects to complete.

I am neither a lawyer nor a constitutional scholar, so I do not have the expertise to know whether legislative actions by Congress and the states can bestow the mantle of eminent domain upon private parties who meet the conditions spelled out in the preceding pages. But unless we argue that only public employees have the skills required to identify and implement blight-removing redevelopment, allowing private entities into this arena seems to fulfill the same public purpose for which public agencies have long been granted the right of eminent domain.

12. Put the Genies of Toxic Mortgages and Opaque Derivatives Transactions Back in the Bottle

Housing prices were bound to go up once local land-use policies made it impossible for builders to supply the number of homes consumers were willing and able to buy at the prices that existed before the overregulation of the local land supply. But housing prices would never have gone as high or continued to climb for as long without the powerful boosts made possible by

- lowering regulatory standards that encouraged the insurance and purchase of poorly underwritten mortgages by quasi-governmental agencies;
- packaging mortgages into securities and sold to investors worldwide by investment banking houses that earned large fees on the trillions of dollars of those securities without investing any of their own money; and
- selling complex and hard-to-track credit-default swap agreements tied to mortgage-backed securities or derivatives of the mortgage-backed securities insured against the risk of defaults on securities containing the mortgages. (Traded over-the-counter, along with other derivative instruments that were largely not only unregulated but also not available for scrutiny, these mortgage-back securities were created and bought in huge packages by those who believed they were hedged or protected against default risks. The result was a spree of highly leveraged funneling of money into mortgages issued to people without the income to make the payments required in the fine print of those mortgages.)

The mortgages themselves were at the bottom of the pile of mortgage-related indiscretions that finally lit the fuse that ignited the explosion and nearly destroyed the financial structures of the United States and many of its trading partners. Safeguards that had been put in place during the 1930s to protect against issuing mortgages that saddled homeowners with debt their incomes could not support, and principals that exceeded the market value of their homes, were stripped away in an effort to constantly boost the rate of home-ownership. Many of the mortgages that backed internationally marketed securities had been poorly underwritten and called for payments that were initially low to draw in gullible borrowers. The time would come for many borrowers when they would find their payments rising in future years to the point where they could only meet them by refinancing their homes for more than the value of the mortgage on their houses.

To protect borrowers and ultimately the public against the inevitable day of reckoning set up by these mortgages, the federal government must reinstitute sound appraisal standards and business terms, and enable mortgage-backed securities to be pulled apart to permit the renegotiation of individual mortgages in danger of default. As this is written, the Obama administration and Congress are working on such regulations. At a minimum, here is what they must require:

1. The appraisal of a property to be mortgaged by a loan that will be insured or purchased by federal agencies must be independently prepared and checked for validity before the loan can be approved for insurance or resale to governmentally supported agencies.
2. A loan application must provide evidence of a reasonable expectation that the income of the borrower can support the principal and interest costs called for under the mortgage.
3. The number of interest-only loans should be limited. And "teaser rates" that escalate future mortgage interest rates must be outlawed.
4. Just as the government can pass and enforce laws that require markings on bullets to allow law enforcement officers to track down the gun from which the bullets were fired, in much the same way, every individual mortgage bundled into a securitized package must be identified so it can easily and inexpensively be retrieved, its full loan history can be identified, and every individual mortgage can be renegotiated, paid off, or resold.
5. All fees, commissions, and sales charges paid or accrued to brokers, loan servicing organizations, or other entities compensated for the closing of the mortgage must be fully revealed.

There needs to be sunlight. There needs to be transparency so the sunlight can illuminate what is within. My suggestions are offered to make the whole business of securitization less murky. But attention must also be paid to reducing the incentives to take imprudent risks. One way to discourage over-the-top risk packaging—and, indeed, perhaps eliminate or at least reduce the likelihood that investment bankers will continue to price mortgage-backed securities so the price does not reflect the risks they contain—is to disallow such securities issued by any entity that does not have something of its own at stake in the security. Unless the folks who buy and repackage mortgages have some of their own money tied up in the security comprising the repackaged mortgages, it will be hard to for them to resist the temptation to price securities too low and sell them too high.

Now consider the billions of bailout dollars that the federal government pumped into firms like American International Group (AIG) to make good on the derivatives that had been sold with inadequate backing. The bailout is solid proof that all such instruments must be regulated and traded on exchanges that will facilitate transparency. The issuer of a derivative promises the buyer to offset the buyer's loss on a specified asset, say a mortgage, should the value of that asset change to cause the buyer to lose money. Derivatives serve a useful economic function in that they permit the buyer of the derivative to hedge the bet he has made on an asset. But if the issuer of the derivative cannot make good on the promise to make the buyer whole, then like the owner of an insurance policy that cannot pay off, it's "tough luck" for the buyer.

That is exactly what would have happened to Goldman Sachs and other firms that bought derivatives from AIG, except that the federal government stepped in to bail out AIG—the Fed stepped in because AIG and Goldman Sachs were deemed "too big to fail." There is no doubt that the bailouts of those "too big to fail" were necessary to prevent the entire financial structure from crumbling. But the bailout was costly for the U.S. taxpayers. Although it prevented the financial system from crumbling, the Fed could not prevent it from being significantly weakened. Realizing that they could not be sure the derivatives would protect them against loss, lenders became hesitant to issue credit at a time the economy could least afford to see the supply of credit dry up. Never again should the federal government allow itself or the nation to face the need to bail out the issuers of derivatives.

The federal government should adopt regulations requiring the issuers of derivatives to have sufficient capital to deliver what they have agreed. Derivatives trading should be limited to exchanges where such transactions can be observed and the regulations requiring sufficient back-up capital will be enforced. The alternative to requiring that derivatives, including credit-default swaps, be federally regulated and their trading made transparent should not be to allow such transactions to continue to be made in secret. If a workable system for transparency and regulation cannot be achieved, then the suggestion first made by the famous financier George Soros should be made the law of the land—all such transactions should be declared illegal.

Simply following the recommendations summarized in the preceding pages of this chapter will not eliminate the naturally occurring up-and-down cycles of housing prices, in particular, or real estate cycles in general. What can be achieved through these recommendations is a significant reduction of the amplitudes of such cycles. Over time, a reduction in housing price swings will result from the new regulations, and that will tamp down long-term mortgage interest rates. This result will go at least part way to enabling more people to own homes without also blowing up the price of housing until the bubble bursts.

13. A Fix-It, Don't Stop-It Civic Culture

The recommendations in this chapter are not perfect, one-shot solutions to the wrongs of urban policy described in the preceding seven chapters of this book. These recommendations should be revised, amended, and appended as they are followed. Whether and how well they are carried out, improved, and added to will depend ultimately on the spirit and will of America's urban citizenry. There was a time when urban Americans saw change and development as progress and good. In recent decades, in some of America's greatest and still-growing urban places, the attitudes that might be considered a civic culture have shifted—to the other extreme. In many places the civic culture reflected by those who attend the workshops that local planners set up when they start a planning process, and the citizens who speak out at public hearings before their elected and appointed officials, call for stopping development and keeping our public and private spaces they way they are—or were.

Merely stopping what we do not like will in time leave us with an increasingly large accumulation of urban structures and infrastructure that do not improve the lives of residents or the productivity of workers and investors. Building cities is a never-ending process. Stopping that process will result in the gradual but sure deterioration of urban life and work. The civic culture should support and demand policies that guide developers and builders to fix what is wrong with cities at costs that urban residents and businesses can more than pay from the benefits received. To achieve this will require an open-minded willingness to compromise, the acceptance of some change, and the expectation of ingenious solutions to become part of the civic culture. The rewards will far surpass the results of a civic culture that attempts to settle for the preservation of what we have now and how we go about trying to keep it that way.

NOTES

CHAPTER 1   CONSTRAINTS ON HOUSING
ADDITIONS ESCALATE PRICES

1. Floyd Norris, "Housing Market's Upside: Affordability," *New York Times*, March 7, 2009.
2. Ira S. Lowry and Bruce W. Ferguson, *Development Regulation and Housing Affordability* (Washington, DC: Urban Land Institute, 1992).
3. Ibid., 8.
4. Stephen Malpezzi, Gregory Chun, and Richard Green, "New Place to Place Housing Price Indexes for U.S Metropolitan Areas, and Their Determinants: An Application of Housing Indicators," Wisconsin-Madison CULER working papers 96–07, University of Wisconsin Center for Urban Land Economic Research (1996).
5. Joseph Gyourko, Christopher Mayer, and Todd Sinai, "Superstar Cities" (The Wharton School, University of Pennsylvania), June 16, 2006.
6. A Chow statistical test conducted with the data shown in the figure indicates that it would not be invalid to conclude that the trend or path of relative prices of new detached single-family homes diverged or broke in 1998.
7. The R square for the correlation was .6561, hence the trend was found to be statistically significant.
8. Edward L. Glaeser, Joseph Gyourko, and Albert Saiz, "Housing Supply and Housing Bubbles," July 16, 2008, draft of an article forthcoming in the *Journal of Urban Economics*.
9. Peter S. Goodman, "Homeowners Feel the Pinch of Lost Equity," New York Times, November 8, 2007.
10. David C. Wheelock, "The Federal Response to Home Mortgage Distress: Lessons from the Great Depression," The Federal Reserve Bank of St. Louis Review 90, no. 3 (May/June 2008): 133–148.
11. Standard & Poor's Residential Real Estate Indicators, October 2008, http://www2 .standardandpoors.com/spf/pdf/index/200810_Residential_Real_Estate_Indicators .pdf.
12. Richard K. Green and Susan M. Wachter, "The American Mortgage in Historical and International Context," Journal of Economic Perspectives 19 (Fall 2005): 93–114.
13. Ibid.
14. Ibid.

CHAPTER 2   VITALITY FROM GROWTH AND FREEDOM TO CHANGE

1. John M. Quigley, Steven Raphael, and Eugene Smolensky, "Homelessness in America: Homelessness in California," Working Paper No. #99–001, Institute of Business and Economic Research, Fisher Center for Real Estate and Urban Economics, University of California, Berkeley (Rev. March 2000).

2. Natalia Siniavskaia, "Housing's Contribution to State Economies at the Peak of the Boom," NAHB HousingEconomics.com, March 28, 2008. http://www.nahb.org/generic.aspx? sectionID=734&genericContentID=92268&channelID=311.

3. For an interesting study of the effect of clustering on office rents, see Maarten Jennen and Dirk Brounen, "The Effect of Clustering on Office Rents: Evidence from the Amsterdam Market," *Real Estate Economics* 37, no. 2 (Summer 2009): 185–208.

4. For a recent discussion of the difference between urbanization and localization economies, see Stephen Malpezzi, Kiat-Ying Seah, and James D. Shilling, "Is It What We Do or How We Do It? New Evidence on Agglomeration Economies and Metropolitan Growth," *Real Estate Economics, Journal of the American Real Estate and Urban Economics Association* 32, no. 2 (Summer 2004): 270. (The article not only fulfills the promise of its title but is also an excellent compendium of the literature on urban agglomeration.)

5. Rosina Moreno, Raffaele Paci, and Stefano Usai, "Geographical and Sectoral Clusters of Innovation in Europe," *Annals of Regional Science* 39, no. 4 (December 2005): 715.

6. Anthony Downs, "California's Inland Empire," *California Counts*, Public Policy Institute of California 7, no. 2 (November 2005): 3.

7. Ibid., 4.

8. Thomas Jefferson, *Notes on the State of Virginia* (1784). http://etext.virginia.edu/toc/ modeng/public/JefVirg.html.

9. Hernando de Soto, *The Mystery of Capital: Why Capitalism Triumphs in the West and Fails Everywhere Else* (New York: Basic Books, 2000).

10. Alben W. Barkley, *That Reminds Me* (New York: Doubleday, 1954), 45.

11. Thomas S. Allen, "Low Bridge, Everybody Down" (1905).

12. William Cronon, *Nature's Metropolis: Chicago and the Great West* (New York: Norton, 1991), 9.

13. Richard Melancthon Hurd, *Principles of City Land Values*, (New York: The Record and Guide, 1911), 145.

14. Homer Hoyt, "The Effect of the Automobile on Patterns of Urban Growth," *Traffic Quarterly* (1962). Republished in Homer Hoyt, According to Hoyt: *Fifty Years of Homer Hoyt* (Washington, DC: Homer Hoyt, 1966).

CHAPTER 3 ENCOURAGING THE EXPANSION OF LAND USE . . . AND CONSTRAINING IT

1. Henry George, *Progress and Poverty* (New York: Robert Schalkenbach Foundation, 1879), 390.

2. United States Dept. of Agriculture, Agricultural Research Service, "Chronological history by decade from the creation of USDA in 1862 until 2000," http://www.ars.usda.gov/is/ timeline/1880chron.htm?pf=1. While George garnered more votes than Teddy Roosevelt, one of his opponents in that race, his candidacy also split the reform vote so that a Tammany hack won the race.

3. Charles Abrams, *The City Is the Frontier* (New York: Harper & Row, 1965), 3.

4. *Village of Euclid v. Ambler Realty Co.* 272 U.S. 365 (1926).

5. Ibid., 394–395.

6. Richard H. Chused, "Euclid's Historical Imagery," *Case Western Law Review* 4 (Summer 2001): 60.

7. Bernard H. Siegan, *Land Use Without Zoning* (Lexington, MA: Lexington Books, 1972).

8. Eliza Hall, "Divide and Sprawl, Decline and Fall: A Comparative Critique of Euclidean Zoning," *University of Pittsburgh Law Review* 68 (Summer 2007): 916.

9. Ibid., 943.

10. Ibid., 923, quoting *Ambler Realty Co. v. Village of Euclid (Euclid I)*, 297 F. 307, 313 (N.D. Ohio 1924).

11. Nina J. Gruen and Claude Gruen, "Housing Policy and Class Integration," The Western Regional Science Association, *Annals of Regional Science* (December 1975): 109.

12. In 1956 Charles Tiebout famously wrote (*Journal of Political Economy* 64, no. 5 [1956]: 416–424) that households "vote with their feet" to find housing locations that provide the combination of services and taxes that suit their own priorities. His model of human behavior has become a much-used tool for analysts concerned with public finance and the provision of public goods. I suggest that, over time, the way that neighborhoods change in housing quality, price, and type is determined not only by how people vote with their feet in response to the availability of public goods and costs but also with at least equal strength by the way they vote in response to the alternatives of privately provided housing and amenity opportunities and costs as well as the social environment of the options open to them within the neighborhoods of the region.

13. *Golden v. Planning Board of Ramapo*, 285 N.E. 2D 291 (1972).

14. *Northern District of California v. 75S* Supp. 574 (1974).

15. *Village of Belle Terre v. Boraas* 416 U.S. 1 (1974).

16. Eran Ben-Joseph, "Subdivision Regulations: Practices and Attitudes" (Working paper, Lincoln Institute of Land Policy, Cambridge, MA. Lincoln Institute product code WP03EB1).

17. Ethan Fishman, "Not Compassionate, Not Conservative," *The American Scholar* (Winter 2007): 49.

18. U.S. Dept. of Labor, Bureau of Labor Statistics, "100 Years of U.S. Consumer Spending," Report #991 (May 2006). http://www.bls.gov/opub/uscs/titlepage.pdf.

19. The concept of rent seeking was first laid out by Gordon Tullock in "Welfare Costs of Tariffs, Monopolies, and Theft," *Western Economic Journal* 5 (June 1967): 224–232. The term "rent seeking" was coined by Krueger in 1964. A. O. Krueger, "The Political Economy of the Rent-Seeking Economy," American Economic Review 63 (1964).

20. William A. Fischel, *The Homevoter Hypothesis* (Cambridge, MA: Harvard University Press, 2001).

CHAPTER 4   HOUSING MARKET STRUCTURE

1. Alfred Kuhn, *The Study of Society, A Unified Approach*. (Homewood, IL: Richard D. Irwin, Inc. and The Dorsey Press, Inc., 1963).

2. In 2000, 35 percent of New York's population was foreign born, with another 2 percent born in Puerto Rico and U.S. protectorates. "New York City, NY Census 2000 Demographic Profile Highlights," http://factfinder.census.gov.

3. Henry James, *Washington Square* (1880; Mineola, NY: Dover Publications, 1998), 20.

4. For more details on this shift, see Janet L. Abu-Lughod, *New York, Chicago, Los Angeles: America's Global Cities* (Minneapolis: University of Minnesota Press, 1999), 41.

5. Riis's best-known photographs came out in an 1889 edition of *Scribner's Magazine* and then in book form: Jacob Riis, *How the Other Half Lives* (New York: Scribner's, 1890).

6. For a good description of filtering, see Ira S. Lowry, "Filtering and Housing Standards: A Conceptual Analysis," *Land Economics* 4 (November 1960): 362–370.

7. An exceptionally insightful exception to the failure of many to recognize this critical role of the slums was an article that appeared in 1959. J. R. Seeley, "The Slums: Its Nature, Use and Uses," *Journal of the American Institute of Planners* (February 1959).

CHAPTER 5   HOW NEIGHBORHOODS CHANGE, WHY OCCUPANTS CHANGE NEIGHBORHOODS

1. Robert D. Putnam, *Making Democracy Work* (Princeton, NJ: Princeton University Press, 1993), 171.
2. Alvin L. Schorr, "Slums and Social Insecurity," U.S. Department of Health, Education, and Welfare, Social Security Administration Research Report No. 1 (Washington, D.C., 1963).
3. Mabel L. Walker, *Urban Blight and Slums* (Cambridge, MA: Harvard University Press, 1938).
4. Alvin H. Hansen, "Urban Redevelopment and Housing," Planning Pamphlets (December 1941).
5. Housing Act of 1949. Public Law 171, 81st Congr., 1st sess., sec. 12.
6. Claude Gruen, "Urban Renewal's Role in the Genesis of Tomorrow's Slums," *Land Economics* 39, no. 3 (August 1963): 285–291.
7. Martin Anderson, *The Federal Bulldozer: A Critical Analysis of Urban Renewal, 1949–1962* (Cambridge, MA: MIT Press, 1964).
8. *New York Times*, December 22, 2002, 3.
9. Richard F. Babcock, *The Zoning Game* (Madison: University of Wisconsin Press, 1969), 3.
10. *San Francisco Chronicle*, December 4, 2006.
11. In the school year 2006–2007, Sacred Heart Cathedral Preparatory School was 31.6 percent Asian, 3.6 percent black, 10 percent Latino, 33 percent white, and 21 percent multiracial.
12. Nina J. Gruen and Claude Gruen, *Low and Moderate Income Housing in the Suburbs* (New York: Praeger Publishers, 1972), 29–33.
13. Ibid., 33.
14. Herbert Gans, *The Levittowners: Ways of Life and Politics in a New Suburban Community* (New York: Vintage Books, 1969), 167.
15. National Commission on Urban Problems, *Building the American City* (New York: Praeger, 1969), 82–83.
16. U.S. Census Bureau, "Selected Historical Decennial Census Population and Housing Counts," 1993. http://www.census.gov/popest/archives/1990s/popclockest.txt.
17. Bureau of Labor Statistics, Shelter Consumer Price Index, U.S. City Average. Available at http://data.bls.gov.
18. U.S. Census Bureau, "Population, Housing Units, Area Measurements, and Density, 1790–2000," http://www.census.gov/prod/cen2000/phc3-us-pt1.pdf#page=44.
19. Ibid.

CHAPTER 6   THE TURN AGAINST EXPANSION AND GROWTH

1. Richard F. Babcock, *Zoning Game: Municipal Practices and Policies* (Madison: University of Wisconsin Press, 1969), 4.
2. Gay Talese, "On the Bridge," *The New Yorker*, December 2002, 65.
3. Ibid.
4. Ibid.
5. Ibid., 66.
6. Richard E. Foglesong, *Planning the Capitalist City* (Princeton, NJ: Princeton University Press, 1986), 286.
7. Ibid., 257.
8. Ibid.
9. U.S. Census Bureau, "American Housing Survey National Tables: 2001." http://www.census.gov/hhes/www/housing/ahs/ahs01_2000wts/ahs01_2000wts.html.

10. *Construction Industry Association of Sonoma County, et al. v. The City of Petaluma*, No. 74–2100, 522 F.2d 897 (9th Cir. 1975).

11. *Golden v. Planning Board of Town of Ramapo*, 285 N.E. 2d 291 (N.Y. 1971).

12. Robert H. Freilich, *From Sprawl to Smart Growth* (Chicago: American Bar Association, 1999).

13. Ibid., 43.

14. Ibid., 46.

15. *Golden v. Planning Board of the Town of Ramapo*, No. 525–1970 (Sup. Ct., Rockland County, Nov. 19, 1970).

16. *Golden v. Planning Board of the Town of Ramapo*, New York State Court of Appeals, 1972, 37 a.d. 2d at 243, N.Y.S. 2d at 186.

17. *Golden v. Planning Board of the Town of Ramapo*, 30 N.Y. 2d 359, 334 N.Y.S. 2d 138, 285 N.E. 2d 291 (1972), appeal dismissed, 409 U.S. 1003 (1972).

18. Claude Gruen, "The Economics of Petaluma: Unconstitutional Regional Socio-Economic Impacts," in *Management and Control of Growth*, vol. 2, ed. Randall W. Scott, David J. Brower, and Dallas D. Minor (Washington, DC: Urban Land Institute, 1975), 175

19. Ibid., 176.

20. For tables showing the calculations and a fuller discussion of the forecast impacts, see ibid., 173–186.

21. See "Findings of Fact and Conclusions of Law," reported at 375 F. Supp. 574 (1975); U.S. District Court, N.D. California, "Petaluma: The Case Decision" in *Management and Control of Growth*, vol. 2, ed. Randall W. Scott, David J. Brower, and Dallas D. Minor (Washington D.C.: Urban Land Institute, 1975), 135.

22. Construction Industry Association of Sonoma County, a California nonprofit corporation, et al., *Plaintiffs-Appellees, v. The City of Petaluma, a California Charter City, Defendants-Appellants.* United States Court of Appeals for the Ninth Circuit, October 2, 1975, 8 ERC 1001; 5 Envtl. L. Rep. 20; 522 F.2d 897.

CHAPTER 7   SUBURBANIZATION AND SPRAWL

1. Robert H. Freilich, *From Sprawl to Smart Growth* (Chicago: American Bar Association, 1999), 107.

2. Lawrence Livingston Jr., "Confessions of a City Planner," *San Francisco Sunday Examiner/Chronicle*, May 25, 1980, 6–12.

3. "Overview of the California Environmental Review and Permit Approval Process," Governor's Office of Planning and Research, Sacramento, CA.

4. In California, the state imposes a sales tax but returns a portion of the tax to the municipality where the sale took place.

5. Livingston, "Confessions," 12.

6. John Kenneth Galbraith, *The Affluent Society* (Boston: Houghton Mifflin, 1958), 9.

7. Ibid., 138.

8. U.S. Department of Commerce, Bureau of the Census, County and City Data Book 1972, 648.

9. Palo Alto Comprehensive Plan 1976, Library of Congress Catalog Card Number 76–12775, 15.

10. County and City Data Book 1972, 648.

11. City of Palo Alto Economic Resources at a Glance and Real Estate Infolink Multiple Listing Services (2003).

12. "Joseph Eichler (1900–1974) was a California-based . . . , residential real estate developer known for building homes in the Modernist style. Between 1950 and 1974, his

company, Eichler Homes, built over 11,000 homes in northern California and three communities in southern California, . . . which came to be known as Eichlers. . . . Unlike many developers of the day, Joseph Eichler was a social visionary and commissioned designs primarily for middle-class Americans. One of his stated aims was to construct inclusive and diverse planned communities, ideally featuring integrated parks and community centers. Eichler, unlike most builders at the time, established a nondiscrimination policy and offered homes for sale to anyone of any religion or race. In 1958, he resigned from the National Association of Home Builders when they refused to support a nondiscrimination policy." http://en.wikipedia.org/wiki/Joseph_Eichler.

13. Palo Alto Comprehensive Plan and City; City of Palo Alto at a Glance and The Association of Bay Area Governments. http://www.bayareacensus.ca.gov/cities/PaloAlto70.htm/ and http://www.cityofpaloalto.org/visiting/news/details.asp?NewsID=596&TargetID=52.

14. Livingston, "Confessions," 12 (emphasis added).

15. Ibid.

16. William L. C. Wheaton and Morton J. Schussheim, *The Costs of Municipal Services in Residential Areas* (Washington, DC: Department of Commerce, 1955).

17. Real Estate Research Corporation, "The Costs of Sprawl" (Washington, DC: U.S. Government Printing Office, 1974).

18. Alan Altshuler, "Review of the Costs of Sprawl," *Journal of the American Institute of Planners* (April 1977): 207–209.

19. Robert Burchell, David Listokin, Anthony Downs, and Catherine Galley, "The Activities and Benefits of Smart Growth," *Wharton Real Estate Review* (Spring 2002): 86–93.

20. Several years ago, in testimony before the California legislature, I made the strongest case I could for changing the law that directs a portion of sales taxes to the cities or regions where the auto mall, retail center, or store is located to become a system that allocates the portion of the sales tax on a per-capita basis. The committee members listened to that portion of my testimony in stony silence. After the hearing, several of the state legislators told me in private that although they understood the public good that would come from a reallocation of sales taxes that would make municipalities more hospitable to housing construction, they believed the public would not support such a change in the tax codes.

21. Yoram Shiftan, "The Use of Activity-Based Modeling to Analyze the Effect of Land-Use Policies on Travel Behavior," *Annals of Regional Science* 42, no. 1 (March 2008): 79–97.

22. Yair Mundlak, "Economic Growth: Lessons from Two Centuries of American Agriculture," *Journal of Economic Literature* 43 (December 2005): 1018.

23. Gruen Gruen + Associates, "Land for Agriculture and Urban Development: The Case for Balance" An analysis conducted for the Coalition of Labor and Business of Stanislaus County (June 1990).

24. Jonathan Levine, *Zoned Out: Regulation, Markets and Choices in Transportation and Metropolitan Land Use* (Washington, DC: Resources for the Future Press, 2005), 1.

25. *Village of Euclid v. Ambler Realty Co.*, 272 U.S. 365, 47 S.Ct. 114, 71 L.Ed. 303.

26. Levine, *Zoned Out*, 45.

CHAPTER 8   URBAN POLICIES FOR THE NEW ECONOMY

1. Lewis Mumford, *The Highway and the City* (New York: Mentor Books, 1963), 244.

2. Ibid., 245.

3. Richard O. Baumbach Jr. and William E. Borah, *The Second Battle of New Orleans: A History of the Vieux Carre Riverfront-Expressway Controversy* (Fayetteville: University of Alabama Press, 1981).

4. Robert Bruegmann, *Sprawl: A Compact History* (Chicago: University of Chicago Press, 2005), 131.
5. Ibid., 132.
6. Marcycruz de Leon, Thomas M. Fullerton Jr., Brian W. Kelley, and Angel L. Molina Jr., "Infrastructure Tolls in Texas: Evidence from the Borderplex," *Texas Business Review* (University of Texas at Austin, Bureau of Business Research, IC2 Institute, April 2009): 4.
7. Cody Lyon, "Appeals Court Rules for Atlantic Yards Project," *Real Estate New York* 28, no. 3 (May/June 2009): 14.

GLOSSARY

agglomeration. A cluster of diverse uses.

agglomeration economies. The positive influences that enhance the productive power of producers; the benefits that can be enjoyed by residents simply because they locate within an urban area that has a large and diverse population base (urban agglomeration economies) and contains clusters of proximate uses whose activities are mutually supportive (location agglomeration). The benefits provided by agglomeration economies are externalities.

amenities. Structures and natural features in nature or activities that make nearby places more pleasant and desirable.

amicus brief. A written argument to a court by a lawyer representing a party not initially named in the litigation who wishes to support one of the litigants as "a friend of the court."

assessment district. An area within which property owners have voted to be taxed for the funding of public facilities such as lighting or sewage, or for the provision of services such as fire or police protection.

average. The most frequently used measure of central tendency or concentration is the arithmetic mean. The mean, or average, is the sum of all the values in a data set divided by the total number of observations or data points.

blight. Substandard deteriorated structures in a neighborhood where market conditions make the updating of the properties to more valuable and desirable uses infeasible.

bundle of services. All of the utility-providing or detracting features, such as the desirability of neighbors; accessibility to work, shopping, and recreational venues; shelter; and other features that make a residence more or less commodious and that accompany the rental or ownership of a dwelling.

capitalized value. The present worth of a real estate asset, such as a home or land, calculated by dividing the expected annual net income stream by an interest rate thought to be reflective of the risk associated with the expectation of the income stream and the rate of return obtainable from other investments.

code. A systematically arranged and comprehensive collection of laws; a planning code. Codes are typically enacted by state or federal legislatures.

collateral. An asset pledged as security for a debt, such as the deed of ownership to a house that is pledged for mortgage payments.

comparative advantages. Differences in the availability of resources, labor, agglomeration economies, or other factors that enhance innovation and productivity or decrease the costs of the economic activities within a geographic area.

covenant. A promise to do or not do something with property, such as to limit occupancy to certain users or to prohibit certain kinds of uses or structures.

critical mass. The scale and diversity of complementary activities great enough to trigger agglomeration economies that produce comparative advantages.

cross-elasticity of demand. A measure of the change in the purchases of one good that results from the price change of another good. If, for example, the price of housing goes up in one neighborhood (a positive change) causing the quantity of housing purchased in another neighborhood to increase (also a positive rate of change), as some buyers shift from the first neighborhood to the second and some homeowners sell their home in the first neighborhood to move to the second, then the ratio between the two is positive (a positive price change divided by a positive change in purchases). In such situations the cross-elasticity is said to be positive, indicating there is some substitutability between the neighborhoods. Conversely, if the price of housing in the first neighborhood decreases, which causes the quantity of houses purchased in the other neighborhood to increase, then the cross-elasticity is negative, suggesting that the two neighborhood are complementary to each other.

default. Failure to pay a debt on the date pledged. A mortgage lender will declare the mortgage in default when payments are not paid when due.

depression. A severe downturn in the gross domestic product for a sustained period, usually a decline of at least 10 percent for more than six months.

disamenities. Developments, human activities, or naturally occurring phenomena that make adjacent or nearby locations undesirable by emitting unpleasant, dangerous, or otherwise undesirable effects.

eminent domain. The right of public entities to acquire private property with just compensation but without the consent of the owner.

entitlement. The granting by land use–regulating authorities of permission to develop real estate with specified uses; that is, entitled land is ready to be developed.

equity. The total value of an asset minus any outstanding debts.

exactions. Fees imposed as a condition of approval for development.

excess profits. Returns on the capital and entrepreneurial inputs into a business that are greater than the returns that would be necessary to sustain the business under competitive conditions.

externalities. Benefits received (positive externalities) or undesirable or inconvenient impositions (negative externalities) that are outside the market transactions in which goods and services are purchased. Positive externalities, or amenities, are frequently public goods that are best provided by public entities or regulated private firms. Similarly, many negative externalities, or disamenities, are best prevented by laws and public services.

face value of a mortgage. The principal sum due the lender by the borrower stipulated in a mortgage.

fair market value. The price in cash or its equivalent that a typically motivated and knowledgeable buyer would pay an equally knowledgeable seller for a property at its most probable use after a reasonable time is allowed for the exposure of the property in an open, orderly market.

farm subsidies. Payments by the government to farmers in return for producing or not producing specified crops and livestock.

feedback. A feedback system of information or communication involves mutual cause–effect relationships. A response that increases or supports the initial effect is referred to as positive feedback. A response that diminishes or extinguishes the initial effect is referred to as negative feedback. The thermostat on your wall is an example of a feedback system. If the temperature goes up beyond the degree of heat you have set, the heating system will be turned off (negative feedback). If the temperature drops below the setting, then the heat is turned on (positive feedback).

filtration. The process by which the movement of households within and between neighborhoods interacts with supply conditions to determine the price and quality of houses in the submarkets of urban regions, which we refer to as neighborhoods.

foreclosure. The redemption of ownership in a property by the mortgagee for the failure of the borrower to meet the terms of the mortgage.

G.I. Bill (officially titled Servicemen's Readjustment Act of 1944). Legislation originally passed by the U.S. Congress in 1944 to provide benefits, such as tuition for educational institutions and eligibility for low interest mortgages, to returning servicemen and women.

home. One's place of residence.

house. A residential structure.

household. The individuals living together in a dwelling unit.

inclusionary zoning. The requirement that private housing developers sell a portion of the residential units they build at prices set at a percentage of the income of households whose incomes are less than specified maximums. In some cases developers are allowed to make cash payments to public agencies in lieu of providing the below-market residential units.

in-fill sites. Small pieces of property that have remained vacant in neighborhoods where most of the once-vacant land has been developed.

inflation. The increase in the general level of prices for goods and services.

Iron Law of Wages. The theory originally suggested by Thomas Malthus and accepted by David Ricardo that held that an increase in the wages of working people would in time be offset by increases in population.

leapfrog development. A pattern of development in which vacant land is left undeveloped between existing and new construction.

leverage. The use of borrowed funds to purchase more of something than could be obtained with one's available cash. Overleveraging extends borrowing to the point that there is a significant risk that the borrowed funds cannot be repaid.

margin. The additional cost or revenue contributed by one more unit.

median. One type of average found by arranging data values from smallest to largest and then selecting the one in the middle.

metropolitan area. Generally refers to the geographic entities defined by the U.S. Office of Management and Budget (OMB) and utilized by the U.S. Bureau of the Census for its statistical reports. Each metropolitan area consists of an urban core of at least fifty thousand inhabitants and one or more counties containing the core urban area, as well as any adjacent counties that have a high degree of social and economic integration with the urban core, as measured by commutation to work.

monopoly. The advantage gained by the seller of a product when the absence of competition from other sellers of similar products permits a sufficient degree of control of the price charged to enable the seller to earn a higher profit than would be earned if a competitive supply of the product were available.

mortgage. The conveyance of a property as security for the repayment of a debt.

mortgage broker. An agent who sells mortgages, usually on a commission basis.

multiplier. The ratio by which an initial expenditure or output for a good or service creates additional jobs and incomes through the stream of purchases induced by the initial transactions. The ratio is also known as the multiplier effect.

option. The purchase of an agreement under which the buyer has the right to subsequently purchase an asset at a specified price. Often developers option land to purchase within a time period they believe will enable them to entitle the property for an intended use.

ordinance. A law typically enacted by a city or county.

political economy. The study of human behavior that allocates scarce means between alternative uses; the way this behavior is influenced by the laws and social constraints imposed by governing institutions.

present value. The discounted value of a future stream of money calculated looking forward from a point in time.

recession. A decline in the gross domestic product sustained for at least two consecutive quarters.

refinance. To replace an existing debt, such as a mortgage, with a new debt instrument that increases the size of the original debt or changes the terms of the original debt to stretch out the payments or decrease the interest rate.

rent seeking. The increase in the value of something that would exist at a lower value if it were not for the shortage created by those who have thereby increased the value of property or another asset or service. Examples of rent seeking include the producers of a good who petition their government to raise tariffs to keep out foreign-made goods so they can charge more for their products. Similarly, if the property owners of a neighborhood or city facing increasing residential demands can preclude the building of additional housing units on vacant land in their jurisdiction, they have been successful in causing the value of existing housing units to increase.

residual land value. The amount of value that land can support. It is calculated by capitalizing the income that remains from the expected future flow after deducting the competitive returns that could be expected for the capital and entrepreneurship of development on the land from the present value of the net operating income expected from the use of the property. The residual value of the vacant land or building is the amount of money that a would-be developer can afford to pay for vacant land that will be used as a site for a new building, or for an existing building that will be remodeled, to earn an acceptable profit on the entire project.

single-room occupancy. Multistory building containing small rooms providing housing for single individuals, sometimes pejoratively referred to as "flop houses."

slum clearance. The removal of deteriorated substandard housing referred to as slums. Initially the demolition of slum neighborhoods and their replacement with low-rent public housing was authorized by the Federal Housing Act of 1937.

sprawl. Low-density, spread-out development outside of the urban core.

subjective value. The worth put on something by an individual based on personally held priorities of what provides satisfaction so that no two people need agree on the worth. This contrasts with the value placed on something traded in a market transaction where the worth is quantified objectively by the price of the transaction.

subprime mortgage. A loan with real estate, usually a residential dwelling, as collateral issued to a buyer whose income and or credit history would suggest that the lender is accepting a significant risk that the borrower may not be able to comply with the repayment provisions of the loan.

suburbs. The formerly mainly agricultural land and open space outside of cities developed by nonfarmers who often commuted to urban places to work, until the suburban areas developed workplaces.

supply elasticity. The responsiveness of producers (the suppliers of a product) to changes in the price of that product; the percent change in supply or number of units produced divided by the percent change in the price to which producers are responding.

tenement. Multifamily dwelling usually with three stories, although some "dumbbell" tenements were taller. Rented to poor working-class families, they had a minimum of space, ventilation, and light and had no indoor toilets. Many tenements were built in New York between 1833 and 1901 and provided housing for the immigrants who came to that city in the nineteenth and early twentieth centuries.

tranche. Assets grouped together within a security, usually based on similar risk ratings. For example, mortgages judged as being similar in terms of the risk of default are combined for sale as a single mortgage-backed security.

unincorporated area. Territory usually under the jurisdiction of a county that has not been granted a charter or the right to form a separate municipal government.

urban. Human settlements with nonagricultural economic bases with the density and type of residential structures historically associated with cities rather than rural farming communities.

urban extension or urban limit line. A geographical boundary established by land use authorities that prohibits nonfarming development beyond the specified border.

zoning maps. Drawings delineating the geographic boundaries within which similar land use regulations apply. Such maps are typically included in the general plans of urban areas that also contain descriptions of the development restrictions, land uses, densities, and design parameters specified by locally applicable ordinances.

INDEX

ABOUT THE AUTHOR

For more than forty years as principal economist of Gruen Gruen + Associates, Dr. Claude Gruen has led studies and provided consulting to serve the economic interests of federal, state, and local land-use policymakers, investors, and property owners. He has lectured at universities and public forums and has published extensively in the fields of urban economics and land-use policy.